A Sentence of Exile

The Palestine/Israel Conflict
1897–1977

A Sentence of Exile

The Palestine/Israel Conflict 1897–1977

David Waines

THE MEDINA PRESS

Wilmette, Illinois
1977

Copyright © 1977 by David Waines
A Publication of Medina Press
P.O. Box 125, Wilmette, Illinois 60091.

LCC: 77-73083

ISBN   0-914456-14-8 (clothbound edition)
ISBN   0-914456-15-6 (paperback edition)

All rights reserved.

David Waines is Lecturer on the History of the
Middle East, University of Lancaster,
England.

TO NAHED

WHO HAS SHARED THE

STRUGGLE

Table of Contents

	PAGE
PREFACE	ix
INTRODUCTION	3
CHAPTER 1 Imperial Friendships	11
CHAPTER 2 Palestine: The Waste Land?	29
CHAPTER 3 A Game of Nations	39
CHAPTER 4 Confrontation	46
CHAPTER 5 The Horns of a Dilemma	53
CHAPTER 6 The Palestine Rebellion 1936-1939	71
CHAPTER 7 Zionist Countermoves	85
CHAPTER 8 End of the Mandate	95
CHAPTER 9 The Palestinian Diaspora	105
CHAPTER 10 The Palestinians Within	120
CHAPTER 11 Pax Israelica	139
CHAPTER 12 Whither Palestine?	171
THE END IS PROLOGUE	195
BIBLIOGRAPHY AND NOTES	213
INDEX	223

Preface

Six years ago the original version of this book appeared entitled *The Unholy War*. The present volume is a revised, enlarged and updated account of that earlier work. New material has been added to some chapters (especially Five and Ten) while the last third of the original book has been entirely rewritten.

I have called it *A Sentence of Exile.* The phrase, appropriately Biblical, seemed to me to describe best the judgement that others, from politicians to propagandists, have imposed upon the Palestinian people. The Palestine problem is entering its eighth decade. Although there are now some positive signs that the Palestinians have, through their own unremitting sacrifices, succeeded to a degree in having that sentence repealed, there is hardly a single observer today who can look dispassionately at the conflict and say, "The end is in sight."

Cairo, Egypt
1976

A Sentence of Exile

The Palestine/Israel Conflict
1897-1977

Introduction

All too often we assume that our first awareness of a problem is indicative of the time it came into being. This was the position I found myself in when I went to the Sudan in 1957 as a student. I was already an "armchair politician" and, like most North Americans, I knew at least a little about the hard-working band of pioneers who, led by David Ben Gurion, had created Israel as a model democratic state amid the backwardness and poverty of the Arab Middle East. The Suez crisis was just over, and like most in the West I admired the skill and tenacity of the young Israeli Army.

It is, of course, no fault of the armchair politician that his analysis of a current international problem must be based on the information available in daily newspapers or on the television news where he can see the replay action of a battle which may have occurred only hours before in some far away, instant graveyard.

An example is the Arab-Israeli War of June 1967. Television cameramen followed the battle across the empty wastes of the Sinai Desert and up the slopes of the Golan Heights. The Security Council debates on the crisis were telecast live and seemed to place us right in the heart of international diplomacy. How long will it be before the roving cameraman in the United Nations also captures on film the drama of political arm-twisting in the corridors? The magazines too had their function, providing "in depth" analyses of the causes and significance of the crisis as well as background sketches of some of the leading characters, including the now-deceased President Gamal Abdel Nasser, General Moshe Dayan and Ahmad Shukayri.

We were then bombarded with a flood of "instant" books on the war. Incredible as it may seem, the first one appeared only days after the battle had ended! Other, more thoughtful books followed, skillfully dissecting the war hour by hour. This massive output of analysis and opinion could have provided a clearer understanding of the entire Arab-Israeli conflict. Instead, it produced an ever more confusing and perplexing picture of the situation.

It is important to know why this is so. In the first place, the June war was not seen in its historical context. It is understandable that limitations of time and space in the television and newspaper coverage did not permit a reflective backward glance to the very roots of the conflict. The "instant" books made the same omissions.

The basic causes of the June war are not to be found in the weeks immediately prior to the crisis. The causes lie partly in the aftermath of the Suez crisis of 1956 when Britain, France and Israel invaded Egypt, and partly in the Arab-Israeli War of 1948 which followed the creation of the State of Israel. It may well be that an enduring solution to the Arab-Israeli dilemma will not be found by turning the clock back to May 1967, to 1956 or even to 1948. To *understand* the problem, we must revert to its basic roots.

This leads to a second point, a subtle but important difference in terminology. In North America we speak of the Arab-Israeli conflict. In the Arab world they speak only of the Palestine Problem. This does not mean that the Arabs generally disclaim interest in the conflict. Far from it. It means rather that the core of the problem is viewed from a different perspective.

In any bitter controversy each side believes it holds a monopoly on the truth. This is human and understandable. In each subjective argument there is an element of objective truth which gives substance to the interpretation of each side.

For example, my Sudanese friends at the University of Khartoum were vexed by my attitude over Suez (naïve, they called it), and I was puzzled by theirs. One explained to me that the crisis was a conspiracy between British and French imperialism and their Israeli protégé. The British wanted to repossess the Suez Canal, the French wanted to overthrow Nasser because of his assistance to the Algerians rebelling against the tyranny of French rule, and Israel was bent upon another reckless adventure of expansion. I didn't see the crisis in that light at all. Besides, the idea of a conspiracy seemed quite ludicrous and why would Israel want to expand into the Sinai Desert of all places?

It mattered little that time would prove my friends substantially correct. It is now accepted that a conspiracy did exist between the three invading powers. Even Prime Minister Ben Gurion had at

INTRODUCTION

the time claimed before the Israeli Parliament that, by attacking Sinai, Israel had not invaded *Egypt proper*, but had merely *liberated* part of the ancient Jewish homeland. Nevertheless, the confrontation revealed to me that not only could divergent views be held concerning the same events, but also that these views could be voiced with a deep conviction because these things mattered in their lives. When a Sudanese student spoke to me of imperialism and colonialism, he was reminding me that Britain had only recently relinquished her rule over his country. That was an experience in which I had had no share and I could not then grasp the fine combination of intellectual appraisal and emotional involvement.

From the Arab perspective the Palestine Problem is simply the displacement of the inhabitants of Palestine under conditions of British colonial rule by another people, Zionists, who were fired with a political ideology which threatened the status of the Arab community. After 1948 and the creation of the State of Israel, the conflict remained essentially "the struggle of an indigenous population against the occupation of part of its normal territory by foreigners."[1] This is the substance of the Arab position, and it is cast strictly in terms of the fate and the struggle of the people of Palestine. All other elements of the broader Arab-Israeli conflict stem from this. But again, faced as we are with the half-real world of the news media and the effects of time and distance on our powers of perception, the subjective interpretation of the Palestinian case has become distorted and unreal. The consequence is that even the substance of their story has been kicked into oblivion.

Nevertheless, Palestinians are what the problem is all about. And this book is about the problem of Palestine.

The Sudan was a good place to begin one's education on the Middle East. Jordan 1962 was a good place to continue. In the summer of that year, I had intended merely to spend a leisurely six-week vacation in Lebanon, Syria and Jordan. But 1962 was a year of dramatic upheaval. Caught there as a bystander I was

[1] *Israel and the Arabs* by Maxime Rodinson, Penguin Special, London (1968).

soon swept into the maelstrom of events causing me to prolong my stay well into 1963. The Royalist Regime in Yemen had just been toppled by the Republicans, who had chased the royal head of state and his tribesmen north into the inaccessible mountains. Iraq witnessed a coup d'etat, and I myself nearly witnessed one in Damascus which I had left scarcely two days earlier.

It was in Jordan, however, that the greatest tension seemed to be concentrated. Everywhere one encountered Palestinians, that embittered remnant of a people who had once inhabited the land now known as Israel. At that time they made up more than half of King Hussein's kingdom and represented a potential threat to both his person and his throne. The relationship between the king and the Palestinians was an odd love-hate affair. He bore the stigma of his grandfather's "betrayal" when, after the 1948 war, King Abdullah had tried to make a deal with the Israelis. His efforts cost him his life; he was assassinated by a Palestinian youth in a Jerusalem mosque. King Hussein could expect no less were he to follow on the same path. On the other hand, he was regarded as a courageous and modest ruler. His country was not inherently wealthy like several of the oil kingdoms, but he had nursed and pushed it toward economic viability. Though the ultimate authority in his kindgom, he was not aloof like most monarchs. Often he would visit his ministers in their homes and he could be seen driving his own car through the streets of Amman.

When I first arrived in Amman I was exhausted. It had been a seven-hour car trip from Beirut, across the mountains down to the shimmering garden city of Damascus, and then through the stifling mid-afternoon heat to Amman. A Jordanian border guard had suggested a hotel in Amman where he told our taxi driver to leave me. It was clean and cool and after a shower I went in search of a good meal. I was too shy to speak Arabic except with those who, I was sure, did not understand English.

This is how it came about that as I was haltingly asking a porter about a restaurant two boys, who looked like students, approached me, one saying: "*Ta' ma'na, badna nakul kamaan.*" (Come with us, we too are going to eat.)

"*Shukran,*" I replied and followed them toward the door.

"You're American," the one said pleasantly, in English.

INTRODUCTION

"Canadian," I politely corrected him, noting ruefully how quickly he had spotted my appalling accent.

"You speak Arabic very well," he said. Relieved by his generosity, I confessed he had come along just as I was running out of appropriate phrases with the porter. The ice was broken and I spent the rest of the evening with Khalil and Jelal.

When we stepped into the street the sun had already gone down and a cool breeze was blowing in from the desert. The restaurant was some distance from the hotel and, as we walked, I learned that my companions were students in the Faculty of Engineering at the American University of Beirut. They had come to Amman to visit friends for the weekend. Both were tall and lean, dark of complexion and each spoke with a quiet intensity and purpose, but not without humor, as I soon learned.

The restaurant they chose was called Ali Baba. Inside it looked like an oriental rogues' gallery with imaginative portraits of the forty thieves spaced at intervals around the walls. The picture of Ali Baba hung in the place of honor above the doorway.

"You know the tale of Ali Baba and his gang of thieves," said Jelal. Of course. What child has not read the Tales of the Arabian Nights with Ali Baba and Aladdin and his magic lamp?

"How many thieves were in the band?" asked Khalil, smiling quietly.

"Forty," I replied without hesitation.

This aroused their glee and they told me to count the portraits. I had counted down one wall when I noticed something out of context — on the back wall of the restaurant, in a space slightly above and between two of the thieves, I spotted a different picture. Whether out of malice or respect, I know not, the proprietor had placed a framed photograph of the king, making him a so-called forty-first "thief." This is when I realized that my companions must be Palestinians.

Their story was simple. Khalil, the son of a minor official of the Palestinian Government, was born in Jaffa and Jelal, a doctor's son, in Haifa. The boys were about eight years old when their families were forced to flee from the terrors of the war in 1948. These two families were more fortunate than hundreds of thousands of their countrymen who had spent the years since the war in refugee camps. Khalil's father found employment in a ministry of the Jordanian Government, and Jelal's father was able to set up a medical practice in Amman even though he had lost all the land his family had owned near Haifa. Fate had brought Khalil and Jelal to the same school in Amman and now they were on Point-4 American Government Aid Scholarships at the American University in Beirut.

Our conversation was to the point: a capsule of the Palestine Problem.

"Why did you choose your particular line of study, and what of the future?" I asked them.

"One day Palestine will need professional men and engineers will be called upon to help build that future."

"But you live in Jordan now. Is this not your country?"

"We live in Jordan, it's true, but Palestine is our home as it has been our fathers' and their fathers' before them."

My next question was: "How do you expect to go back to your home, to Palestine, or rather to Israel?"

"One day the world will acknowledge the injustice done to our people, and we shall return."

This was their fundamental article of faith: "We shall return." Never again did I see Jelal or Khalil after that night in Amman.

From the capital I traveled the length of the West Bank of Jordan. Strange places soon became familiar: Tulkarm, Nablus, Ramallah. The well-known names of Jerusalem, Hebron, Jericho and Bethlehem assumed an altogether different reality for me from the images of these ancient places which I had retained since childhood. Wherever I talked with Palestinians, whether in a coffee shop in Jerusalem, a schoolroom in Tulkarm, a private home in Nablus or a refugee camp in Jericho, I heard the same phrase: "We shall return." It echoed down the rocky hills and through the green valleys.

Their poets too, even the least among them, tried to capture the sense of loss which sustained the passion for their return. These are the words of a native of Jaffa, an exile gazing from a height of land on the West Bank toward the gray expanse of the Mediterranean he had once known so well:

INTRODUCTION

> Wounded shore! Vainly fluttering before my eyes!
> You are ever in my heart.
> Not in humiliation will I return,
> Will you, liberated, welcome me back?
> My hands outstretched to you
> Fall wearily beneath the weight of longing.
> When I weep, lamenting my loss
> I weep for myself and you.

These words came back to me as I again sat in the gracious lounge of the Grand Hotel in Ramallah. Five years had passed. It was September 1967, two months after the June War and Ramallah, like the entire West Bank of Jordan, was occupied by the Israeli Army. The man who had written the above lines sat across from me. Kamal Nasser was perhaps forty, with thinning black hair, a tanned face and deep brown eyes which animated his conversation as he endlessly lit one cigarette after another. He had led an active life on the Jordanian political scene, in journalism, in parliament and in prison. He spoke softly and intensely of the Arab defeat.

"We have been humiliated by this disaster. The morale of our people has been shattered, and yet we shall pick up the pieces and begin again. The Arab leaders have let us down, Nasser, Hussein and the rest. Our faith in the United Nations' ability to solve this problem has been misplaced; perhaps we were too naïve in believing in its power. Now we shall have to fall back upon our own resources; we shall resist the Israeli occupation peacefully as long as we can, in whatever form we can. But somehow I believe that this is what Winston Churchill once said — not the end, nor the beginning of the end, but rather the end of the beginning. The beginning of the revival of our people, the Palestinians."

That was Kamal Nasser in 1967. Shortly thereafter, he was expelled by the Israelis from the West Bank. In exile he became one of the political leaders of Fateh. In April, 1973, he was murdered by Israeli agents at his home in Beirut. Two other Fateh leaders, Muhammad Yusuf Najjar and Kamal Adwan were gunned down in the same operation. All three were deeply mourned by Palestinians, particularly those in the occupied territories.

Time will tell whether the Palestinians are at the beginning of the end or at the end of the beginning. In any event, the June war of 1967 and the Israeli occupation of the rest of Mandated Palestine brought the Palestinian people back to center stage. In the past, their script was written by other hands. Others attempt to do so until the present. On the eve of the civil war in Jordan in September, 1970, Yassir Arafat declared, "Everyone wants to sweep us under the rug. But we are not dust yet." An audacious remark, perhaps, but what a cost was Black September in Jordan. And who could foretell that just five years later in the Lebanon Palestinians would be dragged into the bloodiest civil war of modern times? Add to this the incessant Israeli air and ground and sea attacks upon their guerilla bases and refugee camps. Palestinians appeared at times to be engulfed in a tidal wave of violence. Nevertheless, all these seasons of malevolent storms could not blot out a persistent ray of light. Seven years after the humiliation of June 1967 a Palestinian addressed the United Nations General Assembly in acknowledgement of the international community's recognition of his people's rights to repatriation, self-determination and independence. This is not a small achievement. Only when these rights are fulfilled will the Palestinian be freed from his sentence of exile.

1

Imperial Friendships

One version has it that the Six Day War of June 1967 began in 1897, the year Theodore Herzl founded the World Zionist Organization. Zionism however, at least in the abstract, initially had nothing to do with either the Arabs or the Middle East. Zionists were preoccupied with the growing menace of anti-Semitism on the Continent, a disease which had reached alarming proportions during the last quarter of the nineteenth century.

European imperialism, which had already afflicted the Middle East for some time, would continue to be a painful reality to the peoples of the Arab world. France achieved a foothold in North Africa by seizing Algeria in the eighteen-thirties, and then Tunisia in 1881. In 1882 Great Britain "temporarily" occupied Egypt to secure the Suez Canal, that vital artery of the imperial lifeline joining Britain to Gibraltar, Malta, Cyprus, Aden and thence to India. The occupation did not end completely until King Farouk's overthrow in 1952.

Between Herzl's 1897 activities and the end of World War I, Zionist nationalist ideals had forged a bond of common purpose with the imperial strategy of the British Government. The attention of each was focused on Palestine. The bond which linked their purpose was the Balfour Declaration. Issued in November 1917, the declaration was as momentous a document as the idea which inspired it. When Zionists brought to England their incredible scheme for the solution of "the Jewish problem," a Jewish national home, the outcome was highly speculative. No one could have foreseen the irony that was to unfold: the eve of the fiftieth anniversary of the Balfour Declaration occurred in the very year that Zionism's child, the State of Israel, was again at war with the Arabs. At the same time the last outpost of the British Empire in the Middle East was being abandoned in Aden. British imperialism died ungracefully, but the Palestine Problem remains a dangerous issue.

The story begins with the rise of Zionism in the late nineteenth century as an answer to the secular problem of anti-Semitism which itself was a product of European Christianity. Hatred of the Jew had for centuries been a part of Church propaganda and, although not effective everywhere, it did reach the highest ranks of the clergy. Men such as St. John Chrysostom, St. Bernard and Peter the Venerable count among those who had added their voice to the traditional Christian indictment of the Jew for the death of Christ. To kill a Jew in the twelfth century was regarded as a virtue — an excess of virtue. Peter the Venerable once said: "God does not wish to annihilate the Jew. He must be made to suffer fearful torments, and be preserved for greater ignominy, for an existence more bitter than death." The Jew was despised as the living symbol of God's wrath for his crime of deicide. Christianity's rationalization of the persecution of the Jew evolved over the centuries into a social and political persecution based on racial theories.

During the nineteenth century, in the wake of the liberalizing spirit of the French Revolution, the Jew in Western Europe found himself emancipated from centuries of bondage, and allowed to become an assimilated member of the country he inhabited. Nevertheless, modern or political anti-Semitism derived in the same century from persons who saw in the Jewish emancipation all that was offensive in the liberal revolutionary movements. It was believed that the Jews were a people apart — a people who did not belong as full participants of European society.

The Western European Jews who continued to struggle against these currents were firmly convinced that the final answer to "the Jewish problem" lay in their genuine freedom and assimilation within their own society be it French, English, or German.

In Central and Eastern Europe, on the other hand, the ideas of emancipation were not to take root. No practical improvement had occurred in the medieval condition of urban Jewish ghettos. The impoverished rural townlets within the Pale of Settlement, that prison house created by czarist Russia for the majority of its Jewish inhabitants, fared little better. In these Jewish communities spiritual sustenance compensated somehow (if anything could) for physical privation. But when Czar Alexander II fell victim to an assassin's bullet there was no refuge, even in prayer, from the officially inspired torrent of violence and terror which marked Russian vengeance against an alleged Jewish conspiracy. Anti-Jewish pogroms swept over Russia on an unprecedented scale. Pogroms were a sadly familiar part of Russian Jewish life. Odessa during Easter of 1871 had been the scene of the worst outbreak in recent memory, but 1881 was a year of crisis for many Jews. The extent of the violence — nearly 150 cities and villages witnessed pogroms — and the fact that the usual illiterate rabble was now supported by men of status, including government officials, added a new dimension to the horror.

Mobs, like packs of ravenous wolves, stormed and pillaged Jewish shops, homes, schools and synagogues. The press stoked the fires of hatred with horrendous accounts of every imaginable sin, deceit and wickedness ascribed to Jews. Books were written to prove that Jews drank the blood of Christian children. In this cauldron of fear and hate the venom of man's unreason boiled over.

The new wave of repression was officially marked by the so-called May Laws of 1882 of which Chaim Weizmann later wrote: "It seemed that the whole cumbersome machinery of the vast Russian Empire was created for the sole purpose of inventing and amplifying rules and regulations for the hedging in of the existence of its Jewish subjects until it became something that was neither life nor death."

The very year of the infamous May Laws saw the appearance of another document in which one Russian Jew, Leo Pinsker, penned his response to the terrible dilemma of his people. In a small pamphlet entitled *Auto-Emancipation*,[11] Pinsker stated that the Jews must emancipate themselves from their political disabilities, establishing for themselves a nation with all the usual attributes: a common language, common customs and a common land from which no foreign master could expel them. Although he considered Palestine a reasonable location, Pinsker was more conscious of articulating the dangers inherent in Jewish minority status anywhere in the world. The national home, therefore, "might form a small territory in North America, or a sovereign *pashalik* in Asiatic Turkey recognized by the Porte and the other Powers as neutral." It was the first coherent and reasoned statement for the rebirth of Zion.

Two alternatives to the Jews' position seemed possible. The Jew of Western Europe saw his solution in assimilation as an equal member of his own society. The idea of a Jewish nation might be repugnant to him, for he regarded Jews as sharing only their religion in common. The Jew of Eastern Europe seized upon the nationalist ideal by which he would mold his own destiny within a Jewish nation dependent upon no one but himself.

The specific form of the Jewish problem which Zionism emerged to resolve was the ghetto life in Russia and Eastern Europe. Zionists therefore championed Jewish nationalism and at the same time rejected the efforts of the western Jew to assimilate within Gentile society, or to be emancipated on Gentile terms.

The founder of the Zionist movement, Theodore Herzl (1860-1904) summed up the aim and motivation of Jewish nationalism in these words: "Let the sovereignty be granted us over a portion of the globe large enough to satisfy the rightful requirements of a nation; the rest we shall manage ourselves."

Herzl, a Hungarian Jew educated in Vienna, was a lawyer by training and a journalist by profession. His impressive face was set off by piercing eyes and a fine nose; a black beard, which tumbled from his cheeks onto his chest, seemed almost to precede him as he walked. In 1891 he was appointed Paris correspondent of the Vienna newspaper, the *Neue Freie Presse*. For some years he had been concerned with the Jewish question and anti-Semitism. In 1894, while covering the famous trial of a Jewish officer of the French Army, Alfred Dreyfus, he was appalled by the overt anti-Semitism which it stirred up. The experience compelled him to compose during the following summer *Der Judenstat* (The Jewish State), the first major formulation of the Zionist thesis.[2]

In one week of feverish, anguished writing Herzl produced his ideas for the Jewish State. Unaware that Pinsker had anticipated him, especially with regard to the concept of the Jewish State, Herzl's own work was nevertheless more detailed and daring than his predecessor's. He was convinced that anti-Semitism anywhere, in any form, was an immutable force which the Jews could learn to use to their own advantage. For the Jewish masses the solution to the Jewish question must be a national one; the Jews as one people must possess their own land as a nation.

Like Pinsker, Herzl was at first vague about the precise global location of the Jewish state. In *Der Judenstat* he mentions both Argentina and Palestine as possible sites. Initially the motivation to a "return to Zion" played only a small role in the minds of early Zionists. They were more strongly imbued with the spirit and concepts of European nationalism of the late nineteenth century than the traditional Jewish ideals of the return from exile to the Holy Land. Zionism was the secularization of the Jewish messianic ideal of the redemption as a confrontation between man and God. Professor A.R. Taylor observes in his *Prelude to Israel* that "in their search for the support of all Jews, the Zionists employed the romantic idea of the 'return', a concept which holds emotional appeal for all Jews. It was thus that Zionism became mistakenly confused with Judaism, but this did not alter the essentially secular character of the Zionist movement."[13] Zionism was the Jewish quest for a kingdom in this world and was viewed as the confrontation between the Jew and the world, specifically the Gentile world. And this world, as Herzl shrewdly perceived, held the keys to that kingdom.

Herzl insisted that the first step toward the attainment of Jewish sovereignty was to secure international recognition of the Jews' right to colonize some "neutral piece of land" which could be developed, without let or hindrance, into the Jewish state. He argued that it would be fruitless to infiltrate immigrants into a particular land, for the process would continue only until "the inevitable moment when the native population feels itself threatened" and protests against further immigration. "Immigration," concluded Herzl, "is consequently futile unless based upon an assured supremacy."

Herzl immediately anticipated and then quickly ignored the one major obstacle confronting the successful creation of the Jewish state. He was aware that this "neutral" land would possess an indigenous population which might oppose the mass immigration of Jews. The potential threat of native resistance would therefore be overcome by an "assured supremacy" guaranteed the Zionists by one or more European powers.

This is the only reference in Herzl's work to a native population; nevertheless, it is important. Herzl was no longer groping with the problem of the Jew and anti-Semite alone. A third party, unobtrusively, had become involved. Herzl pondered the question at the very time he was writing *The Jewish State*. In his diary he observed that should Palestine one day become the Jewish state it would be necessary to spirit the penniless population across the frontier by denying it employment.[4]

This crude response to the "native problem" reflected Herzl's simplistic view of his European environment. "The universality with which Herzl applied his concept of anti-Semitism to all non-Jewish peoples made it impossible from the very beginning for the Zionists to seek truly loyal allies," Dr. Hanna Arendt has written. "His notion of reality as an eternal, unchanging, hostile structure — all *goyim* [Gentiles] everlastingly against all Jews — made the identification of hard-boiledness with realism plausible because it rendered any empirical analysis of actual political factors seemingly superfluous."[5]

Most Zionists after Herzl shared his point of view. Their failure to dispense with, or even alter, this basically irrational proposition was a precipitating factor of conflict when that proposition was applied to the situation in Palestine. If, for example, the Arab were *a priori* part of a hostile environment, then genuine cooperation and understanding between Arab and Jew would become impossible or, at best, exceedingly difficult. Since the Arabs' assumed hostility could not be turned to advantage as anti-Jewish sentiment in Europe could, then the Arab simply had to be excluded. Herzl was not a prophet, but his words were later to be tragically mirrored in certain Zionist activities in Palestine when all Arab labor was excluded from Jewish-owned land and enterprises.

Herzl's greatest contribution to Zionism lay less in his literary output than in the demonic energy he poured into the World Zionist Organization of which he was the founder and first president. In August 1897, he convened a congress of Zionists in Basle, Switzerland. In the intervening years between writing *The Jewish State* and the Basle Congress he had become convinced, largely through his contacts with Jewry in Eastern Europe, that Palestine must become *the* site of the Jewish State. Because of

IMPERIAL FRIENDSHIPS

this the Congress determined the aim of Zionism to be "to create for the Jewish people a home in Palestine secured by public law." The official program was set out in four points:

1) The promotion of Jewish colonization of Palestine by Jewish agricultural and industrial workers;
2) The establishment of an organization to bind world Jewry by means of institutions in each country inhabited by Jews;
3) The strengthening of Jewish national sentiment;
4) The acquisition of government consent to the attainment of Zionist aims.

Herzl had used the word "state," the Congress the word "home" in deference to the objections of many Jews to the idea of a Jewish nation. Herzl expressed himself untroubled by semantics since he assumed devoted Zionists would in any case read "state" for "home."

The rest of Herzl's life was spent trying to obtain his international charter of recognition for the Zionist program. He may have been aware that death was stalking him (he died prematurely in 1904) as he journeyed frantically across Europe to the Middle East cajoling heads of states and empires alike to lend their support. His approaches to German Kaiser Wilhelm II and Sultan Abdul Hamid of Turkey earned him only discreet courtesies from the one, and a decoration (second class) — in some obscure Ottoman order — from the other. After these unsuccessful efforts he entered into negotiations with the British Government.

Herzl had given some thought also to the strategic importance of Palestine in the event that Britain might one day be forced from her occupation of Egypt. In his diary he wrote: "[the English] would then be obliged to seek out another road to India in place of the Suez Canal, which would then be lost to them, or at least rendered insecure. In that event a modern Jewish Palestine would resolve their difficulty."[16]

Palestine was not available for Jewish colonization when Herzl commenced his negotiations with British Foreign Secretary Joseph Chamberlain in 1903, and so he suggested that Cyprus, al-Arish and the Sinai Peninsula be granted to the Zionists. He believed that these areas could be used by the Jewish people as a rallying point in the vicinity of Palestine, which could then, in time, be taken by force.

Chamberlain listened patiently to his guest who must have appeared as a Jewish version of Cecil Rhodes, an imperialist giant whom Herzl greatly admired. Rhodes' own last words in fact would have made a fitting epitaph for Herzl: "So little done, so much to do." Chamberlain, however, was not attracted to the Cyprus plan. Herzl's recollection was that the foreign secretary's office was like a junk shop whose manager was not quite sure whether some unusual article was in the stockroom. "He's going to take a look and see if England happens to have anything in stock for the Jewish people," Herzl thought to himself. Chamberlain rummaged through a stack of papers and picked out a map, the predominant color of which was red, indicating British imperial acquisitions. After a moment's thought he addressed Herzl: "I say, my good fellow, how about Uganda?"

Herzl was by now desperate for any territory and he accepted the idea as a temporary location. The Sixth Zionist Congress of 1903 rejected the scheme out of hand.

Herzl's diplomatic efforts ended in failure. The next year he was dead. His last testament was a fictional account of the future Jewish State which he titled *Altneuland* (Oldnewland). The book described Herzl's vision of a New Society in which Christian, Muslim and Jew would live in personal freedom and tolerance. In one of its passages, a European asks an Arab inhabitant of the new Jewish State why he doesn't consider the Jew an intruder. The Arab replies: "Would you regard those as intruders and robbers who don't take anything from you but give you something? The Jews have enriched us, why should we be angry at them? They live with us like brothers, why should we not love them?"

Time was to prove that reality wore a different mask from Herzl's vision of the future. Many years later, when Britain was committed to the establishment of the Jewish National Home in Palestine, a European reporter asked the Arab mayor of Nablus what he imagined to be the aims of the Zionist movement. "To take Palestine," the mayor answered simply. Part of the tragedy of modern Palestine was that the Arabs grasped the full implication of the Zionist movement even before many Zionists admitted it frankly to themselves.

Where Herzl had failed, another man was to succeed. Chaim Weizmann came to England from Russia in 1904 at the age of thirty convinced that there lay the strongest potential sympathy for the Zionist cause.[17] Weizmann's sole companion during his first days in London was the kindly Jewish tailor with whom he lodged in Sidney Street. He felt alone and insignificant amid the crowds of London's streets and soon took himself to the quieter life of Manchester where he shed the cloak of solitude. Through local Zionist circles and a post as chemist at the university, he made his first real acquaintance with English life. Ultimately he enjoyed an intimacy with many of England's leading figures in politics and journalism. Among them was C.P. Scott, editor of the influential *Manchester Guardian*, who introduced him to David Lloyd George, a member of the cabinet and future prime minister of Great Britain. By 1907 Weizmann was the leading figure in the Zionist movement, devoted to fulfilling Herzl's political work and to encouraging the actual physical occupation of the land of Palestine by Jewish settlers.

Shortly, two other important Zionists, Sokolov and Tshlenov, joined him from the Continent. Their task was to convert British Jewry to Zionism and to cultivate friendship for the Zionist cause among the highest ranks of His Majesty's Government. The Zionist leaders had easy access to the corridors of power in Whitehall and met often with ministers of the Crown and ranking civil servants in the intimacy of their carpeted, book-lined bureaux. In the end their labors were rewarded, although Gentile enthusiasts were to support their program for a variety of motives, some humorously engaging, others devilish in their effect.

Some saw the restoration of the Jew to Palestine as the fulfillment of biblical prophecy; others were moved by a sense of guilt stemming from a subconscious anti-Semitism. Still other Gentile Zionists confused Zionism with liberalism; the Jewish problem demanded a solution and the most just approach may have appeared to be the national or racial one advocated by the Zionists as against the more genuinely liberal view of the assimilationists. In later years there were more sophisticated arguments suggesting that a Zionist presence in the Middle East was "good" for civilization (European), that the Jews would introduce democracy, modern technology to that unstable part of the world, and generally protect European interests, the Suez Canal in particular. After the June War, Israeli, European and American interests became so closely allied that in France the still anti-Semitic fascists could shout *"Vive l'Israël, à bas les Juifs,"* while right-wing American newspapers carried a host of letters on the theme of defending Israel as the "bastion of Americanism and democracy in the Middle East, the only ally we can rely on."

Zionism made little actual headway until the outbreak of World War I in 1914, when Turkey joined the German side against the Allies. British Prime Minister Asquith remarked that the Ottoman Empire had committed suicide and consequently the policy toward Ottoman Turkey and her Arab provinces had to be reevaluated.

Hostile Ottoman forces in Palestine rendered vulnerable the British occupation of Egypt and the security of the Suez Canal. A Turkish attack on the canal in the early months of the war (February 1915) while unsuccessful, confirmed this view. Moreover, Britain was in stiff economic competition with France for a dominant position in Syria. On the eve of war, Britain and France had concluded separate agreements with Germany which effectively partitioned the Ottoman Arab provinces into economic spheres of influence. Britain's aims were twofold: *first*, to prevent the expansion of any rival European influence into the Persian Gulf and Lower Iraq, and *second*, to secure an outlet on the Mediterranean Sea (preferably at Haifa) as a railhead for a line connecting the gulf with the sea. Therefore, either the control or the neutralization of Palestine with a British naval base close to Egypt would provide a buffer zone to protect the Suez Canal and make Britain the supreme naval force in the entire Mediterranean. French financial, religious and national interests, on the other hand, were striving for exclusive control of the whole of Syria, including Palestine.

World War I was a boon to the Zionist cause, Britain and France needed friends and were ready to bargain in order to get them. It so happened that they bargained with the Zionists and the Arabs at the same time, leading both to believe that the European Allies were on their side.

In the meantime, Weizmann had been considering a line of approach to complement British interests. If Britain were to secure a foothold in Palestine and then encourage Jewish settlement there, the Jews could, he wrote in a letter to C.P. Scott, "develop the country, bring back civilization to it and *form a very effective guard for the Suez Canal.*"[181] Later he thought that if Britain did not want to acquire Palestine as a permanent protectorate the Jews should take over the country under temporary British rule.

By the spring of 1916 the British Government began to give serious consideration to official recognition of the Zionist program. Several factors determined their thinking. These were the difficult months of the war, Britain began to sound out her Allies' reactions to the Zionists' aims bearing in mind that a favorable reception might win over the Jewish populations of Eastern Europe and the United States more positively to the Allied side. Other motives were also apparent. Britain had by then abandoned all pretensions of her "hands off Syria" policy of 1912, and now challenged France's determination to secure undivided control of the area. Military considerations also hastened the need to forestall mutual suspicions between the two allies by formally recognizing each other's spheres of influence.

In October 1915 London informed Paris of her efforts to draw the Arabs to the Allied side against Turkey. France was anxious to have a voice in any agreement which might otherwise be used to the detriment of her own interests in Syria. The two governments decided to settle their claims to the Ottoman Arab provinces by dividing Syria (including Lebanon and Palestine) and Iraq into spheres of influence. The details of the partition were worked out by Sir Mark Sykes, the War Office's leading expert on the Middle East and M. Georges-Picot, who had served as French consul in Beirut before the war.

During the bargaining sessions the British negotiator pressed for the inclusion of Palestine in her sphere. After intensive discussions which nearly exhausted the negotiators, it was finally agreed that the area should be placed under an international regime. Britain received the port of Haifa and a vast zone bordering directly upon the proposed internationalized area, considerably increasing her power in the region of southern Syria. The bulk of the Sykes-Picot agreement, concluded in March 1916, related to railway rights in Syria and Iraq, indicating the concern of the two parties to give diplomatic sanction to their economic and strategic interests.

British Prime Minister Lloyd George was unhappy with the proposed internationalization of Palestine, a view shared by the Zionists. It is quite possible that, as Dr. Frischwasser Ra'anan suggests, "the decision to replace international government by British rule over Palestine was the mainspring behind the policy leading to the Balfour Declaration."[9] As sponsor of the Jewish National Home, Britain would be the logical choice as trustee.

By the fall of 1916 the Zionists were ready to present their program to the British Government. In October they submitted a memorandum to the Foreign Office in which specific mention of a future Jewish state was not included, but where the suggested provisions for the existing Jewish community in Palestine and for the Jewish community-to-be would give the Jews a preferential position in the form of a quasi-government under the suzerainty of either Britain or France. A charter company (originally Herzl's idea) would be incorporated possessing vast powers such as the control of immigration, the right of preemption of Crown lands and the acquisition of all or any concessions which the suzerain government might grant them.

Zionists justified these preferential powers on two grounds: *first,* that the Jewish population of Palestine (which at the time was 10 percent of the total) constituted a distinct national unit, and *second,* that the remaining Arab population "being too small, too poor, and too little trained to make rapid progress, requires the introduction of a new and progressive element in the population, desirous of devoting all its energies and capital to the work of colonization on modern lines."[10]

In the Zionist field of vision the Arab never appeared in sharp focus as a human being of flesh and blood, but rather as a blurred and shadowy figure, indistinct and unreal, a political factor of negligible importance. Herzl would have had the Arab population *"spirited* across the frontier." The verb itself is suggestive. They were also regarded as too small (although 90 percent of the total population), too poor and backward to merit attention. The Zionist motto at the time crystallized the attitude: "Give us, a people without a land, a land without people." The Arab peasant in his field or on the hillside and the artisan in his shop simply did not exist.

The claim of privileged rights for the present and future Jewish inhabitants of Palestine was quite natural. If Palestine were decreed empty of inhabitants, then such rights which Jews would enjoy would not be beyond the common advantage of others, there being no others in this case. But if the embarrassing subject of the Arab population were raised, then the privileges could be shown to benefit the entire population, Arab and Jew, by "the introduction of a new and progressive element" into the country.

Such crusading sentiment was common to nineteenth century colonialist propaganda. The French had argued that their occupation of Algeria would open the continent to "culture and civilization" and the Englishman in Egypt was convinced that his mission was to save Egyptian society. In neither case was the Algerian or Egyptian persuaded that these European civilizing missions were worth the price of domination and occupation.

In any event, the narrow nationalistic Zionist viewpoint demanded the application of a double standard of judgment, one for themselves and the other for the Arabs. For example, in the light of the final formula of the Balfour Declaration, it is interesting to note the distinction which the Zionists drew between Jewish and Arab rights in Palestine. According to their memorandum all inhabitants "regardless of denomination, religion or nationality" should be guaranteed equality of "civic rights" while the Jewish population should enjoy "civic, *political,* and community rights." No Zionist proposal ever mentioned political rights pertaining to the Arabs. The same omission was made in the Balfour Declaration. Zionists protested that such rights for the Arabs were taken for granted. If so, why not take them for granted in their own case? But a more fundamental question is: should political rights ever be taken for granted?

The attitudes of prominent Zionists merely underlined the point. In one of the frequent informal meetings between British officials and Zionists, Sir Mark Sykes interviewed the Jewish leaders on the details of their program. He raised the possibility of an Arab challenge to the Zionist claims. Weizmann retorted that "the Jews are returning to Palestine for the purpose of re-creating the Jewish nation and of remaining Jews in the complete sense, and not to be turned into Arabs, Druze or even Englishmen."[11] Weizmann's remark was clarified by the observation he made at about the same time to the effect that the Zionist movement was similar to the French colonial enterprise in Tunisia. "What the French could do in Tunisia," he said, "the Jews would do in Palestine with Jewish will, Jewish money, Jewish power and Jewish enthusiasm."[12]

The French colonial regimes in North Africa (and the attitudes of the French *colons*) were, however, not noted for generous consideration of the local Arab population.

At that same informal gathering of British civil servants and Zionists, Sykes suggested that Sokolov meet with M. Georges-Picot, the French diplomat, to secure his country's support for their program. Georges-Picot also raised the question of Jewish relations with the Arabs, and Sokolov replied that "no serious opposition would be encountered from the Arabs because they had never regarded Palestine as an important center, particularly in light of the fact that an Arab dominion was to be set up elsewhere."[13]

On the assumption that Arabs considered Palestine relatively unimportant, the winds of change were blowing favorably for the Zionists and all seemed well, save for one element of opposition which, if not unexpected, was at least untimely. It was becoming evident in anti-Zionist Jewish circles that the British Government was about ready to declare some sort of open support for the Zionists. This provoked a protest from D.L. Alexander and Claude Montefiore, respectively president of the Board of Deputies of British Jews and president of the Anglo-Jewish Association. In the name of their Conjoint Committee a manifesto of protest appeared in the London *Times,* May 24, 1917. They attacked the political theories of Zionism as a threat to the religious basis of Judaism because a secular Jewish nationality based on some obscure principle of race or ethnic peculiarity "would not be Jewish in any spiritual sense."

Moreover, the Zionist demands for certain special rights in Palestine which the Arabs would not enjoy was contrary to the principle of equal rights for all religious denominations which Jews in Europe and North America claimed as vital for themselves. If Zionists were to disregard this principle in Palestine, Jews the world over would be convicted of having appealed to it "for purely selfish motives."

The letter ended with the prophetic words that the Zionist scheme was the more inadmissible because it would involve them "in the bitterest feuds with their neighbors of other races and religions," and would "find deplorable echoes throughout the Orient." As a foretaste of the conflict ahead in Palestine, these words had a strange harmony with later Arab warnings. Similar protests were heard from anti-Zionist Jews and non-Jews alike in France and Italy; but their governments too were now virtually committed to the Zionist cause.

The Zionists next got down to the business of drafting their own formula for the declaration. Every word was carefully scrutinized and each phrase weighed for the correct shade of meaning. Possibly no document in diplomatic history has been subjected to such minute attention. After three separate efforts one formula was chosen which covered the essential ground and dealt with the main proposals presented in their memorandum.

The formula was presented to His Majesty's Government on July 8, 1917. It called upon the government to recognize the whole of Palestine as the national home of the Jewish people; the area east of the Jordan River, Transjordan as it was known, was implied in the request. With regard to the Zionists' privileged position in Palestine, the government was to grant "internal autonomy to the Jewish nationality in Palestine, freedom of immigration for Jews, and the establishment of a Jewish National Colonizing Corporation for the resettlement and economic development of the country." While the term "national home" was used instead of "state," the two had become virtually interchangeable. Jewish sovereignty over Palestine was the Zionists' ultimate goal, as Weizmann spelled out to a special congress of the English Federation of Zionists in May of the same year.

Within the cabinet the Zionists could count on the firm

support of Prime Minister Lloyd George, Foreign Secretary Lord Balfour, and Lords Milner and Cecil. The most incisive criticism came from the only Jew in the cabinet, Sir Edwin Montagu, who was the secretary of state for India. Sir Edwin was the son of Samuel Montagu, a devout and active Orthodox Jew and the founder of one of London's most important private banks. The younger Montagu's only nationalism was English, and he felt that loyalty to another nationalist cause was tantamount to treason to his native land. His opposition ran along the lines of the Conjoint Committee's protest. If a Jewish national home were created, he asked, how could he negotiate with "the peoples of India on behalf of His Majesty's Government if the world had just been told that His Majesty's Government regarded his national home as being in Turkish territory?" Zionists held him largely responsible for the failure of their draft being accepted substantially as it was. Weizmann, in fact, expressed his bewilderment at the attention the British Government gave to a "handful of assimilated Jews."

The Zionist draft was consequently modified by a cabinet committee. Like the original, the amended draft made no mention of the Arab population, but the crucial phrase "National Home" was retained. In the final version the Arabs were alluded to as "the existing non-Jewish communities," and the only safeguards they were given pertained to their civil and religious rights. A leading Zionist, Jacob de Haas, who had a hand in drafting the declaration, later admitted that the phrase "political rights" was deliberately omitted to distinguish Jewish "rights" from Arab "claims." Since the Arabs had not been consulted on the matter, they were in effect being told what "claims" they were entitled to and, by omission, what "rights" they would not receive.[14]

The final version was dispatched by the cabinet to Washington to be worked over by Zionists there, and then submitted to President Wilson for his approval. Only slightly revised, the formula was returned to London and was issued by the war cabinet. It was contained in a letter from Lord Balfour to Lord Walter Rothschild on November 2, 1917:

His Majesty's Government view with favor the establishment

in Palestine of a national home for the Jewish people, and will use their best endeavors to facilitate the achievement of this object, it being clearly understood that nothing shall be done which may prejudice the civil and religious rights of the existing non-Jewish communities in Palestine, or the rights and political status enjoyed by Jews in any other country.

The Balfour Declaration, as it became known, was the product of many hands, minds and months of labor. Despite Zionist participation in its composition, some were less than satisfied. Weizmann records that he was disappointed in the final emasculated version. The original Zionist formula had said that *all* of Palestine should be made the Jewish National Home. In Balfour's version the phrase read "the establishment *in* Palestine" of the national home, meaning *in part* of Palestine. Weizmann's second objection was that the final version "introduced the subject of 'the civil religious rights of the existing non-Jewish communities' in such a fashion as to impute possible oppressive intentions to the Jews, and can be interpreted to mean such limitations on our work as completely to cripple it."[15] The point was, of course, that it should have been unnecessary even to mention the rights of the indigenous population. Preoccupied as they were with obtaining sufficient conditions for the national home, Zionists like Weizmann never seriously considered whether the problem they were attempting to solve would necessarily raise other problems — such as how to deal with the inhabitants of Palestine — which demanded immediate, if only tentative, solutions.

There was instead an awareness of realities, the implications of the declaration being understood by its authors which made a verbal sleight-of-hand politically expedient. Arthur Balfour clearly wanted to see a Jewish state established.

Balfour, the earnest politician, had first been introduced to Zionism during the 1906 general election when he stood as the Conservative candidate in the Clayton division of North Manchester. Charles Dreyfus, a leading industrialist and chairman of both the Manchester Conservative Committee and the local Zionist Society, introduced Chaim Weizmann to Balfour in the course of the campaign. Balfour listened with patient interest to Weizmann's argument, delivered in a difficult and heavy accent. Nevertheless his eloquent and impassioned narrative of the historic longing of the Jews to rebuild their life in Palestine touched the philosopher in Balfour. The two men did not meet again until the beginning of the war, when Balfour, then First Lord of the Admiralty, greeted Weizmann warmly, saying: "You know, I believe that when the guns stop firing you may get your Jerusalem."

However, Balfour, the pragmatic statesman, was aware that the Zionist goal might be made more difficult if precise terminology was employed or if the eventuality of a Jewish state was prematurely discussed in public.[16] Hence the retention of the vague term "Jewish national home" in the declaration. If the Jewish State were the ultimate intention, what then of the promised safeguards of Arab rights? Again, Arthur Balfour was not unmindful of the possible repercussions of a premeditated policy of support for Zionist pretentions in Palestine. In a memorandum written in August 1919, Balfour stated that the Arabs of Palestine would not be consulted concerning their future. "The four Great Powers," he wrote, "are committed to Zionism, and Zionism, be it right or wrong, good or bad, is rooted in age-long tradition, in present needs and future hopes of far profounder import than the desires and prejudices of the 700,000 Arabs who now inhabit that ancient land."[17]

2

Palestine: The Waste Land?

Palestine in history was the fertile bridge between Asia and Africa, the crossroads of three continents and the land of three faiths. The natural endowments of the land, its geographical position and its religious associations attracted many peoples and invaders from the ancient Hebrews, through the Greeks and Romans, the Byzantines, Persians and finally the Arabs.

From the middle of the seventh century Palestine belonged to the Islamic world, at first by the simple act of conquest, and then by degrees, as Islam, the vital cultural force and Arabic, the language of Islamic religious and secular literature, were woven into the fabric of the everyday life of the people.

In the brief space of four years the Muslim armies swept out of their desert fortress in Arabia and overran Iraq, Syria and Palestine. The imperial armies of Byzantium in the west and of Persia in the east, weakened by their own bloody struggle for supremacy in the area, crumbled before the onslaught. Palestine fell before a two-pronged thrust. Amr ibn al-As, one of the most valiant warriors and eminent political figures of early Islam, attacked Palestine from the south via Aqaba and Gaza. Pressing northward after two swift victories against Byzantine forces, he suddenly encountered stiff resistance from the enemy. Amr was in desperate straits until assistance miraculously appeared from an unexpected quarter. The most formidable Arab general of the day, Khalid ibn al-Walid, had been chasing Persians up the Euphrates valley and out of Iraq when he heard of Amr's plight. He force-marched his troops across one thousand trackless, blistering miles of the Syrian desert, joined up with Amr near Jerusalem and routed a vastly superior Byzantine Army. A new chapter in Palestine's long history was about to begin.

Islam and the empire spread rapidly westward across north Africa from Egypt to Morocco, into Spain and eastward beyond Persia into the depths of Central Asia. In this mighty arch of empire, Palestine seemed an insignificant keystone, although it formed the important land bridge between the eastern and western halves.

In a richer, and deeper sense too, this ancient land became part of the Islamic world. After Mecca, the birthplace of the Prophet Muhammad, and Medina his second home, Jerusalem is regarded as the third holiest city in Islam. It is said that one night the angel Gabriel appeared before Muhammad with a white mare and ordered him to mount and follow. The Prophet's nocturnal ride took him to Jerusalem where, on the site of the rock believed to be part of the ruins of Solomon's Temple, he was raised into heaven. In 691 A.D. the Caliph Abd al-Malik erected a cupola over this spot. Known as the Dome of the Rock, this building remains today the finest piece of architecture in the Old City. The sanctity of Jerusalem is well expressed in the tradition related by Ka'b ibn Ahbar, an early Jewish convert to Islam, that each night 70,000 angels descend from heaven to intercede for the pardon of those who have come to the Holy City to pray. It was this same Ka'b who suggested that a mosque be built on the site of the ancient Temple of Solomon.

The Christian and Jewish populations lived in peace with their Muslim rulers. As possessors of their own divinely revealed scriptures, they were respected as People of the Book. They enjoyed certain privileges as protected minorities, although they were also obliged to pay special taxes. Many converted to Islam and over the centuries slowly became Arabized. Palestine enjoyed its claim to be the land of three faiths. Ironically, the two bitterest periods of enmity which Palestine has witnessed came about as the result of European intrusion. The first was during the Crusades when Jews were massacred in Jerusalem and Tiberias by the invading Christian armies. Jews and Muslims were brothers-in-exile until the Crusaders were finally driven from the Middle East. The second occasion came after World War I when Christian and Muslim Arabs of Palestine allied in their struggle against the British Mandate and its policy of a Jewish National Home. Today the Arab struggle against Israel is seen by the Arabs as a fight to liberate a part of their homeland from foreign occupation.

At the dawning of the nineteenth century Palestine was, as it had been for centuries, Arab in character, an integral part socially, economically and politically of the Fertile Crescent which included Syria, Lebanon and Iraq. At that time the Fertile Crescent as a whole comprised several provinces of the Ottoman Empire. The administrative divisions of Palestine, for example, reflected the political integration. West of the Jordan River, the northern half of Palestine was part of the Vilayet of Beirut; the southern half was known as the Sanjak of Jerusalem and was governed directly from Constantinople (the Istanbul of modern Turkey). The area east of the Jordan was part of the Vilayet of Damascus. Palestine, in fact, was regarded by the Arabs as southern Syria.

The country's main source of wealth was the fertile land which supported a peasantry engaged in the traditional methods of cultivation. A fertile coastal plain, varying in width, stretched from Gaza in the south to Acre in the north. There the belt of green described a gentle curve from the Plain of Acre to the Plain of Esdraelon resting between the Carmel range of mountains and the Galilean hills to the Vale of Jezreel which approached the Jordan River south of Lake Tiberias.

There are no glossy colored photographs of Palestine dating from the early nineteenth century. Fortunately, however, the English produced men and women who were not content with the beauties of their own sceptered isle. Lady Hester Stanhope, a remarkable Englishwoman who gratified a lust for adventure with a life of travel, visited Palestine in 1810. In her diary she recorded the variety of plain and mountain, hill and valley, river and lake which the country presented to her admiring eye. "The luxuriance of vegetation is not to be described," she wrote. "Fruits of all sorts from the banana down to the blackberry are abundant. The banks of the rivers are clothed naturally with oleander and flowering shrubs."

Laurence Oliphant wrote in 1883 that the Plain of Esdraelon, where a Beirut family had large holdings, "is at this moment in a high state of cultivation. It looks today like a huge green lake of waving wheat, with its village-crowned mounds rising from it like islands and it presents one of the most striking pictures of luxurious fertility which it is possible to conceive." The terraced cultivation of Judea moved John Brinton to exclaim in 1891: "Here is one more among the thousand proofs of the ancient prosperity of the land." The words of an anonymous scribe are preserved in the Bible: Palestine in ancient times was a land "flowing with milk and honey," a phrase which has become symbolic for abundance and plenty. In more precise language Lady Stanhope described the Arab orchards near Jaffa as containing "lemon, orange, almond, peach, apple, pomegranate and other trees." These were the milk and honey of the inhabitants.

But Palestine presented another aspect. The Jordan River might be bordered with oleander and flowering shrubs, but the hills which rose on either side of the valley were stark, barren and inhospitable to man or beast. South of the Judean Plateau the Negev Desert ran as far as the eye could see and lost itself in the empty wastes of Sinai. Apart from a small nomadic population, the desert supported no permanent settlements. Only in recent times have modern men and machines dared to tame this natural wilderness.

The peasant worked the land by traditional means, the hand hoe and bullock-drawn plow, and in normal times his labors yielded a harvest of plenty. Some years there was want, for a plague of locusts could bring destruction to a field of wheat more swifty than invasion by enemy infantry. Through times of plenty and want the peasant lived by the simple ethic that he would take from the soil what God had given him, and give to others from what he had. By 1900 the picture had changed very little, although a few citrus growers had begun to import motorized pumps to irrigate their orchards. The products of the land, the citrus fruits and the cereal grains were shipped to all parts of Syria. The famous olive oil soap of Nablus and Jaffa, which was used for ritual purposes, also reached wide markets in the Muslim Near East. Other home industries operated, but on a much smaller scale. Clothing, carpets and rugs were made by workers in their homes or in small workshops in the towns. Silk worms were cultivated at Acre. Objects of piety carved from olive wood or made from imported mother-of-pearl were to be found in the artisan shops of Jerusalem. Wine was produced in Christian monasteries and in Jewish settlements established by Baron Edmund Rothschild at the end of the last century. For the modest needs of the times, Palestine was remarkably self-sufficient.

Although the country was overwhelmingly rural in character, the urban population comprised members of the landowning class, the religious hierarchies, professional people, artisans, trade merchants and shopkeepers. The educated were few. Christians enjoyed the facilities of European mission schools, but for their higher education they would travel to Beirut to attend either the American Protestant College or the French Collège Saint-Joseph. Muslims pursued higher learning mainly in the traditional Islamic sciences of theology, philosophy, language and literature at either the metropolis of Constantinople or at the famous 900-year-old University of al-Azhar in Cairo. The vast majority of the population was Muslim, while important concentrations of Arab Christians lived in Jerusalem, Nazareth and Bethlehem. Arab Jews resided in Jerusalem, Safad and Tiberias.

At the outbreak of World War I Palestinians were neither a separate people nor a nation. As Arabs and subjects of the Ottoman sultan they did exist *in* Palestine, the land which was their home and where their forefathers had for centuries past lived and left their graves.

Palestine was neither desolate nor uninhabited.

Even Balfour was to admit that Palestinians had their "desires and prejudices," many of which they shared with their fellow Arabs in Syria, Lebanon, Iraq and Egypt. The Arabs' view of the world and the part they sought to play in it were products of a historical situation molded in the previous century both by forces within the Arab community and by the broader cultural encounter with the West. These factors conditioned the Arabs' reaction to post-war developments and to Zionist aims.

By the middle of the eighteenth century the Ottoman Empire, which included the Arab provinces in Egypt and the Fertile Crescent, had begun its decline. The weakening of the military, economic and moral fibers of the empire was occasioned by the rapid technological advances being made in various European countries which were then able to increase their diplomatic and commercial influence at Constantinople. At the same time, the weakening of the central authority meant that Constantinople could no longer command the undivided loyalty of its citizens, nor act as the main focus of solidarity.

Local forces in the Fertile Crescent began to assert their autonomy, although nominally acting in the sultan's interests. Moreover, Ottoman Christians began to cultivate an interest in their own Christian and Arab heritage. While these movements struck at the traditional principles of solidarity of the empire, the Arab provinces themselves remained completely isolated from the ferment of new ideas. They were oblivious to any threat of rising European power and secure in a complacent belief in the superiority of their own inner, yet static, resources.

This atmosphere of blissful complacency was rudely shattered by the sudden and unexpected invasion of Egypt by Napoleon in 1798, and his abortive attack on Palestine in the following year. By this act Napoleon unleashed a tidal wave of new ideas — military, political and socio-economic — on traditional Mediterranean life. He gave birth to what one writer has called the "Arab rediscovery of Europe." From the time of the French invasion to the decade of the eighteen-seventies the Arab world was uprooted from its isolation, and embroiled in European cultural and political rivalries.

In Egypt Muhammad Ali made the initial response to the European presence, aiming to build a viable state patterned along current western models. Small missions of students were sent to Europe to study the new techniques. Schools of engineering, medicine, pharmaceutics, minerology and agriculture were founded. A school of translation was entrusted with the task of providing Arabic versions of (largely) French and Italian "textbooks." Western ideas filtered into Arab society through channels opened by Muhammad Ali. An Arab image of the Western world began to take concrete form.

Of no less importance in this process of acculturation was the effect of the narratives of Arab travelers to Europe who described and attempted to interpret western society for Arab readers. These impressions of European social and political institutions gradually became a part of the mainstream of Arab cultural awareness. The principle of constitutionalism, or the rule of law as against the rule of the autocrat, captured their attention as it embodied the concepts of justice, equality and freedom. Admiration was also expressed for various welfare, economic and cultural institutions such as hospitals, corporations, libraries and museums, associations which were organized on the initiative of private individuals or groups.

The organizational basis of European society was emphasized in all of the travelers' accounts, and to it they attributed the success of European society. It was believed that Arabs could achieve similar success by adopting western patterns of organization and the superiority of European technology and organization was openly acknowledged. On the other hand, some of them expressed a natural defensiveness because they did not concede the *inherent* superiority of all facets of western culture. Rather, they urged the adoption of what was genuinely strong in order to recapture the earlier moment of the Islamic world's greatness.

By 1870 a generally favorable and comprehensive image of the Western world had been transmitted to the Arab world, for the most part by devout Muslims such as Rifa'a Tahtawi of Egypt and Khayr ad-Din of Tunisia. Christians too, particularly in the Fertile Crescent, were contributing significantly to the Arab awakening. That area of Turkish rule had been opened up to western missionaries and commercial enterprises during the decade of the eighteen-thirties under the enlightened rule of Muhammad Ali's son Ibrahim Pasha.

French and American mission schools were established alongside government-financed institutions. The new wave of learning produced some men of outstanding literary talent who dedicated themselves to the revival of the humanistic spirit in Arabic literature and language. Butrus Bustani compiled a two-volume Arabic dictionary and completed six volumes of an encyclopedia which was continued by other members of his family after his death. Mar'un an-Naqqash, who was influenced by the Italian theater, wrote and produced the first Arabic play and thus introduced a new art form into Arabic literature. The first political novel in Arabic was written by Francis Marrash on the themes of liberty, equality and social justice.

Finally, the historical novels of Jurji Zaydan recalled the romance of the Arab past in the manner of Sir Walter Scott in his Waverley novels. Muslims were late in joining this new movement of self-expression and it was not until 1857 that Muslims first associated with Christians in the Syrian Scientific Society which was founded in that year.

The climate of revival and awakening in the Arab world was accompanied by an intensified European interest in its political developments. Britain, for example, played a leading role in driving Ibrahim Pasha from Syria in 1840. Fourteen years later the Crimean War was fought partly to decide the conflicting interests of Britain, France and Russia in the area. Again in 1860, civil disturbances in Lebanon brought about European intervention and the occupation of the country by French troops. The opening of the Suez Canal in 1869 suddenly provided easy access to European imperial domains in the Far East and served to embroil the entire Mediterranean seaboard in the arena of European politico-economic rivalry. Indeed, Britain finally occupied Egypt in 1882, ostensibly to safeguard her own and French financial interests. In 1899 the Sudan was also occupied by Britain. The French seized what they could of the North African coast – Tunisia in 1881, Libya and Morocco in 1912.

Events after 1870 seemed to accelerate. The spirit of Arab renaissance, Arab awareness of a New World and the tightening grip of western influence combined to complicate the problems of Ottoman Sultan Abdul Hamid. The empire was threatened, at least potentially, from within should the Arab revival assume a more political and anti-Turkish direction. From without, the empire was definitely threatened by ever increasing European pressures.

The sultan's Arab subjects were confronted with their own dilemma. Between 1870 and the outbreak of war in 1914, Syria was pregnant with various shades of nationalist sentiment. Christians tended to identify with the idea of an independent and greater Syria in which all citizens of the Arab nation shared a common cultural bond irrespective of inherited religious beliefs. Muslims were equally conscious of their Arab heritage, but they were hesitant to sever their religious ties with the sultan and the empire. The Young Turk revolution against Abdul Hamid in 1908 raised their hopes that equal rights for all Arabs, whether Christian or Muslim, could be secured within a decentralized empire. But when the Young Turks themselves retreated into a narrow racist pan-Turkism they unwittingly reinforced the Arabs' consciousness of their own identity.

Secret political societies were formed in which Palestinians played a role. For these activities some of them were later executed by the Turks. The aim of these groups was complete independence. Their call went out to all Arabs — Muslim, Christian and Jew — to unite and break away from Ottoman control. Still the tension of loyalties remained. Would the focus of solidarity be the Turkish Empire or the Arab Nation, Islam or Arabism? The final and decisive step was not taken until 1918 when, as British Prime Minister Asquith had foreseen at the beginning of the war, the Ottoman Empire committed suicide. There was, by then, no alternative to nationalism. With the empire gone the problem of Turkey was replaced by the problem of European imperialism.

The "Arab rediscovery of Europe" opened new vistas to Arab imagination, new visions for the future. Arab society, adopting the organizational patterns of the European nations, could achieve similar successes. This was the vision. But the contact with Europe had brought another and altogether undesirable circumstance: domination and occupation. All of North Africa had fallen under European control, and France and Britain were keenly competing for the rest of the Arab world, particularly the Fertile Crescent.

The wartime generation of Arabs was alive to the dangers of further European encroachment. They had been deeply influenced by the ideas and career of the revolutionary activist and religious thinker, Jamal ad-Din al-Afghani (1838-1897).

Al-Afghani had a passionate spirit and was a fiery orator. His energies were phenomenal. He had been involved in the politics of Afghanistan, studied among Indian Muslims and was the founder and leader of a secret society of young Egyptians who were discontented with the growing European influence over their country. When he was expelled for these activities, he moved to Paris where he edited a newspaper calling for resistance to the European presence in the Middle East. From Paris he traveled to Russia and England, ending his days in Constantinople as a forced "guest" of the sultan. Al-Afghani's theme was the same wherever he went: Muslim peoples had allowed themselves to be ruled by reactionary autocrats whose misgovernment made them prey to the unbridled ambitions of the European powers. He attributed the deplorable weakness of the Muslim world to the loss of religious solidarity which had once led them to embrace half the world. But solidarity could also be embedded in the national language, the means of transmitting the Arab national heritage. Religious solidarity was, in fact, national solidarity and vice versa. Al-Afghani's appeal went out to all, from the intellectual to the humblest peasant. To the latter he cried: "Wretched peasant, you break the heart of the earth to feed yourself and your family. Why do you not break the heart of your oppressor who eats the fruit of your labor?"

Al-Afghani had struck the one chord in harmony with the deepest aspiration of all Arabs: to recapture and reconstruct their national independence — their freedom from Turkish and European control. For many Arabs the war opened the door of promise and fulfillment. The result was an unlocked Pandora's box.

3

A Game of Nations

At one point in her journey through Wonderland, Alice joins the Hatter, the March Hare and the Doormouse for tea. It was a Mad Tea Party. Alice was offended by the scatter-brained behavior of her hosts. Conversation always seemed to run in circles. "Why don't you say what you mean?" the March Hare asked.

"I do," Alice hastily replied. "At least — at least I mean what I say — that's the same thing you know."

"Not the same a bit!" said the Hatter. "Why you might just as well say that 'I see what I eat' is the same thing as 'I eat what I see'."

In the innocent world of fantasy the consequences of a character's actions are only as serious as the author's imagination permits. In the arena of international politics the failure to say what you mean might be construed as deceit; the failure to mean what you say might be interpreted as hypocrisy. The repercussions of either could be momentous. For Palestine they were tragic.

During the First World War, Britain and the Arabs reached an understanding on their respective wartime aims. The understanding was contained in an exchange of diplomatic notes between Sir Henry McMahon, the British high commissioner in Egypt, and Sherif Hussein ibn Ali, the paramount leader in the Arabian peninsula who controlled the Hijaz and the holy places of Mecca and Medina. McMahon expressed his government's sympathy with "the aspirations of her friends the Arabs," and its desire to see "the liberation of the Arab peoples from the Turkish yoke." Hussein stressed the determination of the Arab nation "to assert its right to live, gain its freedom and administer its own affairs in name and in fact."

As a result of reports reaching London of anti-Turkish unrest in Syria, the British Government was anxious to draw the support of "the Arab nation" to the Allied side. Once Turkey had joined the Germans, Arab support became imperative, even if only passively given. The ideals of Arab liberation and independence were therefore necessarily linked in the British view with the practical objective of destroying Turkey. After some hesitation Sherif Hussein raised a revolt against the Turk in the Arabian peninsula. Regardless of the value attached to Arab cooperation with the Allies during the war, when that conflict ended the belief was widespread among all Arabs that they were about to realize their dream of liberation.

It was during this period that a slightly built, blue-eyed Englishman stepped into the pages of history immortalized by his own brilliant prose and the eulogies of his biographers. The man was Thomas Edward Lawrence, the "Lawrence of Arabia" of fact and fancy. A complex creature, Lawrence was a competent linguist and scholar, an expert on crusader fortifications, an errant soldier and adventurer, and an arrogant romantic. Lawrence is best remembered for what he wished to be remembered: his daring exploits during the Arab revolt of 1916, the story of which he recounts with passionate vividness in his *Seven Pillars of Wisdom*. During the post-war peace negotiations in London and Paris, he was the constant companion of his comrade-in-arms Prince Faysal, King Hussein's son. Faysal's sole contact with the bewildering world of international political maneuvering was through Lawrence, his interpreter. Although he was mentor and confidant to a man who had come to seek independence for his people, Lawrence was not the anti-colonialist which his more fervent admirers, like Lowell Thomas, have wished to make of him. He believed deeply in the greatness of England and empire and held what were, at best, uncharitable opinions of "native" peoples. He was also the francophobe who had once declared that if the Arab revolt were successful, England could "biff the French out of all hope in Syria." Lawrence died only to triumph over obscurity through the labors of his publicists. His effect on the course of actual events in the Middle East was negligible.

By 1918 the relationship between the Arabs and the Allies

had changed. Britain and France concluded their secret pact, the Sykes-Picot agreement of 1916, which, by dividing the Fertile Crescent into spheres of European influence, set the Allies' aims completely at odds with Arab aspirations. The goals of Britain and France did not stem from sudden inspiration, but from the pre-war rivalry of the two nations in which the Middle East assumed an ever increasing importance. The Arab leaders, although suspicious of Allied intentions, failed to comprehend the competitive and expansionist significance of the interests of France and Britain in their lands. The destruction of Turkey, and with it the Ottoman Empire, suited western imperialist interests better than the Arabs' desires for independence.

The diplomatic partition of the Arab East gave way to a military partition which became effective in the last years of the war. Between December 1916 and December 1917, el-Arish, Rafa, Beersheba and Jerusalem were occupied by British forces under General Allenby. A second British expedition had overrun the Turkish position in Iraq. By October 1918, Damascus had fallen and the rout of the Turk was almost complete. Palestine was placed under British military rule and Lebanon under the French. The interior of Syria remained under Arab control for two more years by which time the French had occupied Damascus by force.

The Allies kept up the façade of sympathy for Arab aspirations. A temporary embarrassment was caused by the Russian Revolution. In 1917 the Bolsheviks disclosed the details of the Sykes-Picot agreement (to which czarist Russia had been a party) from documents unearthed in the Russian Foreign Office. Hussein promptly demanded an explanation from British officials concerning the alleged division of Syria and Iraq. Early in February 1918, he received a note from the acting British agent in Jedda, J.R. Bassett, who stressed his government's pledge "to stand steadfastly by the Arabs," who were struggling for "liberation" and "unity." Reginald Wingate, McMahon's successor in Cairo, assured Hussein that the Sykes-Picot agreement was not a treaty but only "a record of old conversations and provisional understandings." Hussein remained unconvinced by these vague, not to say mendacious, replies.

The British Government further clarified its position in June

1918, in a reply to a petition presented by seven leading Syrians. Britain's declaration made two points.

First, the future regimes in those areas liberated and occupied by the Allied armies would be "based upon the principle of the consent of the governed." At the time of this declaration the liberated and occupied areas included the southern half of Palestine up to a line running from Jaffa to Jerusalem. The principle of consent of the governed was an important advance on previous declarations since it implied some method of canvassing the peoples' opinion on their political future and then basing the form of government on that expressed view.

Second, the declaration stated that His Majesty's Government was committed to securing the freedom and independence of all other territory still under Turkish control.

These pledges and declarations collectively should have put all Arab apprehensions to rest. But disturbing questions continued to torment the minds of Arab leaders. Would the principle of the consent of the governed be applied to areas not yet "liberated," such as the northern half of Palestine and the rest of the Fertile Crescent? Did "freedom" mean only freedom from Turkish rule, or freedom from all foreign rule? Was "independence" consistent with the rumored establishment of European spheres of influence?

Finally, in an effort to dispel the growing atmosphere of suspicion and disquiet, Britain and France issued a joint declaration on November 7, 1918. The principle of the consent of the governed was reiterated, and the declaration went on to say that "far from wishing to impose this or that system upon the population of those regions, their (France's and Britain's) only concern is to offer such support and efficacious help as will ensure the smooth working of the governments and administrations which those populations will have elected of their own free will."

This was the last wartime pledge made by the Allies to the Arabs. From the McMahon-Hussein correspondence to the Anglo-French declaration, words such as freedom, independence, self-determination were used with an apparent air of sincerity. They were ideals which many Arabs had come to believe reflected what was best in European society. The Arab travelers to Europe during the nineteenth century had never wearied of praising European attitudes toward the rule of law embodying concepts of justice, equality and freedom. There was, therefore, a predisposition or attraction to aspects of western culture. At the same time Arabs could not but evince feelings of loyalty to the familiar and tested values of their own culture and express conviction in the validity of their own heritage. This produced an essentially ambivalent attitude toward the West which revealed the Arabs' lack of self-confidence and an awareness of their weakness in the face of the material superiority of European power.

It would have been difficult enough for some measure of understanding and respect to have been created between the Arabs and the West after the war. But Britain and France could not, or at least did not, give of their best to the Arab peoples. Liberalism was decaying in Europe. Although "Christian" nations, both Britain and France were also giants of empire and of modern technological societies. Hard work and technology had made these nations successful and success implied to Europeans a moral superiority, a morality which was protected by a superior religion. Moreover, Zionism and European civilization had a common denominator, the association with the Old Testament out of which evolved the concept of a Judeo-Christian heritage. Jews had also been active participants in creating the superior civilization which the Europeans claimed for themselves.

On all counts the Arabs were, in their eyes, wholly outside the "civilized" world. Moreover, the inherited prejudices against Islam, both as a culture and a religion, seemed to justify the application of a double standard of judgment. Progressive society abhors the vacuum created by static society, and despite the Arabs' acceptance of the principle of progress, their resistance to assimilation would not be tolerated by the dominating European power. The European could admit the legitimacy of the Arabs' struggle for independence and freedom, but would not concede that they should shoulder the responsibility for freedom gained.

The wartime ideals were substituted for the baser currency of the concept of "a sacred trust of civilization," to quote the phrase from the Covenant of the League of Nations. The Paris Peace Conference approved the Covenant (April 1919) which had piously asserted that it was the "sacred trust of civilization" to assume responsibility for the "well-being and development... of peoples not yet able to stand by themselves under the strenuous conditions of the modern world." The instruments of this sacred mission, a euphemism for imperial ambitions, were the mandates established in the name of the League by Britain in Iraq and Palestine and by France in Syria and Lebanon. The Covenant had stated that the Arab provinces of the defunct Ottoman Empire were provisionally recognized as independent, subject only "to the rendering of administrative advice and assistance by a mandatory." The wishes of the Arabs themselves had to be a "principal consideration" in the selection of the mandatory power.

Arab opinion, however, was known to be almost unanimously for absolute independence and against the separation of Palestine from the rest of Syria. This meant an unqualified rejection of the Zionist program which Britain was sponsoring. Nevertheless, without reference to the finer sentiments of the Covenant, the mandates were imposed on the Arab East. At the same time, the least advanced region of the Arab world, the Arabian peninsula, was judged by civilization fit for the rigors of modern life and was not assigned to the supervision of a mandate.

Professor Hourani of Oxford has observed that from the creation of the mandate system in the Middle East "there sprang a new moral relationship between the West and the Arab peoples..." Each of the regimes set up by Britain and France shared certain characteristics: they were imposed and maintained by force against the expressed opposition of politically articulate sections of the Arab population. Moreover, the rights and aspirations of the subject peoples were never the primary concern of the controlling powers, despite eloquent declarations from London and Paris to the contrary. "It is this imposition of an alien rule upon an unwilling people which is called 'imperialism'... the essence of imperialism is to be found in a moral relationship — that of power and powerlessness — and any material consequences which spring from it are not enough to change it."[11]

It was in Palestine that the mandate system inflicted the deepest wounds and left a legacy of enduring bitterness and enmity. Britain had virtually declared Palestine a political *tabula rasa;* the Zionists called Palestine a land without a people, which amounted to the same thing. British military authorities in Jerusalem had been informed confidentially by London that the Anglo-French Declaration, which had been issued in Jerusalem, was not to be applied to Palestine. Lord Balfour had said privately that "in the case of Palestine we deliberately and rightly decline to accept the principle of self-determination." Palestine was to be molded, fashioned, hammered into any shape desired; the Palestinians counted for nothing.

The tactics of legal argumentation, adopted by Palestinian leaders at the time to demonstrate that the wartime pledges included their people as well, served only to underline the actual weakness of their position. Foreign troops occupied the country and the military administration was in effective control. Britain and the Zionists viewed Palestine through the spectacles of the imperialist and the colonialist, and by doing so invited the inevitable consequence — violence. The Arab of Palestine would, sooner or later, be forced to the violent self-assertion that he was *something,* if only to prove it to himself. He would demand recognition that he was not a "non-Jew," but an Arab, and that he had not only "civil and religious" rights but political rights as well.

In a curious way the Palestine Mandate obscured the initial source of conflict. The Royal Commission, reporting on "disturbances" in Palestine in 1936, described the overall conflict as a clash of Arab and Jewish nationalisms and that it was "fundamentally a conflict between right and right." This judgment overlooked (as it is too often overlooked today) the basic relationship of force upon which the system was based. The terms of the Mandate were worked out between the Zionists and the British Government. The Balfour Declaration was mentioned in the preamble of the document, and Britain was to be "responsible for placing the country under such political, administrative and economic conditions as will secure the establishment of the Jewish National Home." In effect the relationship of force between Britain and the Arabs of Palestine was to be transposed through the introduction of alien Zionist rule.

4

Confrontation

The pattern of conflict in Palestine rapidly crystallized. By 1918 Arab reaction had mounted against the British and their Zionist protégés. During the two years of military administration tension increased to the point where violent Arab riots erupted in the spring of 1920 against British garrisons and Jewish settlements. A court of enquiry reported that the underlying cause of unrest was "a disappointment at the non-fulfillment" of British wartime promises. This was true as far as it went, but popular unrest among the Palestinians seems to have emerged before the war.

Arabs had first encountered Zionist pioneers in the early eighteen-eighties when small groups of young Russian Jews, inspired by the ideals of Leo Pinsker, emigrated to the Holy Land. These newcomers were ill-prepared and poorly financed for the adventure. Many died of disease, some of discouragement. Progress in their settlements was slow and arduous, but for those that remained and survived it was work well done.

Arab reaction to the newcomers was mixed. In some parts of the country cordial relations between Arab and Jew did exist. Jewish settlers required labor and hired Arabs to work their farms, and so Jewish farmer and Arab laborer came to know each other on intimate terms. Arab landowners also came in contact with the new colonists, the one trading his superior knowledge of the land for the other's superior technical skills. It was sometimes found that Arab and Jew owned flocks of sheep in common. Bad times were met in the same spirit as good times. Boundary disputes arose, but were settled over a cup of bitter coffee. Both Arab and Jew faced the common danger of Bedouin raids on their lands, but this was not a threat to their existence.

In other parts of the country developments occurred which bore the seeds of later enmity. In the decade preceding the outbreak of the war the second great wave of Jewish immigrants, the second *aliya* as it is known, brought about 40,000 Jews to Palestine, mainly from Russia and Poland. Most of these men and women were dedicated, militant Zionist idealists. None more so than one David Green, who was to adopt the Hebrew name of Ben Gurion. He and other members of the second *aliya* became prominent figures in the Zionist political elite during the Mandate. It was this group of immigrants which created the image of the pioneer settler, the *halutz*.

Ben Gurion has left a stirring account of his early days in Galilee.[11] He describes the pioneer experience of building new settlements as being "a partner in the act of creation." Always the tough taskmaster, Ben Gurion was supremely Jewish in everything he did. Some have made the comparison with Cecil Rhodes in South Africa, and from a personal comparison Rhodes must come off second best. A man of few vices, David Ben Gurion set out to impart to an unwilling people a stern morality based on an agricultural vocation which was strange to their European tradition and desires. That in large part he succeeded is a testament to the man's physical and spiritual fortitude.

Writing much like an Old Testament prophet, he admonished his pioneer brothers for diluting their farm force with Arab guards. Everything had to be Jewish if it was to be a real and permanent return to the Promised Land. He spared no one, not even the pioneers of his kibbutz at Sejera, in Galilee: "Even here the purity of our aspirations was clouded. The fields were worked, it is true, by Jewish hands, but their watchmen were hired Arabs... Jewish labor, our labor, was the rule; the place was alive with Jewish youngsters — could we entrust all that to strange hands? Was it conceivable that we should be hiring strangers to guard our property and protect our lives?"

The Arab watchmen were "diligent in their work and outstanding for courage and spirit," Ben Gurion wrote. Even so, and despite their excellent qualities, they were nevertheless the foe, and some of the younger men decided that hostilities had to be directed against their watchmen in order to convince the farm supervisor that Jews alone should manage their own affairs. Employing various stratagems, the Zionist pioneers succeeded in having the Arab guards replaced by their own people. The campaign was completed, Ben Gurion recalls, only when the settlement had founded its own permanent militia which, of course, required a sizeable supply of arms. The arms were forthcoming and so, in time, was open conflict between the Jewish settlers and the Arabs.

These developments were not viewed lightly by the Arabs.[121] The implications of Jewish immigration and land purchases began to dawn on them, and the Arabic press warned its readers that a Jewish state was the Zionists' final goal. Anti-Zionist groups sprang up in Jerusalem, Haifa and Nablus, drawing support from the younger, more politically conscious elements. Slowly, popular unrest began to grow. One Arab notable from Jerusalem, who was not unfriendly to the Zionists, warned them that although governments may come and go, "the people are the constant factor; one must come to agreement with the people." For their part, the Zionists realized that there could be no measure of compromise on the questions of immigration and land purchases for on these two pillars their assured supremacy in Palestine would be built.

Zionists were proud Europeans who shared with their Christian fellows what was, at best, a paternalistic attitude toward "native" peoples, at worst open contempt. Perhaps, unlike classical colonial ventures, they did not seek to dominate the native population. But the construction of the National Home made the exclusion of the Arab implicit. Their view of the Arab contained a kind of self-fulfilling prophecy. They assumed the Arab was their enemy, implacably determined to destroy the cherished ideals for which Zionism stood. He had to be resisted at every turn. When the Arab finally turned violently against those who sought to exclude him, possibly even to eliminate him, the original assumption was proven correct and the prophecy fulfilled.

When Zionists attempted to transform their ideals into practice, it seemed to the Arab that their actions gave the lie to the genuineness of those ideals. In his *Road to Jerusalem*, historian Barnet Litvinoff has neatly summarized this Zionist attitude. Theirs was "a ruthless doctrine, calling for monastic self-discipline and cold detachment from environment. The Jews who gloried in the name of socialist worker interpreted brotherhood on a strictly nationalist, or racial basis, for they meant brotherhood with Jew, not with Arab. As they insisted on working the soil with their own hands, since exploitation of others was anathema to them, they excluded the Arabs from their regime... They believed in equality, but for themselves. They lived on Jewish bread raised on Jewish soil that was protected by a Jewish rifle."[131]

Other factors contributed to the disturbances of 1920 which were the initial steps taken toward the establishment of the Jewish National Home. The British cabinet had authorized the Zionist Organization to form its own commission ostensibly for the purpose of carrying on relief work in the Jewish community of Palestine which, like the rest of the population, had been badly hit by the war. The commission's definition of status also made it a representative body of the World Zionist Organization in Palestine to act in an advisory capacity to the military administration on all matters which might effect "the establishment of a national home for the Jewish people in accordance with the (Balfour) Declaration." The Zionist Commission, therefore, had a definite political function and, consequently, ran into difficulties with the military administration which, under international convention, was obliged to preserve the status quo of the occupied country and keep its institutions intact.

Dr. Weizmann, who was head of the commission, recognized the administration's position and also the need to dispel Arab apprehensions concerning the commission's work. He spoke to a group of Arab notables in Jerusalem, saying that "all fears expressed openly or secretly by the Arabs that they are to be ousted from their present position are due either to a fundamental misconception of Zionist aims or to the malicious activities of our common enemies." The inner meaning of Jewish aspirations, he said, was the longing for a moral and spiritual center to bind Jewish tradition of the past with the future. Weizmann, however, addressed himself to a very different purpose in discussions with representatives of the Palestinian Jewish community who expected the imminent creation of the Jewish State. Weizmann argued that since the Jews lacked the power, the time had not yet come to found the state. Instead "we must ask for some strong government, which we may trust to administer our 'state' justly, to take matters under its direction, enable us to develop our abilities, our institutions and our colonies until the time comes when we shall be fit to undertake the administration of the country ourselves."[141] As for the Arabs of Palestine, they were now convinced that they labored under no "fundamental misconception" of Zionist aims.

The Zionist Commission made numerous demands of the military administration in an attempt to alter the status quo. They were successful in having Hebrew recognized as an official language and in setting up a land commission to investigate development prospects of the country. Other demands were rejected as excessive, such as the transfer to the Zionists of some quarter of a million acres of land under state domain. These were the urban and rural properties of German colonists near Jaffa, and even the French-owned Jaffa-Jerusalem railway. The Zionist Commission also sought to increase Jewish participation in the administration (the twenty odd senior executive posts were held by the British, nine of whom were Jews) at a time when no Arab participation was permitted.

Great Arab resentment was caused by the Zionist Commission's opposition to the administration's granting of agricultural loans to farmers. The assets of the Ottoman Agricultural Bank from which the farmers used to obtain cheap credit had been carried away by the Turks when their army was driven from Palestine. In the difficult economic conditions brought about by the war it was imperative that the farmers acquire capital advances in order to rebuild their farms and orchards. The commission demanded that the power of granting loans be entrusted to the Anglo-Palestine Bank, a Zionist enterprise. The administration balked at these demands and the timely intervention of Weizmann caused the matter to be dropped. Further damage to Arab-Jewish relations, however, had already been done.

At the time of the 1920 crisis, the chief administrator, Sir Louis Bols, severely criticized the commission's activities and attitudes in a report to London:

(The Zionist Commission) seek not justice from the military occupant but that in every question in which a Jew is interested discrimination in his favor shall be shown...

It is unnecessary to press my difficulty... in controlling any situation that may arise in the future if I have to deal with a representative of the Jewish community who threatens me with mob law and refuses to accept the constituted forces of law and order...

It is no use saying to the Moslem and Christian elements of the population that our declaration as to the maintenance of the status quo made on our entry into Jerusalem has been observed. Facts witness otherwise: the introduction of the Hebrew tongue as an official language; the setting up of a Jewish judicature; the whole fabric of government of the Zionist Commission of which they are well aware; the special traveling privileges to members of the Zionist Commission; this has firmly and absolutely convinced the non-Jewish elements of our partiality. On the other hand, the Zionist Commission accuse my officers and me of anti-Zionism. The situation is intolerable...[15]

Sir Louis recommended that in the interests of peace the Zionist Commission be abolished. Instead of acting upon this recommendation, the British cabinet decided instead to abolish the military administration! The first British high commissioner, Sir Herbert Samuel, initiated the civil administration of Palestine in July 1920.

Sir Herbert's unenviable task was to give effect to the Balfour Declaration which was then being written into the terms of the Mandate. He was charged with the duty of creating in Palestine such political and economic conditions as would secure the establishment of the Jewish National Home, while at the same time safeguarding the rights of the majority Arab population.

Although he proved to be an extremely able and fair administrator, Sir Herbert's choice as high commissioner was unfair to both the man and the office. As a Jew and a Zionist he had helped draft the Balfour Declaration and subsequently he advised the Zionists on their memorandum which was submitted to the Paris Peace Conference. Highly placed and influential, but also tactful and discreet, he was able to keep the Zionists closely informed as to the likely shape of events in government. His name was brought up casually for the position of high commissioner during the discussions at San Remo when the mandates were apportioned to Britain and France. Lord Balfour's approval was obtained while he was engaged in a tennis match with an Italian delegate. No one seemed unduly alarmed at the possible implications of the recent disturbances in Palestine and Sir Herbert sailed forth to the warm applause of the Zionists, while the Arabs received him with something far less than enthusiasm. When he left Palestine five years later, Zionists had become disillusioned by his even-handed treatment of the Arabs which they called weakness and partiality. In itself, this was a tribute to the man's administration.

5

The Horns of a Dilemma

When Britain abandoned her Mandate over Palestine in 1948, His Majesty's Government was, in effect, absolving itself of any responsibility for its future. To emphasize the point, the British delegation to the United Nations abstained from the debates and the voting on the partition of Palestine. This simple act of withdrawal could not, however, cover up Britain's role and share in creating the tragedy of modern Palestine. Power imposes its own responsibilities and the abdication of her privileged position of authority in Palestine was a result of Britain's failure to fully recognize the responsibility for the burden she had actively sought and secured.

Nearly thirty years before, from the time of Sir Herbert Samuel's civilian administration, it was clear that the first priority of the Balfour Declaration was to be the establishment of a Jewish national home. The declaration was repeated in the introduction to the mandate instrument, and none of its major articles revealed any shift of intention or alteration of this main objective. The mandate document moreover spelled out the *means* by which the national home policy could be implemented. A Jewish agency, that is, an arm of the World Zionist Organization, would advise and cooperate with the British administration in Palestine in all matters, social, political and economic, which would affect the establishment of the Jewish National Home. The British administration would facilitate Jewish immigration and the settlement of Jews on the land. These arrangements were settled through mutual consultation and, like the Balfour Declaration, the mandate document was co-authored by British officials and the Zionists.

Committed to the National Home, Britain also had to face the reality of articulate Palestinian opposition to both her presence and her policy. The time had come to admit that the "non-Jewish" elements of the population were a more tangible factor than the as yet non-existent Jewish population of the National Home. It was evident from the beginning that large-scale Jewish immigration would ultimately lead to an attempt to found a Jewish state. Sir Herbert Samuel had observed before he became Palestine's first high commissioner that the *immediate* creation of a Jewish state would be undemocratic since a minority would rule a majority. Therefore conditions must be fulfilled, including large-scale immigration, he said, in order that "with the minimum of delay the country may become a purely self-governing commonwealth under an established Jewish majority."[11]

Palestinians read the fine print of the mandate policy and it was inconceivable that they would meekly accept the emasculation of the Arab identity of their own land. They had heard an earlier appeal from King Hussein who reminded them that their sacred books and traditions placed upon them the duties of hospitality and tolerance. "Welcome the Jews as brethren," Hussein had said, "and cooperate with them for the common welfare." When Weizmann spoke in Jerusalem to an assembly of Palestinian notables about a cultural and spiritual home for the Jews, one Arab dignitary replied in the words of the famous Muslim tradition: "Your rights are our rights and our obligations are yours."

The essence of the Zionist movement appeared to most Palestinians, however, to be far removed from spiritual values. They thought it best expressed in the words of Jacob Klatzkin, a Zionist theorist, who wrote: "In longing for our land we do not desire to create in Palestine a base for the spiritual values of Judaism. To regain our land is for us an end in itself. Our basic intention, whether consciously or unconsciously, is to deny any conception of Jewish identity based on spiritual values."[12]

Jewish nationalism, therefore, had to be countered on political grounds. Muslim-Christian associations were formed with openly declared political objectives. The associations had appealed in vain to the Paris Peace Conference to allow a Palestinian representative to attend their deliberations. Now an Arab congress was convened in Haifa (December 1921) at which an Arab executive was elected to take the Palestinians' protests directly to the British.

THE HORNS OF A DILEMMA

A second and more serious outbreak of violence had occurred the previous May in Jaffa when Jews were attacked at the government immigration offices. The violence spread to neighboring Jewish settlements and the toll of dead was heavy. The congress sought the abolition of the national home policy, and the formation of a representative national government to direct the affairs of Palestine. The tactics of the congress were to urge radical changes in the proposed terms of the Mandate before it was ratified, in order to protect the rights and interests of 90 percent of the population.

The demands of the congress were rejected by the British colonial secretary, Winston Churchill. Despite his assurances that the obligations entrusted to Britain under the Mandate would be fulfilled with absolute impartiality, the congress was by then fully aware that the Mandate itself was conceived in a partisan spirit. The question of Jewish immigration was central, for the Zionist control of immigration had sparked the Jaffa riots. The Arabs believed that the democratic right of self-government would not be granted until such time as the Jews constituted a majority in the country. Churchill did nothing to discourage this belief.[13]

The British Government had worked itself onto the horns of a nasty dilemma. As mandatory power only two genuine alternatives lay before it: *either* cut off Jewish immigration at a level where the Jews would not be strong enough to aim at or seize statehood, *or* take decisive steps toward the establishment of a Jewish state and accomplish that task before Arab opposition became strong enough to check developments. Either there would be a Jewish state or there would not: it was a situation which Shakespeare's Hamlet would have appreciated.

The official attitude of His Majesty's Government, apart from any private misgivings of individual ministers, was to maintain the stance of impartiality toward both Zionists and Palestinians. Two equal obligations were imposed upon the government: one was to create suitable conditions for the establishment of the Jewish National Home and the other to safeguard the rights of the Arab (the so-called "non-Jewish") population.

At the time this must have seemed the most realistic course to adopt, but translated into policy it was inherently more dangerous than either of the other mutually exclusive alternatives. A declaration of equal obligations was susceptible to attack from two sides. Both the Zionists and the Arabs could, and frequently did, charge Britain with failing to fulfill their own particular part of the bargain. Far more dangerous still was the simple fact that the policy rested on an unrealistic premise. It assumed that, in return for a verbal pledge safeguarding civil and religious rights, the Palestinians, as a people, would submit without question or discussion to a scheme which they had had no hand in creating; that they would, moreover, acquiesce to this scheme which would fundamentally alter the political character of their society, if not extinguish them altogether as a community, *as though that scheme in no way concerned them.*

British policy makers continually viewed the two "obligations" as entirely unrelated to each other. If, however, as events were to prove, fulfilling the one resulted in the impossibility of fulfilling the other, then one obligation was indeed intimately connected with the other.

The Haycraft Commission which investigated the causes of the Jaffa riots naïvely declared that the hostility between the two races, the Jews and the Arabs, could be eased if both sides were prepared to discuss their problems in a reasonable spirit. The basis for such discussion, however, would be that "the Arabs should accept implicitly the declared policy of the government on the subject of the Jewish National Home, and that the Zionist leaders should abandon and repudiate all pretensions that go beyond it."

"What the British were trying to do at the time," a former Jordanian cabinet minister (now living in Jerusalem and therefore requesting anonymity) told me immediately after the June War, "was to offer us a poison brew of their own concoction, assuring us at the same time that the Zionists would not shoot us. In either case we were doomed." He smiled wryly and added: "Today, the Israelis don't say they will shoot us; instead they annex our whole city and then exile our leaders."

The assumption that a dual obligation did exist provided a satisfying interpretation of the political history of the Mandate as simply the struggle between two irreconcilable nationalisms, Jewish and Arab. British observers found this useful for it moved the burden of responsibility for the course and ultimate failure of the Mandate from the shoulders of the mandatory power onto the backs of the two contending parties. The analysis had other ramifications which Zionists seized on. Since the conflict involved only Arab and Jew, then only they could find the solution to it. This bilateral responsibility was then neatly halved by making the basis for a solution the *Palestinians*' acceptance of the British policy of the Jewish National Home.

The argument had an almost mystical allure for the liberal mind because of its appeal to "reason." And so, when the Palestinian rejects British policy, and thereby the basis for a solution to the Arab-Jewish conflict, he is accused of being unreasonable and irrational. Finally, when this improbable syllogism has worked itself out, the Arab is blamed for the failure of a policy which he has not contrived and of a scheme on which he has not been consulted. While it is true that the relationship between the Zionists and the Palestinians aggravated an already difficult situation, the imperialist relationship between Britain and the Arabs was one of power to powerlessness. The official claim of equal obligations was, in the final analysis, an illusion. Consequently, British policy was unintelligible to the very people whom it was intended to convince.

A second Arab congress met in Jerusalem in May 1921. The congress decided to send a delegation to London to campaign against Britain's mandate policy. It was headed by a former mayor of Jerusalem. Musa Kazem Husseini, a venerated patriarch of moderate views and disposition. The Palestinians urged the British Government to introduce a legislative council representative of *all* the people of Palestine including, of course, the present Jewish inhabitants.

A draft constitution was accordingly published in February 1922 by His Majesty's Government, whereby the government would be entrusted to an official executive and a legislative council. The senior executive and commander in chief was the high commissioner who was empowered to give effect to the provisions of the Mandate, namely, the establishment of the Jewish National Home. The legislative council would comprise, in addition to the high commissioner, ten official and twelve non-official members. The officials were to be appointed by the high commissioner and would be exclusively British. The non-official members would be elected: eight from the Muslim community, two from the Christian (Arab) and two from the Jewish.

The proposed constitution was a bitter disappointment to the Arab delegation. It was evident that with the ten official members and the two Jews, the mandate administration would have an absolute majority (twelve out of twenty-two) in the legislative council. In this way it could enforce the national home policy against the wishes of the representatives of the majority of the population. Other provisions removed all possible safeguards for the Arabs. The high commissioner had the right to veto any legislation; he could conduct the business of the council with a quorum of ten which he could always ensure with his own officials; finally, there was the provision that "no ordinance shall be passed which shall be in any way repugnant to or inconsistent with the provisions of the Mandate." This last clause, loosely interpreted, could deny any Palestinian request, legitimate or otherwise, and the council was structured in such a way as to make the denial effective.

Colonial Secretary Winston Churchill used the draft constitution in an attempt to get the Arabs to capitulate completely to the terms of the Mandate. He made it clear to the Arab delegation that the national home policy was not susceptible to change, nor was it subject to discussion. Only the method of safeguarding the Arabs' civil and religious rights was a proper subject of negotiation, and the secretary regarded the proposed legislative council as adequate. Churchill then stated that he could not negotiate *officially* with any delegation which merely "claimed" to represent the wishes of its people.[141] He urged the acceptance of the draft constitution since its object was to provide Palestinians with a "constitutional channel for the expression of their opinions and wishes."

The Arabs were left the option of debating the details of their gradual subordination in Palestine. To accept the proposed council was to accept implicitly the national home policy, and the composition of the council would ensure its fulfillment. Confronted with this constitutional coercion, the Arab delegation felt itself forced to reject Churchill's "concessions." In effect the Arabs told the colonial secretary that "until we see a real practical change in the policy of the British Government we must harbor fears that the intention to create the Jewish National Home is to cause the disappearance or subordination of the Arabic population, culture and language in Palestine." The change never came and fears increased. The issue of a legislative council was raised on two or three other occasions, but came to nothing. Throughout the mandate period the Arab community was governed by the high commissioner and his ten British advisors. For many years two of the top executive positions, the attorney general and the director of immigration, were filled by British Jews who were also Zionists.

The British Government could only offer the Arabs paper assurances that their rights would be protected. But these protestations of goodwill were usually coupled with the thinly veiled threat that no government would ever abandon the Balfour Declaration. British authorities spoke to the Arab with a reassuring liberal voice, but always echoed the menacing commands of self-confident power. The national home policy was never justified to the Arabs beyond the claim that Britain had made a solemn promise to the Zionists. This was incomprehensible to the Palestinians, and any material advantage stemming from mandate rule and Jewish investment in the country was canceled by the multiple dimensions of the threat to the existing Arab community. Palestine was, in fact, governed like any colony of the British Empire and the high commissioner was in benevolent but autocratic command of all he surveyed. Inevitably the people became estranged from the source of authority, a situation which was an encouragement to violence since Palestinians realized they must either endure perpetual submission or break the law.

Westminster had drastically underestimated the depth of Arab feeling. Opposition to the Mandate was dismissed as the work of discontented intellectuals or disgruntled agitators. The Zionists made a similar misjudgment; they attributed the cause of violence to the machinations of upper-class landowners who were anxious to preserve their privileged position in society as well as their feudal hold over the peasantry. Both interpretations are valid only if we are prepared to turn a blind eye to what was really happening among the Arab population.

It was natural that the most politically conscious groups would be the first to express their resentment to the Mandate and it was also natural that opposition would be voiced by the educated few. The members of the congress and the Arab executive were landowners and professional men. The congress abounded with the names of the educated families of the aristocracy, such as Nashashibi, Husseini, Khalidi, Dajani, Tukan and Abd al-Hadi. These leaders would be expected to arouse the population against the foreign ruler and his policy. But it was wrong to assume that peasants were incapable of political judgment or deep feeling, or that their resentment sprang merely from a cultivated religious fanaticism. Fierce Arab opposition could not be reduced to what psychologists might call the collective egoisms of the various elements of society.

The congress was the first body to express the growing sense of Arab community identity against the external threat of the national home policy. Peasant and landlord alike felt their political and material interests were identical. It was a common sight in the villages to find illiterate peasants gathered at the home of one of their educated brethren to hear the newspaper read to them, following which a lively discussion of the major issues of the day would engross all of them. In a largely illiterate society this was the only way of keeping up with the news.

This system of political discussion is as alive as ever. I was sitting some years ago in an open-air café with a group of Jordanian villagers. When they discovered I was Canadian, they bombarded me with questions about "unrest" among the French Canadians in Quebec. I explained as best I could of French desires to preserve the integrity of their culture, to run their own affairs. They were instantly sympathetic. Beside me an older man said: "Your French fight the same struggle we lost; I hope they will not be deprived of their homeland, as we have been." Not surprisingly, one Royal Commission concluded after an intensive survey of rural Palestine that "the Arab peasants and villagers are probably more politically minded than many people of Europe."[5]

Peasants and farmers were actively concerned in their

country's affairs. Peasant parties, organized mainly by lawyers, sprang up throughout Palestine in the mid-twenties. A large conference of about 1,000 farmers was held in tents near Hebron in 1929 and several resolutions were passed relating to their needs and the methods the British administration should adopt to improve their condition.

The growing nationalist movement was further supported by Arab women. In October 1929, a Palestine Arab Women's Congress was held in Jerusalem.[16] Women from all over the country presented reports to the congress on the unsatisfactory conditions in their communities. Resolutions were handed to the high commissioner, and a demonstration against the mandate policy was staged through the streets of the Holy City. It was the first time in Palestine's long history that women had indulged in political activities.

Despite widespread backing from all quarters of the population, Arab leaders realized that without some tangible form of power in Arab hands they could not hope to guide the destiny of their people. The mandatory regime, like all colonial administrations, was rigidly conservative and the British were obsessed with matters of security. Pouring money into educational facilities and social services for the Arab community was considered little better than subsidizing unrest. The government pleaded financial stringency, but at one time when schools were closed down and teachers dismissed for "lack of funds" the treasury actually showed a surplus of six million pounds on its books. Meanwhile, the Jewish community was making rapid progress in all aspects of development under the protection of British colonial rule. The status quo was being altered in their favor. Arabs had to fight on two fronts, both against the British and the Zionists. While the British excluded them from a genuine role in government planning and decision making, the Zionists simply excluded the Arabs from everything.

The Arabs' fear of Zionism was derived from its Jewish exponents in Palestine. Giving evidence before the Haycraft Commission, Dr. Eder, the acting chairman of the Zionist Commission, said that in his view of the Zionist ideal there could only be "one National Home in Palestine, and that a Jewish one, and no equality in the partnership between Jews and Arabs, but a Jewish predominance as soon as the numbers of that race are sufficiently increased."[7] Dr. Eder added his belief that Jews, not Arabs, should have the right to bear arms on the grounds that "this discrimination would tend to improve Arab-Jewish relations."[8]

Harry Sacher, head of the Political Department of the Jewish Agency, told the Shaw Commission in 1929 that political rights could not be granted the Arabs if that meant the immediate establishment of representative democratic institutions. The leader of the Zionist revisionist wing, Vladimir Jabotinksy argued essentially along the same lines: only when a Jewish majority was achieved could parliamentary institutions be introduced so that, as he candidly put it, "the Jewish point of view should always prevail."[8a] Israel Zangwill once suggested that the Arabs of Palestine should be resettled elsewhere in order to liberate the land for Jewish nationalization. At about the same time Chaim Weizmann replied to a reporter's question concerning the problem of the Arab majority: "We expect they won't be in a majority after a few years."[9]

These views were well known to the Arabs. The opinions of Zionist leaders reflected the general attitude of the average Zionist settler toward the Arab. Even the most liberal of the Jewish pioneers would shrug his shoulders and say: "We cannot afford to see the Arabs' point of view."[10] There was, of course, another side to the story. The 12th Zionist Congress in Carlsbad in 1921, passed a resolution reassuring Palestinians that the progress of Jewish colonization would not affect their rights. From time to time similar declarations were repeated. The Arabs, however, could be excused for cynically dismissing such resolutions as better suited to Zionist propaganda needs in Europe rather than its practical ends in Palestine.

Frederick Kisch, head of the Zionist executive in Palestine, conceded that the major weakness of the Jewish Agency was that in its program for cooperation with the Arabs "its fine words were not matched by deeds."[11] The small group known as Brit Shalom, which called for a bi-national Arab-Jewish state, was outside the mainstream of Zionist thinking and influence. Arabs respected the members of Brit Shalom, but they knew their real struggle would be against hard-core Zionists like Ben Gurion.

In fact, no program of cooperation could exist. It was characteristic of the single-mindedness of Zionist leaders to proclaim the universalist principles of their movement while denying their application to the Arabs of Palestine with whom they were in direct and daily contact. Outlining the imperatives of Zionism, Ben Gurion stated that Jewish nationalism was "part of a tremendous movement which involves all of humanity — the world revolution, whose aims are the redemption of man from every form of enslavement, discrimination and exploitation..."[12] But in Palestine where the Arabs struggled against the colonial rule of Britain, Zionism could hardly pretend to be part of that same struggle while claiming the protection of the Balfour Declaration and the Mandate Power.

The Jewish National Home developed along the lines of a sub-national government, a kind of state within a state. The internal affairs of the Jewish community, the Yishuv, were conducted by an elected national council. The Palestine Zionist Executive, later the Jewish Agency, provided the liaison between the mandate administration and the World Zionist Organization (W.Z.O.). The Agency drew upon the political and financial resources of the World Zionist body which functioned in most European countries and in North America. With these resources at hand, the Agency was able, through its various departments, to control efficiently the economy of the Jewish sector of Palestine, as well as build schools and hospitals, direct public works programs and exploit natural resources through government concessions such as the Palestine Electric Corporation.

As early as 1922 the Jewish community possessed its own para-military force, the Haganah. The idea in Weizmann's mind was to select new immigrants carefully for their skills and training to play a role in the militia of the Jewish colonies. In the later years of the Mandate an intelligence service was organized comprising Jewish officials in the Palestine Government who acted as agents. Through its connections with the W.Z.O. the Jewish community was able to exploit worldwide propaganda outlets. Zionism was never the monolithic movement it often appeared to be, but with skillful organization it had remarkable success in shaping favorable public opinion.

One of Zionism's greatest assets was its capacity to tailor its propaganda to particular moments and specific audiences. Jews and Gentiles alike were attracted for a variety of reasons: religious, humanitarian, social, imperial. Even anti-Semites found their own interests could be furthered by cooperation; and there were yet other anti-Semites, like Colonel Richard Meinertzhagen of the British army in Palestine, whose contempt of the Arab was patent, although no more or less so than that of some leading Zionists. Weizmann had once written to Balfour referring to "the subtilities and subterfuges of the Oriental mind . . . the trecherous nature of the Arabs . . . who are superficially clever and quick witted (but who) worship one thing only—power and success."[13] If matters did not always go their way Zionists were confident, with good reason, that a local setback in Palestine could be repaired in Whitehall through its many sympathizers and supporters. In contrast, as British Member of Parliament, Richard Crossman once put it, "the only way the Arabs can get a hearing is through violence." This was unfortunately true, but of no great help to the Palestinians in the long run. Violence begets violence, and as events were to show, the Arabs were far less equipped to sustain the alternative of violence than were either the British or even the Zionists.

Immigration was a top priority of the Jewish Agency. Measured against Zionist aspirations, the level of immigration during the first decade of the Mandate was disappointingly low. Between December 1922 and December 1931 about 87,000 Jews entered Palestine.[14] Annual figures fluctuated considerably owing to uncertain economic conditions both inside and outside the country. In fact, during this same period more than 25,000 Jews actually left Palestine disillusioned, leaving a net in-migration of some 61,000 persons. Measured against Arab expectations, therefore, the incoming tide of aliens did not, initially, materialize. The proportion of Jews to the total population rose from 10% in 1920 to 16% in 1931. In this latter year Jews were still only 8% of the *native* born population, or, to put it another way, they comprised some 77% of all *foreign* born residents.

In a recent and important study on the demographic transformation of Palestine the actual pattern of Jewish settlement has been soberly set against the lavish Zionist ideological claims of vast rural agricultural development supposed to benefit the country as a whole. The author of the study, a prominent American demographer, demonstrates that in 1922 "fully three-fourths of the total Jewish population of the country was concentrated in the central urbanized belt of Palestine, i.e. the Jerusalem-Jaffa districts delineated in the (1922) census."[15] Moreover, in the northern districts of Palestine where Zionists concentrated their efforts on land schemes, 70% of the Jewish inhabitants living in the region were urban based in Haifa, Tiberias and Safad. Jews comprised only 12% of the total population in the entire northern area.

During further phases of immigration "given the increasingly alien character of the Jewish population and the ideologically supported policy of apartheid followed by Zionist organizations, it is not surprising that geographic specialization and concentration persisted."[16] Thus by 1936 when the Jewish population in Palestine had nearly doubled in the preceeding five years alone, still over 68% of Jews were concentrated in the Jerusalem-Jaffa urban belt. Again, in the northern districts Jews were still small minorities everywhere. These developments were decidedly unrevolutionary if judged in terms of the Zionist claims to "the land of Palestine." A largely urban Jewish population was not going to transform an alleged desert into a garden paradise. Nevertheless, the Palestine Government's immigration policy exposed the economy to danger and intensified the already unstable relations between Arab and Jew.

First, immigration was not based on rational principles which took into account the long-range interests of the country as a whole. The only criterion used to judge the immigration level was the vaguely undefined "economic absorptive capacity" of the country. Social, political and psychological factors were disregarded. The most important immigrant category was the labour list. Every six months the British high commissioner would place a specified number of immigration certificates at the disposal of the Zionist Organization. In applying for them Zionists tended, for propaganda purposes, to exaggerate every favourable circumstance to obtain the largest possible number of certificates.[17] As a result the government was under political pressure every six months to provide a large labour schedule. There was no time to make adjustments for the dislocations which were bound to arise from rapid increases in the population. An expert employed by the Jewish Agency in 1927 concluded that "much of the unemployment in the country during 1926 and 1927 was, in fact, the consequence of this hasty and unbalanced flow of Jewish immigration."[18]

Second, immigrants were being admitted at a time when the government was supplying relief work for Jewish labourers already in the country. At the same time the level of Arab employment or unemployment was not taken into account when drawing up the labour list. Two of the British Government's own commissions, the Shaw (1929) and the Hope Simpson (1930), advised more stringent controls of immigration. When Whitehall adopted their advice the result was tantamount to throwing a grenade into an explosives arsenal. The House of Commons witnessed an opposition onslaught on the government's new policy statement. Chaim Weizmann resigned as chief of the W.Z.O. in protest against the government's "whittling away" of the National Home. Combined pressure finally forced Prime Minister Ramsay Mac-Donald to explain away the proposed changes until all the whittled shavings were glued back onto the old policy plank.

Finally, the actual control of immigration was another point of Arab grievance. Effective control was not in the hands of the Palestine Government, which was ostensibly the responsible body, but held by the Zionists themselves. The selection of immigrants, their financing, settlement and allotment of funds was handled entirely by the Zionist Organization, which consequently was invested with the power, but not the corresponding responsibility, for its actions.[19] The all-important labour schedule accounted for 50 percent of total immigration; if the category of labourers' dependents is included, then the Zionists had direct control of nearly 70 percent of all immigration into Palestine. On this subject the Shaw Commission noted that Zionists seemed more concerned with the "political creed" of prospective immigrants than with their particular qualifications.

The ethical aspect of Zionism was expressed in the twin concepts of the conquest of labour and the conquest of land. The conquest of labour was accomplished through the establishment of production, marketing and service cooperatives organized by the Jewish Federation of Labour (Histadrut) which gradually emerged as the most powerful political force in the Yishuv. The conquest of land was accomplished through agricultural colonization, the establishment of communal settlements both by private enterprise and by the Jewish National Fund. Leaders of the Jewish labour movement (the Ben Gurions and the Ben Zvis) were inspired by universal socialist ideals although in practice they pursued a policy of socio-economic apartheid through the exclusion of Arab labour from Jewish enterprises run by the Histadrut and from land bought by the J.N.F. [20]

A picketing campaign was launched against private Jewish agricultural settlements where Arab labour was employed. These were generally the older settlements where good relations had developed between Jewish farmers and Arab labourers. The newspaper *Davar* described the effects of the campaign at one settlement near Jaffa:

> A branch of the labour office has been opened in Beit Vegen. The office has begun an important social activity in which it has been helped also by the contracting office of the Workers' Council of Tel Aviv. During the past five months the position has changed as follows. In place of 200 Arab workers and 50 Jews, the last count gives 200 Hebrew workers and 70 Arab workers in Beit Vegen. The work continues. [21]

Land leased by the J.N.F. prescribed fines for and eventual eviction of Jewish farmers who broke the rule prohibiting the employment of Arab labour.

A more realistic and more genuinely socialist approach would have been for organized Jewish labour to combine with cheap, unorganized Arab labour to raise the general level of wages against the combined interests of Arab and Jewish capitalists. In any event, the Histadrut policy drove even deeper the wedge separating Jew and Arab. In his report Sir John Hope Simpson criticized these practices. The exclusion of Arab labour, he said, was incompatible with the professed sentiments of Zionists that they desired relations of friendship and respect with Arabs. Two communities could not grow up in peace if the indifference of the one fed suspicion and fear in the other. Sir John added that the Histadrut's policy of "persistent and deliberate boycott" of Arab labour was a continuing source of conflict in Palestine.

If Arabs accused Zionists of being alien intruders, Zionists constantly reminded them that it was so.

Zionist conquest of the land was on the one hand a slow, often expensive, and a politically unsatisfactory process; even by 1948 on the eve of the first Palestine war, total Jewish holdings leased and owned comprised only 9-12 percent of all arable land.[22] On the other hand, Zionist colonization, where it was effective, brought the alien settler into the heart of Palestinian life, the village and its peasant inhabitant. Among this rural population there were no "rich" and "poor" classes. The hardship of peasant life and its economic weakness in the face of outside forces made the struggle for survival a common pursuit within an extended family system and a patriarchal distribution of authority. Absentee feudal landlords (some living outside Palestine altogether, for example in Lebanon) held large tracts of land. Their income was derived from rents or from a share of the crop produced by the peasant cultivators. In the past they had produced not only for themselves but also for the governing classes of landlords, tax farmers or the Ottoman state. During the British Mandate the peasantry had to meet the rising consumer demand of the unproductive urban classes for the agricultural produce of the land. Hence the Arab cultivators' role was to provide the largely urban Jewish settler community with the bulk of its food.

This was only one aspect of the growing pressures upon the rural inhabitants. It is true, Zionists purchased the lands they acquired; about 90 percent of the lands purchased between 1922-1932 were from large absentee landowners.[23] But in Palestine, as throughout the Middle East, political power and the ownership of land went together. Therefore, the Arabs feared that should the Jews gain power they would seize the land. The beginnings of Zionist land purchases were inauspicious enough. They led to the eviction of Arab tenants as the land became the inalienable property of the Jewish people. The long range effects of this "extraterritorialization" were perceptively described by Hope Simpson in 1930:

> It ceases to be land from which the Arab can gain any advantage now or in the future. Not only can he never hope to lease or to cultivate it,

but by the stringent provisions of the Jewish National Fund he is deprived forever from employment on that land. [24]

Hope Simpson further observed that the land-man ratio, or land hunger, had worsened by 1930 and that the average size of a peasant family's lot seldom exceeded half of what was judged necessary to maintain "a decent standard of life." Nearly a third of all the peasantry was landless. This was the genesis of its transformation into a proletarian class of unskilled wage labourers. The process was checked, momentarily, by the war in 1948 barely two decades after Hope Simpson's tour of the country. This marked the first phase of the Zionists' conquest of the land by force of arms. The war displaced or deprived of livelihood some 60 percent of the original inhabitants of Palestine. For the remnant of villagers left in Israel after the armistice in 1949 the transformation into unskilled labourers continued. Of this remnant a few could still follow the agricultural life but even by the mid-1960's their annual income was only half that enjoyed by Israeli agriculturalists. [25] The second phase in the conquest of land by force, after the abortive attempt in 1956, was the war of June 1967; details of these developments, however, will be treated later in the story. Suffice it to note here that the conquest of land by arms and the expulsion of the Arab population was but a logical extension of an ideology and practice which excluded the Palestinian from every sphere where cooperation might have built a bridge rather than a wall between the two communities.

Education, for example, was one area in which close contacts between Jewish and Arab youth could have dispelled the atmosphere of alienation. But again separate development was the rule. Jewish and Arab public schools (such as there were of the latter) existed apart. The Jewish school system was only nominally under the control of the Mandate Government's director of education, although it was partly financed from the government's budget. The Arab system, like all aspects of their community, was controlled directly by the government.

The mandate administration proposed the establishment of a British university in the city of Jerusalem to serve as the educational apex of the two public school systems. The Zionist executive informed Sir Ronald Storrs, the author of the scheme, that the Jews would not participate because it "constituted a threat to Hebrew culture in Palestine."[26] The project was dropped and the only university to be constructed in Palestine was the Hebrew University which, while admitting Arab students, meant that higher education, even partially in their own cultural tradition, was not available to the Arabs. The Zionist executive consistently refused to have anything to do with any education program where Hebrew was not the sole language of instruction. An idea for an Arab-Jewish agricultural school was likewise shelved and instead two separate schools were established.

As the wall was erected brick by brick between the Arab and Jewish communities, events dragged each side of the political triangle toward the precipice and over the edge into an abyss of prolonged and violent encounter. Zionists claimed that neither Arab nor Jew should dominate the other, but their actions and policies would lead them logically to seize control of Palestine. Britain originally intended to govern two peoples impartially; but its policy was to allow the Jews wide latitude for development while ruling rather than governing the Arab community. When the crisis came between Britain and the Arabs, Britain opted for repression rather than concession. The Arabs were being asked to accept a European concept of a just solution to its own Jewish problem. In fact the Arabs were being forced to submit to the inequitable consequences of that solution. Sovereignty was a question of destiny and the Arab in his own land could not concede that the reins of his destiny be held forever by foreign hands. Zionists read the future in the same light.

6

The Palestine Rebellion 1936-1939

The early nineteen-thirties were prosperous ones for Palestine, the more remarkable by contrast with the depression into which the world as a whole was plunged. With the expansion of industry and agriculture Jewish immigration increased dramatically. In 1930 the figure was 4,944 immigrants; in 1932, 9,553; in 1933, 30,327; in 1934, 42,359; and in 1935, 61,854. By 1936 Jews comprised 30 percent of the total population. Illegal immigration was on the upswing and any number of ingenious methods were used to bring Jews to the Promised Land. There is the story of enterprising young Palestinian Jewish men who became professional husbands, "marrying" single girls in Europe who wanted easy access to Palestine, "divorcing" them with a handshake once the ship had docked in Haifa.[1]

Nineteen thirty-three began as any other year, but three apparently unrelated incidents, none of them earthshaking on the surface, seemed to portend the tumultuous years which lay ahead. A man died. In the Jewish community elections were held. The high commissioner made a proposal.

When Musa Kazem Husseini died, his moderating influence on the Arab political movement disappeared as well. Respected and accepted by all factions, Musa had led several delegations to England to urge the colonial office to grant representative institutions to Palestine.

With his death the nationalist movement passed completely into the hands of Hajj Amin Husseini, head of the Supreme Muslim Council and Mufti of Jerusalem. A man of medium stature, bearded, and with gentle eyes which concealed a tough and uncompromising disposition, Hajj Amin had received the traditional Muslim education at the Azhar University in Cairo.

His talents were as political as religious for he had been from youth an ardent nationalist. In 1918 he cooperated with the British Army, raising some 2,000 recruits in Palestine in the belief that the Allied promises to the Arabs would be fulfilled. Two years later he was strongly attacking the Zionist policies of the British. Accused of fomenting the 1920 disturbances, Hajj Amin was sentenced to ten years in exile.

High Commissioner Sir Herbert Samuel later pardoned Hajj Amin and appointed him head of the Supreme Muslim Council, which curiously earned him the tag among some Arab elements of being a British agent. The Mufti's bitter attitude toward Britain was accentuated by the disillusionment caused by Prime Minister Ramsay MacDonald's retreat from the recommendations of his own commissions on Palestine which had become short-lived government policy in the White Paper of 1930.

Hajj Amin Husseini now concluded that organized resistance to the Mandate was the only means of bringing about meaningful concessions for the Arabs. He actively discouraged the sale of land to Jews, and the Muslim Supreme Council purchased land in competition with the Jewish National Fund. He also encouraged greater expenditure on education in Muslim religious schools controlled by the Council: 19 percent of its budget was tied up in education as compared to a meager 5 percent allocated by the mandate government from its revenues for the entire country. During the Arab rebellion of 1936-1938 Hajj Amin ruthlessly eliminated his political opponents who advocated a more moderate line with the British. In the long run this was a tactical blunder, for when the rebellion was crushed by the British and the Mufti himself banished forever from Palestine, no effective leadership remained inside the country and the Arab nationalist resistance collapsed.

The second incident was the election in the Jewish community in which the labor group of the Histadrut led by Ben Gurion captured control of the Jewish Agency. It was natural to expect a shift in Zionist strategy from the gradualist approach to Jewish statehood. Zionists believed that the Arabs were no longer strong enough to destroy the position of the Jewish community. The next stage of their strategy was, therefore, to ensure that the relationship of Jewish and Arab forces was such as to preclude the possibility of establishing an Arab state in Palestine. Once the Arabs were unable to frustrate the growth of the Jewish community, then a solution could be reached based upon the premise of effective power being in the hands of the Jews. This, however, required a transition period during which the Jewish minority would exercise organized revolutionary rule over the whole country. The idea was that the state apparatus, the administration and the military establishment would fall into their hands.[21]

Zionists had at last accepted the logic of their scheme for the National Home which would put them on a collision course with the Arabs. The principle of minority rule had previously been rejected, but once granted it became linked with a territorial imperative which implied that the National Home could be Jewish only if the removal of a major part, or all of the Arab population were accomplished. Then the control of the state would pass legitimately into the hands of the majority.

In 1933 the high commissioner, Sir Arthur Wauchope, advocated self-determination by stages for all of Palestine. The final stage called for a legislative council. The details of its composition revealed that the Arabs would have fourteen of twenty-eight seats which ensured the Arab community a greater measure of security than previous proposals. The Arab leaders decided to discuss the question and sent a delegation to London in January 1936, led by Hajj Amin Husseini, who was skeptical of the outcome. The plan had already been denounced by the Zionist Congress in Lucerne, Switzerland, and the Jewish Agency followed suit. In both Houses of Parliament the council scheme was bitterly attacked. The British Government again retreated under pressure, and the plan was withdrawn.

Arab reaction was predictable. No one doubted that the Zionist lobby in London had caused the council proposal to be dropped.

A new element entered the confused picture when a cache of arms consigned to an unidentified Jew were found in barrels of cement at the port of Jaffa. Two thirds of the cement consignment contained a total of 800 rifles and revolvers and an estimated 500,000 rounds of ammunition.

Rumors spread that the Zionist settlements were arming against the Arabs. The peasantry was restive and a spirit of rebellion moved swiftly among them. One Izzadin Qassam acted. Soon there were tales out of the hills of Galilee of the exploits of this romantic figure who led a small band of guerillas against armed Jewish settlements and British garrisons. He scored several successes in about eight months of guerilla activity, harassing armed Jewish camps and even British forts. For the embattled Palestinians he symbolized a love of liberty, a scorn of death, a fresh breeze of idealistic faith and vigor which fanned the smoldering embers of revolt. The British hunted him down as a worthless brigand. Instead he suffered a martyr's death at the hands of his country's oppressors and was mourned by Arabs throughout Palestine.

In April 1936, serious riots erupted in Jaffa in the course of which sixteen Jews and five Arabs were killed. Recently established Arab political parties immediately formed a united front known as the Arab Higher Committee under the leadership of Hajj Amin Husseini. The committee was made up of members from all party factions as well as both religions, Christian and Muslim. It summoned the Arabs to a nationwide strike against the Mandate in order to bring an end to Jewish immigration, land sales to the Jewish National Fund, and finally to bring about the creation of a national government responsible to a representative council. These remained the minimum safeguards for the protection of the Arab community. The high commissioner reacted quickly, enacting drastic regulations, including a curfew, censorship, search-and-arrest-without-warrant and deportation for political undesirables.

The strike began nevertheless as an economic boycott against the Jewish community. Shops in the cities and towns were shuttered and silent.[131] The streets filled with crowds of demonstrators demanding justice for their people and the police were called in to disband them by force. In Nazareth an angry crowd stoned a police contingent which then turned on the demonstrators supported by armed members of the British Loyal Regiment.

The next day at the Damascus Gate in Old Jerusalem, Arab

THE PALESTINE REBELLION 1936-1939

students armed with sticks attacked police near the government offices. The police charged in a flying wedge wielding batons and drove the students into the narrow winding streets of the walled city. A shot fired from a cafe by an unknown assailant felled one policeman. The story was the same in Haifa, Ramleh and Hebron. The district commissioner's office in Gaza was stoned while the population barricaded the main streets for protection against the police and soldiers, who were equipped with Lewis automatic weapons and tear gas.

On May 26 a lively fusillade rang through the night in the gardens and orange groves around Jaffa as soldiers and Arabs engaged each other in a deadly caricature of hide-and-seek. Jaffa continued to defy any pacification attempts by the authorities. The tough and rugged Jaffa boatmen lived in the mass of closely packed houses perched above the port; by day they pelted police patrols with bombs, then vanished among the labyrinth of narrow lanes.

The young men then left the streets to their sisters and elders. They slipped into the hills to join their cousins from the villages who had formed guerilla bands. There was no central organization and yet guerillas sprang up all over Palestine. They had no real knowledge of guerilla tactics yet they blew up bridges in the south, derailed trains at Nablus and Tulkarm, attacked British convoys wherever they were encountered and even shot down an airplane whose pilot was imprudent enough to attempt a ground-level bombing attack. These incidents began to assume the aspects of the Irish Easter Rebellion and, like the Irish, the Arabs were up against the British Empire itself. The British garrison had doubled before the end of May, and redoubled before June was out. Famous regiments like the Cameron and Seaforth Highlanders were transferred to Palestine in battalion strength. Thousands of troops combed the hills for dissidents and R.A.F. fighter planes bombed and strafed the hills where guerillas were suspected of hiding.

The high commissioner took further security measures and increased the penalties for bomb throwing, for firing on soldiers and for the illegal possession of weapons. Collective punishments were imposed on whole towns and villages. In the working-class quarter of Jaffa, 237 tenement houses were blown up on the pretext of initiating a town-planning scheme, thereby increasing the hardships of the growing urban proletariat. House to house searches for guns and ammunition were conducted in the Arab villages. At one location, Kefr Kenna, village women stoned the troops from the rooftops of their homes. The soldiers replied with Lewis guns; miraculously only a young girl of nine was killed.

The secretary-general of the Arab Higher Committee, Auni Abdul Hadi, and forty-nine prominent labor and strike leaders were arrested and interned in a camp on the Egyptian frontier where they promptly set about sabotaging the camp's installations provoking more severe security measures against them. The Arab Higher Committee issued a manifesto urging the non-payment of taxes on the principle of "no taxation without representation." At the same time the committee issued a statement eschewing violence in all forms, claiming that the object of the strike was to recover the Arabs' violated rights. Unorganized and undirected, the violence increased.

There was, however, a lighter side to the wave of unrest. One evening the police received a telephone call from a village near Jerusalem. Two *fellah* had found a Jew wandering in the hills and the villagers wanted the police to come and collect him. The young man, perplexed at having been led to the village and locked in a room, explained to the police that he had been enjoying his customary nocturnal stroll. In the circumstances, the Arab villagers had decided the man must be mad and in his distraught state of mind the confines of a police barracks would be safer for him.

The war of nerves between the high commissioner and the Arab Higher Committee continued through the long, hot Palestinian summer. A large number of labor certificates had been issued to the Jewish Agency in May at the same time as the announcement of another Royal Commission to investigate the causes of the "disturbances." The British Government insisted that the strike end before the commissioners were sent to Palestine, and the Higher Committee demanded at least the

THE PALESTINE REBELLION 1936-1939

cessation of Jewish immigration as a condition for an end to the resistance.

After six months the strike had a telling effect on the Arab community, which could no longer finance the shutdown of the economy. Moreover, it was evident that the guerillas were no match for the superior British forces. The Higher Committee was driven to the wall, and in October the strike was broken without it having won a single concession. The rulers of Iraq, Transjordan and Saudi Arabia had all urged the Arabs of Palestine to end the disorders and trust the good intentions of Great Britain which, they said, "has declared that she will do justice." In November the Royal Commission arrived, spent three months in Palestine and a further six months preparing its report. For nine months an uneasy calm settled over the Holy Land.

The commission's report was issued in July 1937, simultaneously with a Government White Paper adopting the general findings of the report. Its main conclusion was simple: the Palestine Mandate was unworkable. The reason was equally simple: British obligations to the Jews could only be fulfilled by a policy of repression against a resentful Arab population. After twenty years of frustration and indecision the government was forced to concede that there was "an irreconcilable conflict between the aspirations of the Jews and Arabs in Palestine."

It was cold comfort to the Arabs that they had finally scored a point. The commission's decision for a permanent solution to the impasse was that Palestine should be partitioned into sovereign Jewish and Arab states, and a British mandatory zone. The Jewish state would comprise the coastal plain from a point south of Jaffa, thence to Haifa, the whole of Galilee and to the Jezreel Valley. Jaffa would be included in the Arab state which would comprise the rest of Palestine. The mandate zone was designed to include the Holy Places in Jerusalem and Bethlehem, with a corridor leading to the sea.

The concept of partition was consistently rejected by the Arabs for the reason that it was highly prejudicial to their interests. In the first place, the most fertile and developed part of Palestine would fall into the area allotted to the Jewish state where Arabs held title to four times as much land as the Jews, and where seven-eighths of the Arab-owned citrus groves were located. Moreover, the area remaining to the Arab state could never be economically viable. Jaffa would be isolated and a large proportion of Arabs would be placed under Jewish rule.

At the same time the majority of Zionist leaders realized that the formation of a Jewish state in only a part of Palestine and the establishment of an economically backward Arab state adjacent to it was the best means of eventually achieving their aim of a Jewish state in all of Palestine. At the 20th Zionist Congress in Zurich, Ben Gurion had said: "No Zionist can forego the smallest portion of the Land of Israel. Our debate here concerns which of two routes would lead quicker to the common goal." The Zionists anticipated the partition of Palestine and in order to enlarge their territorial claims, armed Jewish settlements — with the help of the Haganah — were being established at the rate of one a month during the course of the Arab rebellion.

Nor did partition extract Great Britain from the horns of the dilemma which it had devised for itself with the Balfour Declaration. The scheme involved the same mutually exclusive alternatives the existence of which the government had denied by professing itself impartially committed to an equal obligation to both Arab and Jew. Professor Hourani has observed that partition was not a middle solution, but in fact a pro-Jewish solution, since, he says: "It conceded the essence of the Jewish claims, although on a smaller scale than they demanded. It involved exactly the same danger to the Arabs, and not even on a smaller scale, since if the Jews once got a foothold it would be difficult to stop them expanding."[4]

A member of the Royal Commission, Sir Laurie Hammond, committed an indiscretion when he said in May 1938, that if the Jews could get sufficient land to meet the immediate requirements of a sovereign power then this would be the first step toward getting back the rest of the country. "It will take many years," he said, "but it will come."[5]

Meanwhile, sporadic Arab resistance was resumed late in the summer of 1937 and the situation once again threatened to deteriorate. The British Government had yet to take a final decision on partition and appointed a technical team to investigate its feasibility. Then came the breaking point.

One morning in September outside a church in Nazareth,

L.Y. Andrews, district commissioner for Galilee, was shot down by four armed men. For weeks the mandate administration had been under pressure from the Jewish Agency and its supporters in England to crack down on the Arab Higher Committee and hold it responsible for the disorders. Popular sentiment against the British, however, was by then too widespread and bitter for the Higher Committee to control it, even had it been so inclined. Nevertheless, Hajj Amin issued a communiqué on the evening of Andrews' murder denouncing it as a senseless, brutal act, which it was since Andrews had been a close friend of a member of the Higher Committee and was respected by the Arab leaders.

Although the Committee was in no way connected with the deed, the administration decided to use the incident as a test of its authority. In a few days some 300 known supporters of the Supreme Muslim Council were arrested and detained while the Higher Committee was declared illegal and dissolved. Members who were caught were deported to the Seychelles. Hajj Amin succeeded in reaching the coast in disguise. A small fishing craft took him to safety in Lebanon. When disorders erupted throughout the country in protest against the wholesale removal of the Arab leaders, the government replied by imposing heavy fines on villages, indiscriminately dynamiting homes and arresting notables and villagers until some 800 prisoners were interned in camps. A few were summarily tried and executed. Of the condemned, one is still remembered today by Palestinians for the lyrics he recited extemporaneously to a fellow inmate the night before he met his death on the gallows:

> Night: let the captive finish his song;
> by dawn his wing shall flutter
> and the hanged one will swing
> in the wind.
>
> Night: slow your pace
> let me pour out my heart to you;
> perhaps you forgot who I am
> and what my troubles are.
>
> Pity how my hours have slipped
> through your hands;

> do not think I weep from fear,
> my tears are for my country...

British army engineers and Jewish laborers worked through the following winter to seal off northern Palestine from neighboring Syria from which the rebels were smuggling arms. A military road was constructed, backed by a system of barbed-wire barriers and supporting defense works. Just as Hadrian's Wall had not kept the barbarian out of England, so rebels managed to filter through the gaps in the frontier lines and melt into anonymity among the friendly and sympathetic village population.

Rebel activity redoubled in the summer of 1938 and well into the fall. In several centers the civil authorities were driven out, police stations destroyed and government offices occupied. Hebron, Beersheba, Jericho, Bethlehem, Ramallah and finally the Old City of Jerusalem felt the direct influence of the insurgents' presence. Then, as superior numbers, training and equipment began to stem the tide of rebellion, the nationalist sub-war spent itself. At the end of the fighting the British had nearly 20,000 troops in Palestine, including eighteen infantry battalions, armored cars and cavalry units, and 700 Royal Air Force personnel. Over 5,000 Arabs died in the fighting. Some 2,000 were wounded and nearly 2,500 were under detention.

The Arab nationalist movement in Palestine collapsed, and was never fully to recover.

Arab leaders were forced to ask themselves what three long years of bitter resistance had accomplished. For the sake of their future they might also have asked themselves *why* they had failed. Despite the common national goal shared alike by the workers and peasants and the upper classes of landowners and religious elite, the Palestinians could not put an end to the scheme for the Jewish National Home. Apart from the structure of the Mandate which favored the rapid growth of the Jewish community over that of the Arab majority, the failure of the nationalist movement can be explained as well by the different perspectives of the Palestinian upper class and the masses.

The upper class, represented by families like the Husseinis and the Nashishibis, sought to resolve the question of political power. Who was to rule Palestine, the British, the Arabs or the Zionists?. Representative democratic institutions would not only have secured the independence of the Palestinian community from the danger of the other two fronts, but would also have served the interests of the Arab upper class which would enjoy the privilege of ruling an independent Palestine. Hence the constant efforts by the Arab leadership to negotiate directly with the British for a democratic constitution.

The reaction of the Palestinian masses in 1929 and again in 1936-1938 was not simply due to an oppressive mandate policy. It also reflected the failure of the Arab leadership to secure from the British meaningful concessions which would have alleviated the increasingly desperate situation of the peasantry. Hence the basis of political action for the masses was incoherent violence. But this violence, welling up from the bottom strata of society, terrified even the Arab leadership since it threatened to sweep them away with the tide as well. In the latest crisis, the Arab leadership tried to soothe the anger of the masses by claiming that Britain would at last recognize the justice of their cause. The failure of the nationalist movement was, in fact, due as much to the inability or unwillingness of the leadership to co-opt the full support of the masses in bringing about the destruction of the Mandate. The effendis could not think in terms of being obligated to the lower classes in the context of a total national struggle. They could only feel some obligation for the lower classes insofar as this did not conflict with their own vital interests.

The full potential of the masses was never exploited by the leadership. The real significance of this failure was not grasped by the Palestinians until after two decades of malignant despair when the Palestinian guerilla groups appeared on the scene to attempt to put together the shattered remnants of their nation.

Meanwhile, Britain had in fact officially acknowledged the implications of its mandate policy and its devastating effect on the Arab community. The partition scheme, too, was officially discarded as impractical owing to the political, administrative and financial difficulties it involved. The moment required a fresh approach to the Palestine Problem — a moment when the world was now poised precariously between war and "peace in our time."

The Arab rebellion had given the entire mandate question world prominence. For the first time Arab governments became involved on the side of the Palestinians both as a moderating force on the local situation and as a pressure on Britain to modify its policy. Fascist Italy engaged in an anti-British propaganda campaign directed at keeping Arab disaffection in Palestine alive. Germany also found the prospects attractive in playing the same game, hoping to weaken the British position in the Middle East. Moreover, however distrustful Palestinians might have been of Germany and Italy *qua* European powers, there emerged a sympathy for Germany as the ideal of a strong and unified nation which shared with the Palestinians a common enemy in Britain, and by extension also the Jews.

The area, however, was too crucial for Britain to allow it to go by default and not make some genuine gesture toward meeting fundamental Arab demands in Palestine. If war broke out in Europe, Arab friendship in the Middle East would be a useful asset, just as it had been in World War I. Against the background of the prevailing international situation, and based upon the conclusions of the most recent of its commissions, the British Government announced its new policy for Palestine in the White Paper of 1939.

The White Paper ruled out the possibility of either an Arab or a Jewish state. The constitutional solution was rather to be found in a Palestinian state in which both peoples would exercise governmental authority; a constitution drafted by Arab, Jewish and British representatives would have to provide for, among other matters, safeguards for the special position of the Jewish National Home. It was envisaged that independence could be achieved in ten years, but it was *conditional upon the development of good relations between the Arab and Jewish communities.* Both Jewish immigration and land purchases were to be subject to restrictions. The level of immigration was placed at an annual high of 15,000 for a period of five years, of which one third was to constitute a contribution toward the solution of the Jewish refugee problem in Europe. After the five years had elapsed, Arab consent to further immigration would have to be obtained. In addition land sales to Jews were restricted in certain areas, prohibited in others.

Most Arab leaders acknowledged that the White Paper went a long way toward removing the threat to Arab national existence in Palestine by ensuring (in theory at least) that a Jewish majority would never be established. There remained, however, a deep-seated suspicion that the policy would be whittled away under pressure from Zionists and their parliamentary sympathizers as had happened all too frequently in the past. For this reason Palestinians were ambivalent in their reactions to the White Paper.

The Jewish Agency on the other hand rejected the government's announcement in the strongest terms as a moral breach of the Mandate, and an illegal abandonment of the national home policy. Zionists vowed never to submit to its provisions, nor permit its implementation. It was, however, Viscount Samuel (formerly Sir Herbert Samuel, the first high commissioner to Palestine), who put his finger squarely on the weakness of the White Paper. Arab sovereignty, he observed, was subject after ten years to Jewish consent, just as further Jewish immigration was subject to Arab consent after five years. Each side was therefore given a veto on the aspirations of the other side and this was supposed to induce each to become friends. Lord Samuel concluded that the British Government apparently assumed that two negatives made a positive, rather than admit that the veto would cripple the whole scheme.

Although Palestinian Arabs had secured certain concessions from Britain, it was far from certain that the concessions were firmly secured. They had paid a heavy price for the new policy. The national movement was in total disrepair, its leaders either deported or under detention. In the early years of World War II, Britain encouraged political émigrés to return to Palestine, but only so they could be kept under close scrutiny and within reach of the authorities. The Supreme Muslim Council fell under complete British supervision. Arabic newspapers were in financial straits and many folded; those which survived suddenly switched to pro-British editorializing, which suggested they were receiving not only government encouragement, but financing as well.

Hajj Amin Husseini was forced to remain outside the country

and spent the war years trying to keep out of reach of the Allied armies. He finally wound up in Germany where he was permitted to meet Hitler and other Nazi leaders. He had reestablished the Arab Higher Committee in Beirut and Damascus and continued to claim that he was speaking in the name of the Palestinian people. He had a considerable following among the Arab masses, but his absence from the local political scene made it difficult for his own Palestine Arab Party to rebuild itself. The National Defense Party of the rival Nashishibi faction was more moderate and prepared to cooperate with Britain on the basis of the White Paper. The mandate administration for its part made no effort to cultivate moderate Arab political opinion for, having already crushed the national uprising, it preferred to take the initiative in Arab affairs and keep the political movements weak. The N.D.P. virtually collapsed after 1941 and the field was left to the smaller and less influential Istiqlal party, which was in any case unable to impose its will on the Arab community.

7

Zionist Countermoves

The option of violence had failed. Twenty years of political struggle culminating in open rebellion had brought the country no closer to independence. By the outbreak of World War II, Palestinians were physically and morally exhausted and the country was beset by a crippling economic depression.

The common denominator of Arab sentiment throughout most of the Middle East by the fall of 1939 was anti-Western, directed especially against Britain and France, the dominating powers in the area for two decades. In Palestine, Arabs had experienced the sustained efforts of the British to aid a foreign people to possess their country. It was impossible, psychologically, for Palestinians to perform a sudden volte-face and embrace the Allied cause in the war. Indeed, Nazi propaganda beamed to the Arab world was effective in Palestine for the simple reason that Germany was the declared enemy of Britain and France. Moreover, while Britain and France had, in Arab eyes, made a mockery of its "sacred trust of civilization," Germany had not been tainted by the same brush. Many regarded Germany as a potential liberator, especially as the early devastating defeats of the Allied forces seemed to herald a Nazi sweep of Europe and North Africa. Some shrewder minds, however, counseled caution for fear of trading one master for another. But there were few who paused to consider that Hitler's diabolical persecution of Jews would force the Zionists to desperate decisions which would make them even more determined to push their aims to fulfillment.

Finally, despite the inevitable community of feeling between the Arabs and Germany, the moment came when the decisive choice had to be made. By 1942 some 9,000 Palestinian Arabs had volunteered for the British Armed Forces, some of whom served actively in Greece and Italy. Palestinians generally had now committed themselves to the Allied war effort.

On the national front, however, little progress was achieved. Owing to the absence of political leadership and factional disputes, Palestinians tended to look to neighboring states for guidance and support. A movement toward Arab unity, strongly supported by Britain, gained momentum in the last stages of the war. In September-October 1944, a general conference of Arab states (including Iraq, Transjordan, Saudi Arabia, Lebanon, Syria and Yemen) met in Alexandria. The outcome was a protocol which led to the founding of the Arab League in the following year. From that time on, major political decisions concerning Arab tactics against the Zionists were taken in Cairo. This development undoubtedly gave the Palestinians an important outlet through which their views reached world opinion, but it did nothing concrete by way of strengthening their community or making it more cohesive. When the final show of strength came, as it was bound to, the Jewish community was far better prepared to seize the option of violence and make it count decisively.

Indeed, the lesson of violence had not been lost on the Zionists. Force would not be discounted if the National Home could not be achieved by political means, and force would be resorted to if and when there occurred a complete breakdown in relations between Britain and the Zionists. In the end, Zionist military tactics skillfully combined with political strategy, weakened Britain's will to govern Palestine. Once Britain resolved to turn Palestine over to the United Nations for disposal, a situation was created in which force alone determined the solution vis-à-vis the Arab population. Zionists had recently accepted the implications of this challenge while, paradoxically, the Arabs who had for a long time correctly read the implications of the Zionist program failed to respond to the challenge.

Ironically, it was the British who gave the Jewish Agency the opportunity to acquire invaluable experience in the military tactics which the Zionists were to employ in undermining mandate rule. During the Arab rebellion the Mandate Government permitted the enlargement of the Jewish Settlement Police, which it also equipped and nominally placed under its control. However,

ZIONIST COUNTERMOVES

the J.S.P. was largely comprised of volunteers from the Haganah, the illegal military arm of the Jewish Agency. Consequently, a legally recognized civil police force was used as a cover for the purposes of an illegal military command.

In May 1938, Orde Wingate, an Englishman with passionate Zionist leanings, organized special night squads of British and Jewish units. Under his brilliant leadership the Haganah received expert training in the latest techniques of guerilla warfare.[11] Haganah volunteers took part in offensive actions against Arab resistance fighters and Wingate's squads operated effectively in such maneuvers alongside British troops in the Galilee region.

In 1941, the Haganah set up an elite commando force called the Palmach. When Britain feared a possible German attack on Palestine, some 600 Palmach members were specially trained by a British military mission to meet this eventuality. The membership of the Haganah numbered about 21,000 men and women in 1937; by 1944 the number had risen sharply to around 37,000, many of whom had seen active service in the Allied armies during the war. It was in September of the same year that the British War Office decided to create a Jewish brigade, actually the result of persistent and repeated Zionist demands for their own fighting units to assist the Allied cause. The Jews of Palestine naturally had no alternative but to join the struggle, in whatever capacity, against the specter of Nazism devouring Europe.

A Jewish fighting force served Zionism in two ways. *First*, the brigade fought in Italy under its own banner (the Star of David which later became the flag of Israel) representing for the Jewish people an important political move toward the recognition of the principle of Jewish statehood. *Second*, as Arthur Koestler notes, the veterans of the Jewish brigade "became the nucleus of the future Israeli Army and a decisive factor in the Arab defeat which amounted to a defeat of British policy."[12] The wartime years had transformed Haganah from an informal home guard into an underground Jewish national army.

The immediate political aim of the Jewish Agency was to bring an end to the restrictions on Jewish immigration and land purchases imposed by the 1939 White Paper. The ultimate goal was set forth by David Ben Gurion, then chairman of the Jewish Agency executive, at a meeting of Zionists at the Biltmore Hotel,

New York, in May 1942. Ben Gurion dismissed any scheme for a bi-national state if this meant offering Arabs equal representation in the government of Palestine. The Biltmore Conference reiterated the basic clarity of purpose always present in political Zionism: the overriding concern of Herzl's Basle program to which all else was subordinated, namely the establishment of Palestine as the Jewish Commonwealth. i.e. the Jewish State. The conference also marked the beginning of an intense campaign to enlist the support of American public opinion and the political leaders of both the Republican and Democratic parties to this end.

In Palestine meanwhile the frustration and bitterness of the Jewish community was mounting against Britain as the provisions of the White Paper were implemented. Illegal immigration was a means of striking a blow to redress the situation. This was, in fact, the chief feature of Jewish activism in Palestine throughout the war. A Committee on Illegal Immigration (Mossad) was formed in 1937 in collaboration with the Haganah High Command. Emissaries were dispatched to Germany and Austria to organize emigration from the European end.

Jon and David Kimche have written an exciting account of these daring operations in their book, *The Secret Roads*. The task of the Mossad emissaries was not necessarily to save Jews from their tragic plight under Nazi tyranny. "That was not their job," write the Kimches. "Their eyes were fixed entirely on Palestine and the British Mandatory. They were looking for young men and women who wanted to go to Palestine because they wanted a national home of their own and were prepared to pioneer, struggle and, if necessary, fight for it. Their interest in those German Jews who turned to Palestine as a haven of refuge, as the next best thing after the United States or the United Kingdom, was secondary to their main purpose."[3]

The program was consistent with overall Zionist strategy. It was also, by all accounts, a great success as approximately 80,000 Jews were brought to Palestine by Mossad. Single-minded purpose, however admirably it is rationalized in terms of results, can still lead to excesses, which in itself is tragic. Mossad activities, for example, forced the Palestine Government in November 1940, to decree that henceforward "illegals" would be transshipped to a British colony for the duration of the war. Two ships, the *Milos* and the *Pacific*, were then intercepted by a British coast guard patrol and the "illegals" were transferred to the *Patria* for deportation to Mauritius. On November 25 the ship blew up and 202 Jewish immigrants and fifty crew and police lost their lives. "It was an open secret," observe the Kimches, "that it had been organized by the Haganah,"[14] but the legend was accepted that the immigrants had committed suicide to bring attention to the plight of the Jewish refugee and the "injustices" of the mandate immigration policy. "By the organizers of the tragedy and their sympathizers, the story of the *Patria*, twisted out of reality, was seized upon for propaganda which had by now become worldwide, for the blackening of the character of the Palestine administration and the motives of its directors."[15] So writes Albert Hyamson, the onetime director of immigration in Palestine, and a man not unsympathetic to the Jewish National Home. The tragedy had the immediate effect desired. The survivors of the *Patria* were allowed to enter Palestine as legal immigrants.

Criticism has been ceaselessly heaped upon Britain and the Mandate Government for gross insensitivity to the Jewish refugee problem before and during the war. It is, therefore, worth recalling the sober strictures of Albert Hyamson concerning the critics of British policy. Palestine, he points out, was not a rich country, but limited in natural resources and space available for development. In the seven pre-war years of the Hitler regime, Palestine received more than 200,000 Jewish immigrants as compared to only 92,000 in the United States, a country which possessed unparalleled riches and resources. Palestine, in fact, absorbed more immigrants from Axis-dominated Europe than any country in the world.

In 1934 and 1935 the position of German Jews was most precarious owing to their increasing number and viciousness of restrictive laws enacted against them by the Nazis. High Commissioner Sir Arthur Wauchope expressed his hope that the Zionist Organization would allot a large proportion of its labor list to Jews in Germany. The Zionists, however, who had complete control over the selection of immigrants, distributed in 1934 only a quarter of the 14,300 certificates to German Jews. The overwhelming majority of certificates were given to Jews of Eastern Europe, especially to Polish Jews.[6] This discrimination may best be explained by the ethnic origin of Palestinian Jewish leadership which was itself largely Eastern European.

These considerations aside, the gradual pre-war and wartime decimation of European Jewry posed the profoundest moral challenge to the governments of those countries which were spared the horrors of Nazi occupation. It was not just indifference which kept the immigration gates of America, Canada and Britain only partially open to Jewish refugees. Awareness of their plight existed. What was lacking was the decency of simple courage to place human life above political expediency. American Zionists, too, tacitly contributed to this moral failure by not openly attacking the restrictive quota system on immigration. Rather, they saw the quota system itself as proof that theirs was the only viable alternative for the Jews of Europe.

Britain's real dilemma in the tragedy of Palestine was that her realization of the hopeless contradiction which the Mandate involved came too late — much too late. It has been said, not unfairly, that if Herzl was the Marxist theoretician of Zionism, Hitler was the Leninist prime mover of the Jewish State.

Jewish activism followed other courses as well. Raids on British arms' depots increased the supply of illegal weapons available to the Jewish community; at the same time, the Haganah became a major purchaser of contraband war material from all over the world. Activism in an extreme form appeared with groups such as the Irgun and the Stern Gang. These groups, it must be stressed, operated independently of the Jewish Agency and the Zionist leadership during most of the war. The two factions differed at first mainly over who was to be regarded as the chief enemy of Jewish statehood. The Irgun thought it was the Arabs, the Sternists the British.[7]

The Irgun's first venture came in July 1938, when two land mines exploded in the Arab fruit market in Haifa, killing seventy-four and wounding 129. Two Freedom Fighters (as the Sternists were later known) in 1944 assassinated Lord Moyne, the British minister-resident in the Middle East and a member of the war cabinet. Both these acts were denounced by the Jewish Agency, although it is also worth noting that David Ben Gurion did little to check the activities of extremists in the early months of the war. Ben Gurion himself was in direct control of small commando groups which were independent of the Haganah high command. The special squads, or P.O.M., initiated attacks on British property and against at least two Arab villages in the Haifa district.

The extremist societies took firm root from 1944 onward. Ideological differences between the Irgun and the Freedom Fighters gradually vanished as each directed its efforts against the mandate regime. As long as the White Paper remained in force, the Jewish community became increasingly passive toward the efforts, albeit feeble, of British authorities to stamp out the extremists' activities. In fact, the real significance of their program lay in their influence on the uncommitted opinion in the Yishuv.

By the summer of 1945 the war had ended and a new Labor government was installed in Britain. The Laborites had shown strong pro-Zionist sympathies at their annual Blackpool conference. A resolution adopted in the party platform suggested that the Arabs be moved out of Palestine as the Jews moved in. The Jewish community eagerly looked to the government's abandonment of the White Paper and the new foreign secretary, Ernest Bevin, was regarded as the champion of their cause. A dedicated socialist, yet unreservedly British, Bevin was sensitive to the nationalist feelings of people everywhere. However, the stresses of the post-war world, Britain's anxiety over the future of Europe and the looming Soviet threat to Berlin all militated against acting in consonance with his socialist principles. Britain's Asian defense strategy put him at odds with Arab nationalists in the Middle East when he tried to bargain for the renewal of treaties with Egypt and Iraq which granted Britain preferential powers in the maintenance of military bases.

Bevin was forced to swim against the rising tide of Arab nationalism. He argued that a unitary state in Palestine would best serve his country's defense needs. This was not unwelcome to the Palestinians, but Bevin, the optimist, believed that a settlement could be negotiated and he was short tempered with those whom he believed viewed problems with blinkers on their eyes. Arabs were no less obstinate than Zionists in pressing their claims, but he allowed himself to commit disastrous indiscretions when angered by the Zionists' insistence that Palestine was the *only* refuge for European Jewry. Bevin was instantly portrayed as a dyed-in-the-wool anti-Semite. Hard pressed by the American administration, he soon lost control over his policy. The ghost which had bedeviled the entire mandate period returned to haunt Bevin; neutrality between Arab and Jew in Palestine was impossible. Anglo-Zionist relations came to an abrupt end.

Jewish public opinion in Palestine was now more than ever favorably disposed toward terrorism as a means of political pressure. In November 1945, Haganah began negotiations for a merger with the Irgun and the Freedom Fighters. For many months their operations were coordinated under Haganah command which concentrated attacks against British installations and personnel.

Mayhem characterized the declining years of the Mandate. The combined efforts of the Haganah and the terrorists demonstrated a degree of ruthlessness and efficiency which gradually sapped Britain's strength and will to remain in Palestine. Increased illegal immigration, coupled with these military tactics added to the pressure from within.

Meanwhile in the United States, Zionist diplomacy aimed at getting the American Government to exert pressure on Whitehall while whipping up public opinion, both Jewish and non-Jewish, to its banner. In the propaganda war for American and Canadian public opinion Zionists held the trump card. Their great strength was that Zionism could be all things to all men. By contrast the appeal of the Palestinian Arab was simple, and seemed to lack depth and meaning. The Arabs had not asked to be ruled as a British colony, and they wished even less to be subordinated to an alien people. All they had sought was the freedom and independence to determine their own future. The argument was unembroidered and direct. Consequently it left no latitude (unlike Zionism) for subtle appeals to American conscience or prejudice. Zionists, moreover, employed organizational techniques to which the Arabs were wholly unaccustomed. As a result, North American public opinion was uninformed of the real situation, in the sense that it was half-informed, and exposed to only one side of the story. For example, a public opinion poll conducted in Canada in 1946 indicated that there was widespread support for free

Jewish immigration into Palestine although the pollsters noted that this did not necessarily indicate a public commitment to Jewish statehood.

Widely based support in the United States from the local to national level was obtained.[181] Pro-Zionist resolutions were passed in thirty-three State legislatures, by the Congress of Industrial Organizations (C.I.O.) and the American Federation of Labor (A.F. of L.), in both the House of Representatives and the Senate, in the Democratic and Republican Conventions during the presidential campaign of 1944, and again during the congressional elections of 1946. In the White House, President Truman was under the impression that the Zionists were primarily interested in securing a haven for Jewish refugees and that statehood was but a secondary and possible future objective. He therefore advanced the proposal to Prime Minister Attlee of Britain that 100,000 Jews be allowed into Palestine. Attlee reminded the president of promises made to the Arabs, and suggested the creation of a joint Anglo-American Commission which could recommend practical avenues of action on the Palestine question. The commission accepted the Truman proposal, but denied that either Arabs or Jews had the exclusive right to establish a state, recommendations which ensured rejection by both.

The scene of the final diplomatic and political battle for Palestine shifted to the United Nations. Anglo-American cooperation had not provided a solution, and the Zionist war of attrition against Britain forced her to confess the failure of the Mandate and to request the United Nations to place the Palestine question on its agenda. The years of wartime Zionist propaganda were about to pay rich dividends.

An eleven nation Special Committee on Palestine was set up by a General Assembly resolution on May 15, 1947. UNSCOP, as it was known, was confronted with the choice of recommending one of two possible alternatives: either independence in some form, or the continuation of the Mandate. Independence was the course chosen and this meant, in effect, the partition of Palestine into independent Jewish and Arab states. The Zionists had achieved a major victory. The next step was to see that the plan was adopted by the General Assembly.

The Arab position was precarious. The Soviet Union, for

reasons of her own, joined with the United States in backing the partition solution. The Arab states combined could not hope for an outright defeat of the scheme, although there remained the chance that it would not obtain the required thirty-two votes which constituted a two-thirds majority of the Assembly. Amid strenuous efforts on the part of the Arabs and Zionists to secure the precious votes, the U.S. moved in to throw her weight behind the Zionists. The crucial votes were with Haiti, Liberia, Ethiopia, China, the Philippines and Greece. The American Government and allied business interests successfully pressured the home governments of Haiti, Liberia and Ethiopia into altering their original anti-partition vote to one of pro-partition. When the final vote was taken on November 29, 1947, the partition resolution passed by thirty-three votes to thirteen, with ten abstentions. It was a momentous decision, or rather recommendation, for it did not confer any legal privilege. It was at best a compromise, and possibly even the best of compromises, but as Benjamin Disraeli once put it, compromise only ends in catastrophe.

Within the Jewish community of Palestine there was widespread satisfaction over the UN decision, although right-wing political parties were angered at the small size of the proposed Jewish State, which even Ben Gurion described as an "irreducible minimum." The General Assembly had declared that the Jewish State should compromise 56 percent of all Palestine, much less than the Jewish Agency's own partition proposal made in August 1946, but far better than the 1937 Royal Commission scheme. From minority status, owning only 6 percent of the total land area of the country, the Jewish community was gratuitously granted possession of the major part of Palestine with a majority (however slight) over the Arabs living within the area of the proposed Jewish State. The resolution further provided for the total withdrawal of British forces by August 1, 1948, and for a UN Palestine Commission which would supervise the transition period to statehood.

The struggle for a separate State of Israel in the midst of the Arab Middle East now entered the last stage. An undeclared state of war has existed ever since.

8

End of the Mandate

It was obvious to everyone that the resolution could not be implemented without resort to force. The United Nations had no means at its disposal, and none of the major powers was prepared to intervene physically. The decision to use force, therefore, would be made in Palestine, where one side would attempt to enforce the resolution, the other to frustrate it.

In the short weeks between the November resolution and the official end of the Mandate, May 15, 1948, public security in Palestine deteriorated to the vanishing point and essential government services were seriously crippled. The outcome of the impending struggle was by no means a foregone conclusion, but several factors seemed to favor the Jewish community over the Arabs.

First, the Jewish National Home had evolved through provisions in the mandate system into a sub-national government able to operate efficiently and to control all aspects of its community life from public works to military preparation. As the Mandate drew to an end, the Jewish Agency was transformed with comparative ease into the governmental machinery of the Jewish State.

Second, the Zionist leadership enjoyed its recent success in forcing Britain to relinquish responsibility over Palestine, capping this with a political victory in the United Nations. The momentum of the struggle on these fronts flowed over into the struggle against the Arab community. The organic unity of the Jewish community, patterned as it was along European lines, made it relatively easy to conscript and mobilize the entire community for war. The best military personnel of the Haganah, especially the elite corps of the Palmach, were British trained. Moreover, tremendous efforts had been made to buy up stocks of arms of all types which were supplemented by local (illegal) armament factories capable of producing light machine guns and ammunition, grenades, mortar shells, Sten guns, flame throwers, anti-tank guns, and the Davidka heavy mortar. In April 1948, an arms agreement had been negotiated with Czechoslovakia and supplies and weapons began to arrive in Palestine by private airplane and small ships. Heavy armor was brought in after the State of Israel was officially declared.

The Arab community, on the other hand, had suffered the weakening and demoralizing effects of British colonial rule. The Mandatory had made little effort to promote the experience of self-government. When the crisis came the Arabs found they could organize effectively only at the local level. Resistance to partition was patterned after the Arab rebellion, sporadically without any central coordinating machinery whatsoever. But 1948 was different from 1938 in significant ways. The Arab leadership was still forced to work from outside Palestine, although the reconstituted Arab Higher Committee was able to establish some local committees in towns and villages with responsibility for fund raising and the recruitment of a kind of home guard for local defense.

More serious, however, was the general demoralization of the Arab peasantry which was the result of the crushing defeat of the nationalist uprising a decade earlier. During the early months following the end of the war in 1945, the peasants remained passive and quiet, making it doubly difficult for Arab leadership to mobilize them to meet the fresh danger. As a consequence, the burden of the struggle was placed on the shoulders of volunteers who infiltrated from neighboring Arab countries. The "liberate Palestine" movement began in January 1948, but even in March the number of participants did not exceed 5,000; too few to cope with the better trained, better equipped and more numerous Haganah. The Army of Liberation, as the volunteers were called, was only suited to static defensive action. This meant occupying the high ground overlooking some of the major roads, sniping at convoys and disrupting communications. Their main activities were centered on the Tel Aviv-Jerusalem and Jerusalem-Hebron roads, which in fact did not endanger the vast majority of Jewish settlements along the coastal plain and in Galilee. There was little active fighting during the first three months of 1948, although Arabs and Jews alike resorted to the customary but irregular methods of intimidation and retaliation by bomb throwing. Despite spiraling violence on both sides there was no evidence of panic within the Arab community.

The Palestinian leaders of the Arab Higher Committee and the Arab League were playing a wait-and-see political game, hoping that the partition scheme would be reviewed and then abandoned. Even the Americans were already having serious second thoughts about the viability of partition, certain as it was to bring about a violent conclusion to the Mandate. On March 19, 1948, the American delegate to the United Nations proposed the suspension of the partition scheme and that it be replaced with a UN trusteeship. Arab tactics, therefore, seemed justified to a degree, although the failure to prepare an adequate military alternative was, in the long run, disastrous. The Jewish Agency's reaction to the unwelcome developments in the UN was to declare on March 23 that, come what may, a provisional Jewish Government would take over as of May 15. In other words, the UN resolution for partition and statehood would be converted into reality through a simple fait accompli. At the end of March the Haganah high command reached the conclusion that "the only solution is to take the initiative into our own hands, to try to achieve a military decision by going over to the offensive."[11]

Meanwhile, the political committee of the Arab League hesitated, and it was not until the end of April that the decision to intervene in Palestine was made. But by that time it was too late to reverse the course of events which were rapidly consuming the Palestinian Arab community.

With the Haganah decision to go over to the offensive, a plan was devised which completely revised previous defense strategy. Known as Plan D, its objective was "to gain control of the area allotted to the Jewish State and defend its borders, and those blocs of Jewish settlements and such Jewish population as were outside those borders, against a regular or para-regular enemy operating from bases outside or inside the area of the Jewish State."[12] The crucial logistical problem for the Zionists was to replace the de jure authority of Britain (which would end on May 15) with the de facto control of successive areas of the country as they were vacated by British troops. Britain's legal "presence" conveniently provided a shield for these operations against possible attack by the regular Arab armies.

In April 1948 Haganah was in full control of all the Jewish fighting forces, including the Irgun group. Haganah was now responsible for all military operations and the Irgun was obliged to submit its plans to the high command for approval. Both the very influential *Ha'aretz* and the popular *Davar*, the leading lights of the Jewish press in Palestine, voiced their satisfaction at the agreement of cooperation.[3]

On April 1, Haganah commenced the first of thirteen military campaigns under Plan D; eight of these were conducted against Arab villages outside the area allotted to the Jewish State.[4] The primary objective was to carve out a corridor between Tel Aviv and Jerusalem, and to isolate the Holy City. Jewish forces attacked Arab villages, expelling the inhabitants and dynamiting homes so that they could not be re-occupied by the enemy. In a few dramatic days some 10,000 to 15,000 Arabs were launched on the road to refugee camps. Later campaigns conducted in the first two weeks of May were designed to capture the entire northern sector of Galilee. Tiberias, for example, was captured on April 18, and some 5,000 more Arabs joined the growing exodus of villagers. On April 12, an attack by the Irgun against the village of Deir Yassin, which lay to the west of Jerusalem, had tragic consequences for the Arab population. All the inhabitants of the village, 254 men, women and children, were mercilessly murdered and their bodies thrown down a well. The pattern was repeated in the Arab quarter of Jerusalem known as Katamon, on April 29.

At the same time Haganah skillfully employed the subtle weapons of psychological warfare to spread fear and panic thus destroying the will to resist frontal attack by its troops. In one such campaign, leaflets were air-dropped over Galilee signed by the Haganah district commander. He threatened that "all people who do not want this war must leave together with their women and children in order to be safe. This is going to be a cruel war with no mercy or compassion."[5] Haganah was true to its word.

The disasters at Deir Yassin and Katamon were rapidly

magnified many times over as rumors of greater atrocities spread among the population. Peasants were not equipped to cope with this invisible enemy called Fear. As news of the fate of those who had been expelled filtered down through the rural grapevine (aided by more threats over Haganah radio), villagers and peasants took to the roads in fear of their lives taking with them what meager possessions they could carry. Few could have known, or scarcely imagined, that they would never return.

The Arab Higher Committee in the meantime was desperately trying to prevent a mass exodus which it knew would destroy Arab morale and thus hinder the defense of the country. Radio broadcasts and communiqués from the various local committees continually urged the Arabs to remain calm, to stay on the land and in their jobs and homes. Palestinians who had already fled were ordered to return and guard their possessions. Arab volunteers offered stubborn, at times valiant resistance, but were really no match for the Palmach commandos. The tide turned decisively by the third week in April when Haifa and then Jaffa were attacked and occupied by Haganah forces. The fall of Haifa was especially tragic since it was one of the "mixed" towns in which Jews and Arabs had lived side by side in comparative amity.[16]

It was Wednesday, April 21. The British commander had ordered his troops to withdraw to positions outside the city. Haganah received forewarning of the retreat (from the British), and quickly occupied the vacated British posts which were strategically located on the hillside overlooking the Arab quarter of Haifa. Some hours before sunset that day, Haganah began a "psychological blitz" using its radio station and mobile vans to warn the Arabs of the dire consequences of resistance. Promises of safe conduct to Arab territory for all who wanted to leave were broadcast along with the threats. Then machine-gun fire and mortar shells were rained down on the Arab sector where the small 350-man home guard prepared to meet a four-pronged Haganah attack. Gunfire continued throughout the night as the Arab defenders fought to hold onto every building and street corner. The smoke from burning buildings and houses forced the inhabitants into the streets and soon crowds of panic-stricken Arabs were streaming for the safety of the harbor. By noon of the next day several thousand had gathered there while the fighting dragged on.

On Thursday morning an emergency committee of five prominent Arab citizens sought the assistance of the British commander, General Stockwell. The general turned down a request that he intervene with his troops to protect Arab lives and property; he also refused to allow Arab reinforcements to enter the city. The reason for this stand was that Stockwell had been in contact with the Haganah commander from whom he had received the terms for the Arab surrender. These terms were not negotiable. If they were not accepted, Stockwell said that he could not be responsible for further Arab casualties. The Arabs were shocked at this display of partisanship and retired to consider their decision.

By noon Arab resistance had collapsed. Much of the town was in ruins and refugees continued to flee to the harbor where British boats evacuated many of them to Acre. The emergency committee bore the heavy burden of decision, while Stockwell and the Haganah waited for an answer to the terms of surrender. The Jewish mayor, Shabatai Levy, pleaded with the committee not to allow the Arabs to evacuate the city. But Haganah was obviously the party in command and the mayor, for all his genuine sympathy at the plight of the Arabs, could not guarantee their safety. Acceptance of the terms of surrender, therefore, would mean absolving the British of responsibility and conceding to the Haganah's fait accompli, while not ensuring the safety of Arab lives and property. The specter of Deir Yassin still haunted Arab minds. Refusal, on the other hand, would mean the loss of more Arab lives.

Elias Koussa, one of the committee members, still recalls their dilemma: "We thought that the only way out was to ask the general to provide us with eighty trucks daily to transport our properties. We knew well enough that he could not provide this transport, and hoped he would eventually resume control of the town, drive out the Haganah forces from the Arab quarters they had occupied and enable the panicked Arabs crowded in the port area to return home. He did neither and so the flight continued."[7]

Over 50,000 refugees were created by the fall of Haifa. Jaffa

END OF THE MANDATE

was taken a week later and Acre early in May. Both were major towns in the proposed Arab state. Scores of Arab villages in both the Jewish and Arab areas were overrun by Haganah forces. By May 15, the date the Jewish Agency proclaimed the State of Israel, over 250,000 Arabs were homeless, fleeing for refuge wherever they could find it.

Major Edgar O'Ballance has described this phase of the struggle in his book *The Arab-Israeli War: 1948:* "It was the Jewish policy to encourage the Arabs to quit their homes, and they used psychological warfare extensively in urging them to do so. Later, as the war wore on, they ejected those Arabs who clung to their villages. This policy, which had such amazing success, had two distinct advantages. First, it gave the Arab countries a vast refugee problem to cope with, which their elementary economy and administrative machinery were in no way capable of attacking, and secondly, it ensured that the Jews had no fifth column in their midst."[18]

Through the campaigns of Haganah, Ben Gurion's "irreducible minimum" had threatened to become an undefined maximum. The secretary-general of the Arab League cabled the secretary-general of the United Nations on May 15 informing him of the decision of the Arab governments to intervene in Palestine "for the sole purpose of restoring peace and security, and of establishing law and order, and to prevent the spread of disorder and lawlessness into neighboring Arab lands and to fill the vacuum created by the termination of the Mandate."

The first phase of the broadened hostilities was generally in favor of the Arabs, despite the lack of military coordination between the Egyptian movement from the south and the Syrian and Lebanese thrusts from the north. King Abdullah of Transjordan was content to use his well-trained Arab Legion troops mainly for the defense of the area allotted to the Arab State. Until the time of the first cease-fire, which went into effect on June 11, the Arab armies (which were roughly equal in number to the Israeli troops) were unable to "fill the vacuum," a task which had been considered relatively easy to accomplish. But, for the moment at least, further Israeli advances were checked.

The four-week truce period was honored more in the breach than the observance. Both sides took advantage of the lull to regroup and rearm, although the Israelis were able to use the respite to far greater advantage than their opponents. Boatloads of arms reached the coast while tanks and other armored vehicles were airlifted from Czechoslovakia and America. With an eye on the battle ahead, some 30,000 Jewish immigrants were brought into the country and immediately deployed in crucial sectors. When the war entered its second phase the Israelis mustered up to 100,000 troops against the combined total of some 30,000 of the Arab armed force.

The day after the first truce ended on July 9, Israeli forces launched an attack on four fronts. This brilliant campaign, later known as The Ten-Day Offensive, put about 1,000 additional square kilometers of Arab territory under Israeli control: fourteen Arab towns and 200 villages in the area of the Jewish State and 112 villages in the Arab districts were captured and occupied, resulting in the expulsion of tens of thousands more Palestinians. These military successes gave Israel a decisive upper hand in the war. Owing to the ineffective efforts of the United Nations to arrange for a satisfactory settlement, the Israeli leaders were determined to press their advantage and force a military solution of their own on the Arabs.

Ben Gurion, who was now Israel's prime minister and commander in chief of the army, had already declared the partition plan dead and had told a *Time* magazine reporter that the expansion of the "tiny state" of Israel was essential in order to accommodate its future population, which he envisaged might reach ten million people.

A second truce brought The Ten-Day Offensive to an end. It was to prove as impermanent as the first. Using the pretext of Egypt's violation of the cease-fire while refusing permission to United Nations observers to verify the allegations, Israel moved 15,000 of her crack troops into Negev and by the middle of October a large concentration of the Egyptian Army was surrounded at Faluja and cut off from its supply lines. New armed settlements were rushed into the area to bolster the claim of Israeli spokesmen to the whole of the Negev. A similar campaign, preceded by accusations of cease-fire violations, was launched against the remnants of the liberation army in Galilee which was swiftly routed. Another large-scale attack on Egyptian positions carried

END OF THE MANDATE

Israeli forces right into Sinai and made further resistance impossible. The Egyptian Government decided to enter into armistice negotiations with Israel.

Negotiations commenced in January 1949, on the island of Rhodes under United Nations mediation with a general Egypt-Israeli Armistice Agreement being signed on February 24. An agreement was also concluded with Lebanon toward the end of March. Transjordan consented to negotiations on February 8. Syria followed suit on March 21. Israel, however, still had territorial ambitions against these last two states and hesitated to make an immediate commitment. In particular, Israel sought to obtain an outlet on the Red Sea at Aqaba. Following the collapse of the Egyptian Army, Israeli units began to push south of the Dead Sea where they skirmished with the Arab Legion in December.

Armistice negotiations with Transjordan began on March 4 while Israeli forces continued their southward thrust, finally reaching Aqaba on March 10. The next day Israel signed an "enduring" cease-fire with Transjordan, but still more territory was seized until King Abdullah was forced to invoke his treaty of alliance with Britain. A small contingent of British troops was dispatched to defend Transjordan, but beyond this gesture neither Britain nor the United States was prepared to act. Anxious to avert renewed hostilities, King Abdullah quietly contacted Israeli officials to work out a final settlement. The Israeli bargaining position was strong and their demands simple: Abdullah would cede to Israel some 110 square miles of territory along the central front west of the Jordan which contained several strategic heights of land and much valuable farmland. The king had no choice but to accept and the armistice was signed on April 3. Negotiations with Syria dragged on for a few more weeks as Israel penetrated inside Syrian territory to force her to relinquish portions of Palestine occupied by Syrian troops. An agreement was concluded in July, 1949.

The Mandate had been buried without honor. With the demise of Palestine, Pax Britannica, too, was virtually dead in the Middle

East. Britain not only lost an imperial foothold, but within a decade her prestige and influence vanished as her remaining Arab allies, Abdullah in Jordan, Farouk in Egypt and Nuri in Iraq were removed either by assassination or revolution. In time, however, these wounds would heal. While the post-war revolutionary trends in the Arab world were only in part a backlash of the Palestine War, that conflict itself sprang from the contradictions and antagonisms inherent in the Palestine Mandate. The Palestine War for its part neither resolved the contradictions nor eased the antagonisms.

Israel was the child of British imperialism and Jewish colonialist-nationalism. There need be no embarrassment about using terms which today evoke much emotion and which have become debased through indiscriminate application. Englishmen and Zionists alike were able to plead the virtues of a Jewish national home in Palestine as benefiting British imperial interests; Zionists also regarded themselves as colonists following in the path of the French in North Africa. It is scarcely surprising, therefore, that in an era of decolonization, such as in our present century, the Palestinian Arabs should deeply resent foreign domination under the Mandate and the gradual implantation of a foreign element which threatened to emasculate the Arab identity of their country: a foreign element, which desired, or rather insisted, that it remain distinct and separate from its neighbors.

Palestinians were forced by circumstances to fight for the survival of their community and they lost. Having lost, they were told, in effect, to accept their lot. For the Palestinian however, it was never a question of whether it was nobler "to suffer the slings and arrows of outrageous fortune." Palestinians, then as now, expressed their bewilderment at the Zionists who denied the Arab in principle the very rights they claimed for themselves: "How can the Jew, who has known suffering and torment in his European home, now treat us as others treated him?"

The years drifted by after the war of 1948. The Palestinians tried to accommodate themselves to their new condition, while at the same time never accepting it. One day, perhaps, they would again take up arms against the sea of troubles which had inundated them.

9

The Palestinian Diaspora

The Palestine War marked the beginning of the end for a generation of Arab political leaders who, for three decades, had struggled to win national sovereignty for their people. Freedom from foreign domination was the primary objective in the struggle against the various mandatory and protectorate powers. The nationalist leaders had the wholehearted support of the Arab people and gradually, under nationalist pressure, the symbols of foreign rule were removed. The Tricolor and the Union Jack no longer flew from public buildings in Arab capitals. In their stead the national flags of independent Arab states were proudly unfurled in air which was now freer than before. Alien high commissioners or governors-general no longer ruled in the name of London or Paris. An Arab now spoke for his people.

All this the Old Order had accomplished. Yet, as the Arab political elite took control of the governments of their countries, the relationship between them and their people underwent change. Various symbols of foreign rule remained and Arabs were aware that their independence was a highly qualified one. The Old Order had purchased independence at the price of treaty arrangements with their former overlords. Britain's Mandate over Iraq ended in 1930, but her position was only modified by a treaty which was to last for twenty-five years and which gave Britain important rights in Iraq's military affairs and foreign policy. Anglo-Egyptian relations were reorganized in 1936 along the same lines. Military bases were maintained in both countries and foreign troops stationed on theoretically independent national soil. Although the last French soldier left Lebanon and Syria in 1946, France retained a privileged status in both countries.

Troops and treaties were viewed by many Arabs as inconsistent with their formal independence. The "mutual assistance" clauses in the treaties were ludicrous enough if one could imagine Iraqi soldiers rushing to the defense of Britain under attack from some third power. The situation appeared quite sinister, on the other hand, if British troops were used in Iraq to spare that country some unspeakable peril known only to the "inner circle" of the cabinet in Whitehall and of absolute irrelevance to anyone in Iraq. Nevertheless, in the name of the Anglo-Iraqi treaty, British forces marched into Baghdad in May 1941, and overthrew the government of Rashid Ali. In February of the following year the British ambassador in Cairo ordered British troops to surround the palace of King Farouk to impress upon His Majesty the choice of leaving the country or of installing a prime minister acceptable to Britain. Even the reactionary and corrupt Farouk could not have devised a better plan to create for himself the image of a martyr to foreign oppression. (Such perhaps is the nature of all mutual assistance agreements, as the Czechs found to their sorrow in the summer of 1968 when Warsaw Pact troops were dispatched to Prague to save the Czechs from themselves. Which party is mutual assistance supposed to assist if not the strongest member of the alliance?)

Unnoticed and unheeded, a younger generation of Arabs had emerged during this first nationalist phase. Many had been educated abroad in the quiet, cloistered colleges of Oxford and Cambridge or in the intellectual beehive of the Sorbonne in cosmopolitan Paris. Others took whatever roads were available for advancement and consequently the lower ranks of the officer corps of the army attracted young men of the new middle class. Their attitude indicated the growing generation gap — an abyss — between them and the Old Order politicians who came under attack for abandoning the Arab mission once independence had been attained. The Old Order had satisfied the national emotion for independence, but the earlier memory of betrayal by Britain and France after World War I soon faded. Close ties with the former rulers suited well the vested interests representing the feudal, commercial and industrial elements of society. These same nationalists were now being held responsible by their younger, angry and erstwhile supporters for continuing social and economic difficulties, and for the failure to gain more complete concessions from the European powers. The material needs of the people also had to be met. The fight against social inequality, poverty and illiteracy was scarcely begun.

The Palestine War of 1948 brought matters to a head. The old civilian and military leaderships were thoroughly discredited and were not equipped to meet the new challenge. The younger generation, however, did not have the political power to effect the changes which the times required.

During that fateful war, a young Egyptian army major sat among his men at Faluja in Palestine. They were surrounded by Israeli troops. Shells fell about them and enemy aircraft buzzed overhead. Food and medical supplies were inadequate and their weapons outdated and worthless. The young major thought to himself: "Here we are in these foxholes, surrounded, and thrust treacherously into a battle for which we are not ready, our lives the playthings of greed, conspiracy and lust which have left us here weaponless under fire." They had fought courageously but were demoralized by the corruption of their own leaders. A brigadier, who was a known trafficker in narcotics, had made a fortune recovering weapons abandoned in the western desert after World War II which he then sold to the Egyptian Government. Rumor had it that King Farouk shared in the profits of this deal.

Four years later, on a particularly humid July night, this same young officer led a group of his colleagues in the officers corps in a coup which overthrew the ruling oligarchy and sent the king into exile. This was Gamal Abdel Nasser, a man destined by humiliating defeat to become a decisive force in contemporary Arab history. The figurehead of the coup, General Muhammad Neguib, summed up the motivation of the Free Officers: "To serve its purpose, the military must be given a worthy government to defend; if the government is manifestly indefensible then the military must either resign itself to the prevailing corruption or intervene in civil affairs."

It is against this background that the intrusion of the military into politics can be understood, not only in Egypt, but also in Syria and later in Iraq.

For others, the Palestine War contained its own bitter lesson. Musa Alami was a Cambridge-educated lawyer who had served as Crown Counsel in the Palestine Government for several years, and in 1945 he sat as representative of Palestine on the Committee of Foreign Ministers which drew up the constitution of the Arab League. To Musa the Arab defeat was a two-edged sword. In Palestine itself, defeat stemmed from the Arabs' fundamental weakness: their lack of preparation, their lack of unity and their lack of arms.

"We proceeded along the lines of previous revolutions while the Jews proceeded along the lines of total war... it was obvious that our aims in the battle were diverse; the aim of the Jews was solely to win."

How did all this come about? Alami's answer is multi-fold. Palestine reflected the condition of the Arab world in general. Disunity on the battlefield was the result of political and military shortcomings and the lethargy of Arab governments, stemming from the absence of popular control because the Arab peoples themselves were weak. While his analysis was critical and frank, he did not underestimate the danger of Israel to the whole Arab nation: "The ambitions of the Jews are not limited to Palestine alone but embrace other parts of the Arab world... the next step will be an attempt to take all of Palestine and then they will proceed according to circumstances — circumstances which they themselves will attempt to create."[11]

As early as 1919 the Zionists had sought at the Paris Peace Conference what they regarded as the minimum territorial requirements of the Jewish National Home. For reasons of economic and defensive viability the Home should include what today is southern Lebanon up to the Litani River, large portions of fertile southern Syria and Transjordan, and an unspecified part of the Sinai peninsula. Israel was still an undefined quantity but Alami and many Arab intellectuals believed in 1948 that, given the chance, Israel would expand: the weakness of the Arab peoples would lead to that temptation.

Musa Alami would have understood Ben Gurion's sentiment when he said that "nowadays wars are not fought just by armies, but rather the whole nation must be mobilized." The Arab

THE PALESTINIAN DIASPORA

nation was no exception. The prescription for weakness was unity and the mobilization of the entire Arab people.

Arab unity or Pan-Arabism has dominated popular political sentiment since World War II. The idea had been the undercurrent of nationalist thinking since World War I, but the Arab-Israeli War lent a sense of urgency for concrete results. The intention of all Arab nationalists was to liberate, unite, revive and reconstruct the Arab world. Their mission was to conduct a campaign against western influence and domination, to build the Arab nation and to adopt revolutionary action against intellectual, moral, social, political and economic evils. Arab Unity is therefore a powerful psychological force and in this sense a political reality and a source of social ferment.

Liberation from British inflence and control was achieved by stages as the treaty system dissolved with accompanying violence, as in Egypt 1954-56, and in Iraq in 1958. After seven bitter years of guerilla warfare the Algerians finally drove out the French, and Algeria became independent in 1962. As colonialism beat its bloody retreat from the desert sands, the United States, haunted by paranoid visions of communism, rushed in to fill the void with guns and pledges gift-wrapped and tied with strings which led straight back to the Pentagon. Arabs generally were unimpressed by the mutual rantings of the two cold war giants, Russia and the United States, and they had no desire to be caught in the web of an ideological struggle which did not concern them.

Besides, the Arabs were preoccupied with their own cold war. Since 1948, the Arab world had been deeply divided and the force of Pan-Arabism greatly dissipated whenever the theme of unity was advocated by different leaders representing different interests.

The Suez crisis of 1956 demonstrated President Nasser's uncanny capacities as a tactician, turning the political tables on his French, British and Israeli adversaries. The union of Syria and Egypt into the United Arab Republic two years later made him the unchallenged leader of the Arab revolutionary movement, but not for long.

In 1958 General Abdul Karim Qasim overthrew the decrepit pro-western regime of Nuri Said in Iraq, and initiated a widely popular program of reform. Qasim became a challenger to Nasser's title of revolutionary leader of the Arabs. Their regimes were at loggerheads and a split in the Arab "left" swiftly developed. Syria pulled out of the United Arab Republic in 1961. Qasim was eliminated in 1963, after which the central issue of Arab leadership was a struggle between the "revolutionaries" led by Nasser and the "reactionaries" who had no acknowledged leader. **This latter group includes the monarchical regimes of Jordan, Saudi Arabia, Morocco and until 1969, Libya when its aged ruler was deposed in an army coup.** The lines between the two warring camps were not, however, always clearly drawn because it was possible (albeit embarrassing) for President Nasser and King Faysal of Saudi Arabia to try and compose their differences over the Republican-Royalist civil war in Yemen.

All these examples of disunity within the Arab family provoked many observers of the Middle East scene to say cynically that nothing unites the Arab states except their collective hatred of Israel, an observation which has become part of the rich western treasury of myths about the Arab world. Professor Malcolm Kerr's more perceptive analysis is that "when the Arabs are in a mood to cooperate, this tends to find expression in an agreement to avoid action on Palestine, but when they choose to quarrel, Palestine policy readily becomes a subject of dispute. The prospect that one Arab government may unilaterally provoke hostilities with Israel arouses fears among others for their own security, or at least for their political reputation."[121]

The accuracy of this analysis is reflected in the theory which was current from the late nineteen-fifties that the Palestine Problem could not be resolved before the fulfillment of the revolution in each Arab country. The economic, social and political transformation of the Arab community, in other words, must precede direct action on the question of Palestine. The focus logically shifted away from Israel and onto the Arab community itself, although this theory was as much a rationalization of the recognized weaknesses in Arab society as it was sound revolutionary strategy. Nevertheless, the decade following the Suez crisis marked a period of rapid economic growth and social change among Israel's neighbors, together with the first abortive attempts at political unity.

THE PALESTINIAN DIASPORA

However, in certain government circles, and among the Arab intelligentsia generally, a deep dilemma had to be faced. The Arab Revolution was committed not only to progress and development but also to the eradication of colonialism from every portion of its national soil. Israel was a *fait colonial*, the creation of which had resulted in the destruction of Palestinian society and the displacement of hundreds of thousands of Arabs from their homes and lands. The Palestinian became to the Arab what the Jew in Europe was to the Christian, a burden of guilt on his conscience. And Palestinians, bereaved of their land, would not permit the burden to be eased.

As a political entity Palestine had disappeared from the map, but the idea survived in the minds and hearts of a people sentenced to exile; an idea, moreover, which is deeply rooted in the land. A poet writes: "In the briar-covered mountains I saw you, a shepherdess without sheep, pursued among the ruins." The shepherdess is the poet's lover, Palestine personified, but without her flock, her own people. The symbol is a simple and honest one which time can neither tarnish nor eradicate.

As well as a *fait colonial*, Israel was a *fait accompli*, with powerful financial and diplomatic support in every major country of the Western world, especially the United States which, after World War II, replaced Britain as the center of Zionist pressure. The western commitment to Israel, like earlier British support for the Jewish National Home, involved the same set of contradictions which had long been inherent components of the conflict. Support for the Jewish State naturally implies acceptance of the historical context out of which the state was born and the ideological foundations upon which it is based.

Statistics reveal the magnitude of the catastrophe which befell the Palestinian community but they do not measure the full enormity of the disaster. Over 750,000 refugees were created by the Palestine War. A third of this number had already fled before the State of Israel was proclaimed in mid-May of 1948. After the first truce Israeli forces drove more than 60,000 Arabs from the Lydda-Ramleh area with little more than the possessions they could carry with them. During the second truce which followed The Ten-Day Offensive tens of thousands of Arabs were sent into exile from the Negev and Galilee before the advancing Israeli Army. As late as the fall of 1950, one year after the armistice agreements, some 7,000 Bedouin tribesmen were expelled from Israel and more Arabs were driven from the Israel-Syrian demilitarized zone in the summer of 1951.

By 1966, the number of refugees had rocketed to almost 1.4 million owing to a very high birthrate. The refugees were scattered in their pathetic hordes throughout the neighboring Arab countries. In 1948 the figures were 280,000 in Arab Palestine, 70,000 in Transjordan, 100,000 in Lebanon, 75,000 in Syria, 190,000 in Gaza, 7,000 in Egypt and 4,000 in Iraq. When King Abdullah of Transjordan annexed Arab Palestine to his kingdom in December 1948, he acquired the Arab refugees from Israeli-occupied Palestine, that is, the State of Israel. By 1950 when the United Nations Relief and Works Agency assumed responsibility for the refugees, about 30 percent of the total were living in sixty organized camps while the remaining 70 percent were scattered in the towns and villages of the host countries.

The other dimension of this exodus of Arabs from their homes and lands was the vast wealth of property they left behind. Some 80 percent of Israel's total land area was land abandoned by the Arab refugees. This abandoned property was one of the greatest contributions toward making Israel a viable state. For example, 350 of the 370 new Jewish settlements established in the five years after independence were on absentee Arab property; 10,000 shops and businesses of all description were left in Israeli hands; half of Israel's citrus groves were on Arab property and in 1951 Arab fruit provided 10 percent of Israel's foreign currency earnings; the olive crop from Arab-owned lands provided Israel's third largest export. A conservative estimate of the total value of abandoned movable property and land came to over 120 million Palestinian pounds, or $336 million.

In 1948 the dimensions of the Palestine Problem suddenly seemed infinite. Humanitarian, economic, political and social questions were all closely linked and progress on one aspect could be impeded by stalemate on another.

The most immediate task was to spare the refugees from the indiscriminate sickle of the Grim Reaper. Without adequate medical supplies, sustenance and shelter, the oncoming winter months, which in the Middle East can be harsh by any standards, threatened to decimate the refugee population. Through the summer of 1948 the Arab governments provided for the Palestinians to the extent their own meager resources would allow. The situation required more drastic measures. Largely as a result of the initiative of the United Nations mediator, Count Folke Bernadotte, interim emergency aid was secured from some European countries and from private relief agencies. The United Nations moved in officially to provide aid through various of its specialized agencies until the UN Relief and Works Agency was established. Nevertheless, refugee relief was regarded as a merely temporary expedient which a formal peace settlement would render unnecessary.

It was of course impossible to wipe out overnight the causes of the conflict which extended back over the preceding half century.

To the international community, to the world at large looking at the Middle East, the question of refugees is primarily a humanitarian problem. To the Arabs, on the other hand, and above all to the Palestinians themselves, the basic configuration is political. The Arab Higher Committee, backed by the Arab League, proclaimed an All-Palestine Government in September 1948, to be centered in Gaza. Its elected president was Hajj Amin Husseini. At a national congress, convened on October 1 in Gaza, it was resolved that "on the basis of the natural and historical rights of the Arab people of Palestine to freedom and independence... we proclaim the establishment of a free and democratic state, working for the realization of the freedom and rights of the people."[131]

It was a hollow proclamation when the so-called Palestinian State was half-occupied by the State of Israel which had been recognized by the two super-powers, Russia and the United States. The Government of Gaza, cut off as it was from the rest of Palestine, made little sense. Moreover, Hajj Amin's political fortunes were spent. The disaster of the Palestine War left him with no credit or credibility and he departed from the scene to become the most widely maligned and villified of the Palestinian leaders. Despite the immediate material needs of the vast majority of its people, the All-Palestine Government nevertheless gave notice that the struggle for the realization of the freedom and rights of the Palestinian people had not been abandoned.

More significant was the move by King Abdullah of Transjordan to annex the remnant of Palestine to his kingdom. Abdullah had been installed as the Prince of Transjordan by the British after World War I. The gesture was supposed to fulfill British promises made to Abdullah's father, King Hussein of the Hijaz, for Arab "independence" as set forth in the McMahon-Hussein correspondence. The desert kingdom was, in any case, an administrative unit under the Palestine Mandate with a special British resident designated to handle all of Abdullah's affairs. When the United Nations resolution recommended the partition of Palestine in November 1947, Abdullah was quick to see the material advantage of adding the proposed Arab State to Transjordan. He initiated secret negotiations with the Zionists as early as November 1947.[4]

His first contacts were with Mrs. Golda Meyerson who, twenty-one years later, as Mrs. Golda Meir, would become Israel's fourth prime minister. Abdullah was anxious to come to an understanding with the Jews and avoid, if possible, a war over Palestine. That nothing materialized was due in part to the strong line adopted by the Arab League, which Abdullah could not openly oppose, and in part by the total lack of Zionist concessions which might have strengthened the king's hand. Even after war had broken out Abdullah was interested in a formal peace with the provisional Government of Israel. Negotiations revealed, however, that Israel was using its military advantage to extract the greatest possible concessions from Abdullah. (Colonel Moshe Dayan was the chief Israeli negotiator in the second round of talks.) Negotiations dragged on in secret for several months until the news leaked out, and Palestinian reaction made a settlement virtually impossible.

King Abdullah made more headway with the Palestinians in implementing his scheme. The shock waves of defeat and humiliation rippled through the whole Palestine community. Palestinian leadership had crumbled and the Arab armies were incapable of pursuing the war to a successful conclusion. The Palestinians needed some form of stable and secure regime and Abdullah offered this with his plan of annexation. The Gaza

Congress, however, appeared as a challenge to his authority. Leaving nothing to chance, Abdullah convened his own Palestine Congress in Amman which denounced the Gaza Government and petitioned the king to place Arab Palestine under his protection. In response to this "request," Abdullah called together a second meeting at Jericho on December 1, 1948, at which time he was proclaimed king of all Palestine. The resolutions of the congress were ratified by the Jordanian Parliament two weeks later and the annexation was formally complete. Annexation evoked loud cries of protest from other Arab governments; Abdullah was accused of trying to liquidate the Palestine Problem, which was in fact the case. The Palestinian delegates to the congress, on the other hand, took the long-term view that the union would not affect their ultimate objective of restoring to Palestinians the rights to their land. The first resolution of the Jericho meeting expressed thanks for the efforts and sacrifices of the Arab governments, and requested their continued support in the fight to save Palestine. Another resolution urged the need for haste in helping the refugees to return to their country.

Palestinians as a whole were encouraged to hope that their rights could be achieved since these rights had been internationally acknowledged. On December 11, 1948, the General Assembly of the United Nations passed a resolution to that effect. Paragraph eleven noted that "refugees wishing to return to their homes and live in peace with their neighbors should be permitted to do so at the earliest practicable date, and that compensation should be paid for the property of those choosing not to return, and for the loss or damage to property..."

Earlier Count Bernadotte, the United Nations mediator, had reported that no settlement could be just or complete if recognition were not accorded to the rights of the Arab refugee to return to the home from which he had been dislodged by the hazards and strategy of the armed conflict. From the beginning, therefore, the principle of the right of return has been for the Palestinians the sine qua non of any settlement. The annual reiteration of this principle in United Nations resolutions has helped keep alive this hope.

Time has, if anything, deepened and intensified the Palestinian refugees' longing to return. Apart from dispensing relief, UNRWA has made repeated efforts to initiate works projects and development programs to help integrate refugees into the economic life of the area on a self-sustaining basis, all in the hope that in this way both the political and practical aspects of the refugee problem might be solved through economic means. The Arab governments were at first extremely reluctant to support the refugees' economic integration, fearing that this would prejudice their right of repatriation to Israel.

There were other practical difficulties as well. First, the host countries, with the exception of Syria, were poor in natural resources and already overpopulated. For example, the influx of refugees into Lebanon increased its population by 10 percent. Jordan alone supported more than half the total number of refugees. It would be difficult for the Arab governments to make fiscal sacrifices on the scale required to integrate the Palestinians, for this would entail holding back on development programs planned for the benefit of their own citizens. In addition, even the largest of the proposed UNRWA works projects would only absorb some 200,000 refugees, a figure slightly greater than the anticipated increase in the refugee population at the time of the projects' completion.

Second, the vast majority of the refugees, or roughly 80 percent of the total, were either farmers or unskilled workers who would have to compete in a market already saturated with farmers and laborers. The more fortunate minority was able to integrate easily and UNRWA provided educational facilities and opportunities for others.

The third, and perhaps most significant factor hindering Palestinian reintegration, was the attitude of the refugees themselves. Henry Labouisse, the then director of UNRWA, reported in February 1957, that the situation was almost unchanged owing to the political aspect of the problem and to deep-seated human emotions. The reason, he said, did not "lie simply in the field of economics. UNRWA can, to be sure, enable some hundreds of refugees to become self-supporting each year — through small agricultural development projects, grants to establish small businesses and the like. But it cannot overcome the fact that the refugees as a whole insist upon the choice provided for them in the General Assembly resolution (December 11, 1948), that is, repatriation or compensation. In the absence of that choice, they bitterly oppose anything which has even the semblance of a permanent settlement elsewhere."

In 1963 I was taken through one of the largest camps in Jordan by a Palestinian friend. This was Jericho, lying near the River Jordan just north of the Dead Sea. Jericho goes back in human memory to the third millenium before Christ and is the place where Joshua fought his bloodiest battle. After 1948 and up to the outbreak of the June War, this ancient spot contained a refugee camp of over 70,000 souls. Today it is desolate and deserted, its inhabitants joining after the war the tens of thousands of new refugees on the east bank of the Jordan.

A minor crisis had seized the camp when we arrived. UNRWA officials were trying to persuade the camp council to permit the whitewashing of the mud huts of their shantytown. If anything could cheer up these one-roomed hovels a fresh daub of white might do it. The council, however, politely declined permission because they feared that any real improvement in their situation would merely add a degree of permanency to their exile. At the time I was shocked at the apparent callousness of the council's position; later, when I had talked with other Palestinians in other camps in Jordan and Lebanon, I began to realize the depth of their sentiment for their former homes and lands. Children who had been born in the camps talked of "home" as though they knew every inch of ground, every tree and bush.

Walid, my companion, was just sixteen years old. He had been born a year before the Palestine War. His father was a schoolteacher in Tulkarm which was located on the armistice line on a height of land overlooking the fertile plain which had fallen to Israel. Walid was fortunate in that his father could provide his brothers and sisters with a normal home life; he had never lived in the camps, although he knew them well. His life had been more complete than the listless monotonous existence of camp life. Nevertheless, he spoke as passionately as his refugee brother about returning, but for another reason. From the roof of his house in Tulkarm, Walid pointed out to me the fields below cultivated by Israeli farmers: "You see that piece of land there, beyond the railway tracks and to the right of that house?

My grandfather owned that house and the land around it. It is good land, is it not? Someday..."

I had heard it all before. We walked down the main street of the town past the cinema and toward the "frontier." A single iron post marked the boundary line. Walid laughed and said: "We play a game with the Israelis." He pulled the stake out of the ground, carried it a few paces forward and drove it into the ground. "Tomorrow, someone from over there will move it back, and then one of us will shift it again." I wondered if their game constituted a violation of the armistice agreements! The Israeli-Jordanian armistice lines in several places had deprived Arab villagers of access to their lands, or had divided Arab towns and villages into two sectors. It was this factor which originally contributed to the high level of "infiltration" into Israeli-held territory after the conclusion of the war.

It was near Jericho that Musa Alami founded his Arab Development Society. Shortly after the war of 1948, Musa and a handful of refugees began their search for underground sources of fresh water in the wasteland of Judea where the experts all agreed that water did not exist. But water was found and slowly, arduously, they began to reclaim the barren land and make it thrive. From their intensive labors a fertile oasis gradually emerged until some 2,000 acres supported refugees in a variety of agricultural enterprises. Refugee orphans are also given vocational training in a special school in this unique Palestinian village.

It is strange to westerners that Musa Alami's triumph did not lessen the desire of the village's inhabitants to see the Palestinian community restored. A later commissioner-general of UNRWA, John Davis, stated in his Annual Report for 1964 that the Palestinians did not see themselves as consciously breaking with their past in order to seek a new life in new surroundings. "The Palestine refugees," he said, "regard themselves, rather, as temporary wards of the international community whom they hold responsible for the upheaval which resulted in their having to leave their homes. As they see it, the international community has a duty to enable them to return to their homes and, meanwhile, to provide for their maintenance and welfare."

Such are the factors hindering the process of Palestinian

integration into the surrounding Arab environment. Other equally important factors have contributed to preventing the repatriation of the exiled Palestinians, thereby prolonging the conflict to the present day. These factors relate to the Israeli perspective of the Palestine Problem.

Under the Mandate for Palestine, the Jewish Agency had never at any time formulated a positive policy of cooperation with the Arab population. Indeed, implicit in Zionist ideology and explicit in practice, the Arabs were excluded from consideration in the functions of the Jewish National Home. Separate development of the Arab and Jewish communities was the rule. Any other arrangement would, in the Zionist view, impair the specifically Jewish character or personality of the National Home.

Palestinians had perceived that in the absence of political power in the hands of their community, the Mandate would be used to change the demographic character of Palestine *as a whole,* and that ultimately, through the mechanics of the imposed Mandate, an alien European (and Jewish) community would assume political control over their land. Thus, from the very beginning, Palestinians demanded representative democratic institutions as the first step to independence, while Zionists insisted that the question of independence be held in abeyance until a Jewish majority was achieved. As a result of war and the Arab exodus, Zionists were left in control of an area 22 percent larger than the partition scheme (they now held 70 percent of the whole of Palestine) with a negligible Arab minority, since only about 150,000 Palestinians remained in what became the State of Israel.

10

The Palestinians Within

The Palestinians were now on the outside, determined in the long run to get back in. The Israelis were equally determined to keep them out. But whereas Israel's military victory had been decisive, there remained the political task of searching for principles on which peace might be based. From a position of military superiority, the young Israeli Government insisted upon direct negotiations with the various Arab governments. It was felt that this would lessen the chances of outside pressures forcing her to make concessions detrimental to her national interests. And above all, Israel's national interests demanded *security*. That was a purely practical necessity, although it gave, in effect, a lower priority to *peace*. The general Israeli attitude was: "We needn't run after peace; peace will come when the Arabs are resigned to our reality." Today, after twenty years, Israel's argument for peace, based on the theory of attrition, has proven as dangerously sterile as the attitude of Arab leaders who have held that if Israel is ignored altogether it would conveniently disappear.

Ironically, after 1948 Israelis found themselves in the same position vis-à-vis the Arab states as the Palestinians had been vis-à-vis the Zionists during the Mandate. It now appeared to the Israelis that the Arabs only wanted to negotiate the details of the emasculation of the Jewish identity of Israel by insisting on the Palestinians' right of return. The Zionist objective of a Jewish state had been achieved. It was not about to be jeopardized by receiving a fifth column of Palestinian refugees within its frontiers. The force of circumstances and the memory of past experience were now more compelling than the will to move decisively toward peace.

However, expediency alone did not determine the framework of Israeli national interests. As an Israeli Government pamphlet entitled *Facts and Figures,* published in 1955, notes: "the State of Israel does not exist for its own sake but as the instrument for the implementation of the Zionist ideal." Since its inception in Basle, Switzerland, eighty years ago, the Zionist ideal has been the promotion of a solution to the problem of anti-Semitism by conferring national status on the Jewish people, which could then re-create its national life within the historic frontiers of Palestine. It is this ideological component of Zionism which has caused Palestinians to fear that the consummation of Zionism is not the State of Israel as established in 1948.

After statehood was attained, Prime Minister Ben Gurion spelled out Israel's continuing mission. In the Introduction to the 1951-1952 *Israel Government Yearbook* Ben Gurion observes that "the cardinal aim of our State is the redemption of the people of Israel, the ingathering of the exiles." For this purpose the organic link between the World Zionist Organization and the Government of the State of Israel was formalized by a status law for the world body in 1952. The W.Z.O. was charged with responsibility for immigration and settlement policy — a unique arrangement whereby a sovereign government delegates such a function to a non-governmental, ideological body. Ben Gurion continued: "A primary and deciding factor in our security is mass immigration in swift tempo." Immigration from the Jewish Diaspora to Israel is therefore defined both in terms of the national interest (security) and of ideology (liquidation of the Diaspora).

Concerning Zionist territorial objectives, Ben Gurion is equally candid. In the 1952-53 *Yearbook* he stated it "must now be said that the State of Israel has been established in only a portion of the Land of Israel." The 1955-56 *Yearbook* reiterates this position: "The creation of the new State by no means derogates from the scope of historic Eretz Israel." A similar theme was echoed with more practical effect by Israeli officials at the time of the Israeli invasion of Egypt in 1956. On the morning of the attack, Walter Eytan, then director general of the Ministry of Foreign Affairs, broadcast that "Israel is not out to wage war or conquer territory; her aim is to defend her security and the lives of her people against the attacks of Egyptian guerilla forces."[1] A week later, in the Knesset, Prime Minister Ben Gurion said "our forces did not infringe upon the territory of the land of Egypt and did not even attempt to do so... Our operations were restricted to the area of the Sinai Peninsula."[2] He spoke of "freeing" Sinai and "liberating" a part of the ancient homeland. These irredentist hopes were quashed at the time by strong pressure from the U.S. Government which reacted in cold fury to the tri-partite invasion of Egypt.

While it is true that there is neither a Zionist nor Israeli concensus on the territorial question, to the Arabs there is little doubt that the campaigns for *aliya* (Jewish immigration) imply a policy of expansion. Immediately after the June war of 1967, with Israeli troops in occupation of Gaza and Jordan's West Bank (the remainder of the former mandated territory of Palestine), a serious debate was joined in Israel on the question of *aliya* in the altered circumstances created by the war. The subject was widely discussed in the Israeli press. The late Prime Minister Levi Eshkol himself referred to the urgent importance of increased immigration as a "pillar of Israel's security."[3] Already parts of the occupied territories (especially the Golan Heights in Syria) have been removed from the bargaining block as new Jewish settlements have been established.

Statehood, from the beginning of Zionist ideology had become smoothly assimilated to the Israeli national interest. Israel's foreign policy was based on the need to preserve the territorial and ethnic integrity of the State, a need which was rationalized in terms of the security policy.

Ideological and pragmatic considerations were evident in Israel's resistance to the early attempts to repatriate the Palestinian refugees. During the first truce period in the '48 war, and before the last major Israeli offensive, Ben Gurion told his cabinet that none of the refugees should be allowed to return. Influential sections of the Hebrew press supported him and all the leading newspapers placed the blame for the Palestinians' flight on the Arab governments and Britain.[4] *Ha-Boqer*, the daily of the General Zionist faction contrived a justification for rejecting repatriation which struck a discordant note with previous propaganda appeals. Israel, it argued, suffered from an unfavorable land population ratio, possessing only 1/100 of the land area of the Middle East and yet 1/60 of its population; nevertheless, Israel was prepared to accept hundreds of thousands of Jewish refugees while the Arab countries with their vast territories were unwilling to integrate their fellow Arabs.[5]

In contrast, one of the prominent themes of Zionist propaganda in the nineteen-twenties and thirties had been that Palestine was sufficiently under-developed and under-populated to support as many as three or four million new Jewish settlers. Suddenly in 1948 the land was too small and congested to welcome back its indigenous inhabitants.

The maximum concession Israel was prepared to make was a partial repatriation of 100,000 refugees on condition that the territorial status quo and the principle of the non-return of the majority of Palestinians were accepted by the Arab governments. Not only the Arabs, but the United Nations and the U.S. Government found the proposal inadequate. Israeli public opinion was also aroused — but not because of its shortcomings; rather because it conceded too much. Foreign Minister Moshe Sharett came under fire from the members of his own party. A commonly heard rebuke of his policy was that the return of any number of Arabs would deprive future Jewish settlers of land.

In June 1949, Ben Gurion replied to a note from President Truman in which the president had described Israel's attitude as a threat to peace. The prime minister repeated his government's position concerning the security risk involved in allowing Arabs to return and he added that on humanitarian grounds alone it would be better to resettle the Palestinians elsewhere, since their homes had been either destroyed or occupied by Jewish immigrants.

Ben Gurion had not exaggerated—Jewish immigrants now poured into Israel. During its first three and a half years the young state absorbed nearly 700,000 new settlers. Israel's population soared by 108 percent. This was indeed "mass immigration in swift tempo." The new social and legal realities rapidly being created in Israel reinforced the argument for the non-return of refugees. Later, Israel abandoned the repatriation issue altogether and the only acceptable solution was the resettlement of Palestinians in Arab countries. In November, 1958, Abba Eban, then

Israel's representative to the United Nations, argued the case before the General Assembly. "The refugees," he said, "are all Arabs. The countries in which they find themselves are Arab countries. Yet the advocates of repatriation contend that these Arab refugees should be settled in a non-Arab country, in the only social and cultural environment which is alien to their background and tradition."[6] In these terms, therefore, repatriation would mean "uprooting" the refugee and "alienating" him from his Arab society. The argument might appear to be Orwellian doubletalk but it does in fact express the basic Zionist postulate; Jew and Arab must each mould his national identity and aspirations separately. Moshe Dayan once expressed the situation more bluntly: "There was a Palestine at one time but it no longer exists. If the Palestinians had wanted to be a national entity they had their chance in 1948."[7]

An opportunity missed was an opportunity lost—for the Palestinians. Nevertheless, that same moment did not resolve an immediate problem for Israel, namely, the presence of "alien" Palestinians who stayed and held onto possession of their lands inside the armistice lines. They were an obstacle to the complete Judaization of the nascent Israeli state. Hence the conquest of the land *within* Israel itself had to resume its tenacious advance.

More than 450,000 acres of land belonging to Palestinians who remained in Israel was seized after 1948. Expulsions and confiscations, continuing until the present day, have been directed solely against those "citizens" of Israel who were not Jewish. (A parenthetical remark is appropriate here. The word citizen is qualified here by quotation marks because the actual rights of citizenship for Israeli Arabs are highly tenuous. The Israeli Law of Return makes it possible for a Jew born anywhere in the world to acquire Israeli citizenship merely by disembarking upon its soil. By contrast, a Palestinian Arab who is born in Israel, is in fact born "stateless," a condition which can be inherited by his children who may also be born in Israel. For the Palestinian Arab, citizenship is not automatically acquired by birth but is determined only at the discretion of the Israeli Minister of the Interior.)[8] Two Christian villages in western Galilee, Kafr Birim and Iqrit, became notorious examples, and by no means isolated ones, of Israeli treatment of Arabs who were prepared to live in the Jewish state. [9] Kafr Birim contained about 950 inhabitants, Iqrit about 500 and their fertile lands combined exceeded 8000 acres. The Israeli army occupied these villages at the end of October 1948. There was no resistance. One Israeli officer, indeed, found friends in Kafr Birim who, many years earlier, had helped him enter Palestine illegally from the Lebanon during the Mandate. The villagers were told to evacuate their homes and take a few days provisions with them until military operations had been concluded in the area. In innocent expectation of their imminent return the villagers removed to another village a few kilometers away. After nearly two years of futile negotiations with Israeli officials these "uprooted" Arabs determined to return and repossess their homes and lands while at the same time appealing to the Supreme Court for a judgement. On July 31, 1951, the court declared that there was no legal impediment to the villagers returning to their property. The military governor thought otherwise and quickly issued an expulsion order. The villagers appealed. The Supreme Court agreed once again to consider the case. Six weeks before the decision was to be handed down the army destroyed all the houses in the villages and the government announced the expropriation of all their lands. A kibbutz and a moshav were established on them for Jewish immigrants from Persia who began to employ the original Arab landowners as wage labourers. For twenty years the villagers of Kafr Birim and Iqrit continued to struggle to have their rights restored. The Israeli government continued to argue that for "security reasons" the villagers could not regain their property. Finally, in 1972, the Arabs offered a compromise. If the lands were registered in their names they would not press further until a peace settlement was reached between Israel and the Arab countries. Golda Meir's government rejected the offer because it did not wish to create a precedent which might encourage other Arabs in Israel to reclaim their lands as well.

In the wake of the 1948 war an intricate series of regulations, ordinances and laws were passed to justify and legalize many similar acts of expulsion and expropriation. [10] Among the most important of these measures are the Absentee Property Regulation

(1948), the Abandoned Areas Ordinance (1948), the Defense (Emergency) Regulations (1945), the Security Zones Regulations (1949), the Cultivation of Waste Lands Ordinance (1949) and the Law for the Requisitioning of Property in Times of Emergency (1949). They were the main instrument by which the Israeli government was able to seize the largest possible area of Arab land and transform it into Jewish ownership and control in perpetuity. A custodian of abandoned (or absentee) property was created. This official could, on the strength of his own personal judgement, declare any movable or immovable Arab property in Israel "abandoned." Other regulations defined the legal relationship between the Arabs and their property. Professor Peretz notes that the absentee property regulations in effect "prevented the return of any Arab, including those who were citizens of Israel, to property abandoned during, or immediately before the war."[11] The definition of an absentee was made so inclusive that a Palestinian who had happened to visit Beirut, or even Nablus or Tulkarm, for a single day during a period covering the last six months of the Mandate up to September 1, 1948 automatically forfeited his rights to his property under Israeli law. These regulations, in fact, created 30,000 "refugees" in Israel itself, persons who had never left the country but who may have gone from their own town or village to another nearby in the course of the hostilities.

Even the severity of these measures did not ease the anxiety of Israeli officials toward the Arab population. Joseph Nahmani, the head of Keren Keymeth from 1935 to 1965, was particularly concerned about the high concentration of Arabs in Galilee:

> Though western Galilee has now been occupied, it still has not been freed of its Arab population, as happened in other parts of the country. There are still fifty-one villages (in 1953) and the city of Nazareth whose inhabitants have not left—in all there are 84,002 Arabs, not counting Acre, controlling 929,549 dunums of land . . . most of them farmers, who make up 45 percent of the Arab minority in the country . . . The Arab minority centered here presents a continual threat to the security of the nation.[12]

The solution, according to Nahmani, was to Judaize the Galilee region by establishing new Jewish centers. First Upper Nazareth was built after all the land available for the future expansion of the Arab city of Nazareth itself had been expropriated. Following Upper Nazareth, the town of Maalot and a number of other Jewish settlements were built. Then in 1961 Israeli authorities announced large expropriations of land belonging to several Arab villages in central Galilee. This move was for the purpose of building the town of Carmiel. Vehement protests on the part of the villagers were of no avail and government promises of compensation with equally rich agricultural land proved false. When Arabs of the neighbouring villages sought permission to move into Carmiel beside their Jewish countrymen they were harshly turned down. As Minister of Housing, Joseph Almogi said in the Israeli parliament, "We didn't build Carmiel to solve the problems of the people in the surrounding area."

As much as anyone. Ibrahim Shabat personifies the problem of the more than 300,000 Israeli Arabs. Shabat was an angry, embittered young man of twenty when the Palestine War broke out. He was born in Tiberias on the Sea of Galilee, an area allotted to the Jewish State under the provisions of the 1947 UN resolution. Tiberias lay close to the Syrian frontier and after the war the district was declared a closed area by the Israeli Government. By then some 80 percent of Israel's Arab citizens were living under a military administration. In a case like that of Ibrahim's family, this meant that the military governor of the northern region was able to refuse them permits to return home from Nazareth where they had sought safety during the war. The permits were refused "on grounds of security." The minister of agriculture then decreed that the family's land was "uncultivated." Since he had the right to ensure that the land was cultivated, he could turn it over to any other party for this purpose. Neighboring Jewish colonies took up the "uncultivated" land.

Ibrahim's only consolation for this high-handed treatment on the part of the government was the fact that 40 percent of the land owned by Arabs living in Israel was expropriated in similar fashion. When compensation was paid (it often was not), payment was made at a time when the Israeli pound was worth a quarter of its previous value and on the basis of 1950 market prices which that year were at a record low.

Ibrahim remained a staunch Arab nationalist even after he became a citizen of Israel. But as the years passed he was ever more concerned with the fate of the Arab minority under the military administration. He learned Hebrew which he now teaches in Arab schools. He joined the Mapam party and became editor of its Arabic magazine, *al-Mirsad.*

I met him in Nazareth in September 1967. He was tall, with flecks of gray hair on his temples. He looked older than his forty years. As we sat one evening at the house of a mutual friend, Ibrahim told me he had joined Mapam because, apart from the Communists, it was the one group which showed genuine concern for the Arab minority and some courage in fighting for their rights. He said: "I came to believe that the best chance for improving our condition lay in the political process. I regard myself a Zionist for there is nothing incompatible with being an Arab and holding Zionist ideals. But the Zionism practiced by the present regime controlled by the Mapai party is tantamount to racial discrimination and, in fact, the relations between Arab and Jew have not improved because of it. We are considered strangers in our own land."

He reserved his bitterest sentiments for Ben Gurion who, he felt, had singlehandedly done more to destroy the Israeli Arab faith in Zionist Government. "Once when I met with Ben Gurion he told me that Israel is the land of the Jewish people and only of the Jews. 'You Arabs,' he said, 'can enjoy the same minority rights here as any other minority group in the world, but you have to face the fact that you live in a Jewish country.' "

Ibrahim Shabat was a broken man who had struggled to find a measure of dignity for his people in an atmosphere which accorded them none. He was not alone.

Aida M_____ was an attractive young woman, a social worker. She spoke to me with a simple intensity about her own impressions. "You must understand that this is not a question of Arab and

Jew. We can and do get along. We have good relations with some Jewish families in Upper Nazareth; many ordinary citizens we know are shocked and sympathetic when they discover the conditions under which we live — with the military government and all it implies. The greatest barrier is perhaps the Jewish ignorance of us as a people and a community, and how we live. Indifference is worse and there is plenty of that too. Worst of all, however, is the negative attitude, the destructive activities of some of the rulers of this country, beginning with Ben Gurion. The military government which he initiated was only abolished in December 1966, but we know that it can be reimposed. For eighteen years we have lived in isolation from the mainstream of Israeli life and consequently Israelis, through no real fault of their own, forget we exist. Many have fought with us to gain us more freedom and for this we are grateful. But the ruling elite set a powerful example for the majority of its citizens, and for many Arabs it is difficult to distinguish between the actions of the government and the attitudes of the Jews. We have proven our loyalty to the land of our forefathers, but the government has never earned our faith in it."

The system of laws upon which the military government was founded was not, in fact, an Israeli invention but rather a device which the British Mandatory used first against the Arabs during the Rebellion of 1936, and thereafter against Jewish terrorists in 1945. There was, however, a certain irony in the way in which it came to be used against the Arab minority in Israel. At a Jewish lawyers' conference held in Tel Aviv in February 1946, many men who were later to rise to prominent positions in the Israeli Government denounced the Mandate Defense Laws in the strongest possible terms. The conference passed a resolution which noted that the laws "undermine law and justice and constitute a grave danger to the life and liberty of the individual and establish a rule of violence without any judicial control."[13] Jacob Shapiro, who later became Israeli attorney general and then minister of justice, declared that even Nazi Germany had not witnessed a comparable system of laws. Yet it was this same system, together with its military courts, which the Israeli Government adopted for its Arab citizens.

The organizational structure of the military government is

quite simple. Under Israeli Defense Laws (1949) pertaining to security areas, the minister of defense appointed military governors for three principal areas: Galilee, the Triangle bordering on Jordan and the Negev, known respectively as the Military Governments North, Central and South. The military governor has extensive powers over the lives of the Arabs who live under his jurisdiction ranging from detention for up to one year without trial or charge, to permanent banishment, confiscation or destruction of property, billeting soldiers and police at the inhabitants' expense and the imposition of curfews. Under Article 125 of the laws large portions of the military government covering most of the northern, all the central and one district of the southern region were declared "closed" areas. This is one of the most oppressive articles in the laws, for the entry into and exit from the closed areas are controlled by means of permits. Freedom of movement can be severely restricted. An Arab who wants to travel outside his village or town must apply for a military permit before he can leave. The permits designate the purpose of the trip and the route to be traveled. No stopovers are allowed. Jewish colonies en route are off limits and the bearer is allowed outside his own area only between the hours of 6 a.m. and 3 p.m. Permits could be refused without reason.[14]

A military court was the only competent body to try offenders of the regulations. The court's verdict could not be questioned for, until 1963, there was no appeal to any civil authority. After that date, appeals could be made to the supreme court but the court, as a general rule, would not interfere with the actions of the military government. The military courts were not obliged to divulge the nature of a security offense, for this itself would be a breach of security.

The Israeli military establishment consistently defended the system on security grounds. In the early days of the State there was unquestionably a need for the apparatus of the military government to watch closely those citizens whose loyalty was open to question. It soon became apparent to the Arabs, and some sections of the Israeli public, however, that the military government was serving interests other than those strictly connected with the security of the State. Like power groups anywhere, the military government had a vested interest in the status quo. The extent of its activities and influence was immense as the state controller noted in his report on the Ministry of Defense in 1959: "The military government interferes in the life of the Arab citizen from the day of his birth to the day of his death. It has the final say in all matters concerning workers, peasants, professional men, merchants, educated men, education and social services. The military government interferes in the registration of births, deaths, and even marriages of the population, in land affairs, and the appointment and dismissal of teachers and civil servants. Often too, it arbitrarily interferes in the affairs of the political parties, political and social activities and the affairs of local and municipal councils."[15] The military governor was, in George Orwell's phrase, Big Brother to the Arab; he could be benevolent or tyrannical, but in either case the Arab was at the mercy of his personal judgment.

The military went unchallenged for nearly a decade, until voices of protest began to be heard among opposition political parties and the intelligentsia. By 1962 a vote in the Knesset to retain the military government passed by only three votes; the next year the majority was cut to one vote. The main charge against the system was that there no longer existed any connection between the effective control of the frontiers and the functions of the military government.

Another charge, which the majority of Arabs believed was true, was that the military government had become the private institution of the ruling Mapai party of Ben Gurion. Sabri Jiryis gives his eyewitness account of a visit to an Arab village in Galilee by a representative of the military governor three days before the elections to the Fifth Knesset (1961). The representative told a general meeting of the village that the government wanted the village to vote for one of the Arab lists affiliated with the Mapai. The election was supervised in such a way as to ensure the "loyalty" of the inhabitants. In another incident, which reached the supreme court, it was established that the military had interfered in the elections of a local council by issuing expulsion orders for two elected members deemed "undesirable" to the military.[16]

The Arab view is colored by an intense suspicion of the Mapai party in particular and of Zionism in general, largely because it is seen to affect them directly. For example, whenever an area has been declared "closed" this has, in many cases, been a prelude to land expropriation and Jewish settlement. In 1962, Shimon Peres, then deputy minister of defense, observed that "it is by making use of Article 125, on which the military government is to a great extent based, that we can directly continue to struggle for Jewish settlement and Jewish immigration... If we are agreed that settlement has a far-reaching political import, we must prevent the creation of a fait accompli (i.e. further Arab settlement) incompatible both with the Zionist concept of the State of Israel and with the law."[17] To the Arab there seemed no end to the process of erosion.

Over the years the military government succeeded only in strengthening the very disaffection it was designed to counteract. It placed a physical barrier between Arab and Jew. Also, it symbolized a far more traumatic reality, namely, the sudden and violent transformation of the Arab community into a defenseless minority. And more, it symbolized the Palestinian's loss of his struggle for national liberation to the alien forces which now firmly ruled the country. He could not identify with the European in control, and the image of the free man across the frontier filled his mind. As an Arab he identified with his brethren in surrounding countries. Emotionally he could remain with the Arab majority of the Middle East, but in day-to-day reality he was fenced into his minority lot. Intense psychological alienation went with his physical isolation, without any compensating factors permitting the development of a national pride, be it Arab or Israeli. Television and radio brought his fellow Arab into his Israeli home from Lebanon, Syria, Jordan and Egypt, but he could not communicate back.

All these factors added to the centrifugal forces tugging him toward the outer perimeter of Israeli life, while the military government seemed designed to keep him there. Israel was the promise of democracy and equality for all which, in time, might have drawn the Arab toward the center. Israel, however, fulfilled the promise with the military government and land expropriation. Hence, democracy became a lie. To the Arab, failure to find a job in the urban Jewish labor market was discrimination; failure to find a place in the Hebrew University of Jerusalem was discrimination; the lack of educational facilities was discrimination. And so it went in all phases of life. Even when there was goodwill on the Jewish side, the Arab was quick to take offense. Sincerity to him was hypocrisy, understanding was paternalism or condescension, indifference was just indifference and hostility was mutual.

By the same token the existence of the military government reinforced the already strong insular attitudes of the Jewish community which were carried over from the mandate period. The Jewish National Home had not been intended for the benefit of the Arab and so the Jewish State was not meant specifically to cater to his particular needs. As for the military government, it was not there to punish crimes the Arabs *had* committed, but for the offenses which they *might* commit if they were not kept in their place. The argument would run: well, as long as the military government is maintained there must be good reason for it. Simplistic reasoning is comforting and relieves the need for deeper and more sympathetic reflection. The stereotype of the Arab remains intact; he is "one of them" and, as such, potentially dangerous. The abolition of the military system was greeted as the triumph of liberalism. It was also the victory for the cooler counsels of expediency. Either way the basic challenge of a non-Jewish minority was left unresolved. For could the Zionists force the pace of Arab assimilation when, in principle, they had consistently opposed Jewish assimilation in the Diaspora?

Nevertheless, within the general democratic framework of Israeli society there were channels through which protest against the injustices of the military government could be made. In Israel's early years, Arab political opposition was neither highly organized, nor articulate, despite the unusually high percentage of Arabs voting in Knesset elections, indicating a keen interest in political issues. In the first place there were no Arab political parties which could galvanize political opinion. After the Palestine War no effective Arab leadership was left in the country. It was several years before the community emerged from the state of shock suffered as a result of the defeat, and adapted itself to the radical new circumstances under which it now lived. In addition, all existing parties in the new state represented various shades of the Zionist ideology and it was unlikely that Arabs could identify with the political views in this spectrum. Moreover none of the major Jewish parties encouraged or even desired Arab membership in their factions.

The sole exception was the Communist party, Maqi, which shortly after the war combined both the Arab and Jewish factions which had operated openly during the Mandate. Maqi has been the only non-Zionist party in Israel to struggle consistently for Arab minority rights. It fought vigorously against discriminatory provisions of the Nationality Law which was complementary to the Law of Return. Under the provisions of the latter law, the right of immigration and citizenship by "return" was conferred on Jews all over the world. Arab residents of Israel, on the other hand, had to prove that they had been citizens of Palestine, which in practice was not easy owing to the very small number of Palestinians who possessed passports or identity cards. Communists also took up the cry against arbitrary arrests, expulsions and destruction of Arab villages, expropriation and the like. Fulminations were directed at the government for their handling of the Kafr Qassim incident, a tragedy which left a deep imprint on the minds of Palestinians in Israel and elsewhere.

On the eve of the Israeli invasion of Egypt on October 29, 1956, a curfew was imposed on several villages in the Little Triangle near the Jordanian border.[18] The Triangle had been under permanent night-time curfew since 1948, but on this occasion it was to be strictly enforced from 5 p.m. to 6 a.m. The village authorities only heard of the curfew a half hour before it was to begin and protests were made to the unit commander that the workers in the fields and nearby villages or more distant spots would have no way of knowing of the curfew. The Mukhtar was assured that all the workers would be allowed safe conduct to their homes. However, in the first hour of the curfew, as the sun was gently setting behind the hills, the men of the Israeli Frontier Force shot forty-nine men, women and children of Kafr Qassim as they returned to their homes. Some weeks passed before the Israeli public became aware of the details. The prime minister ordered an inquiry. Eleven members of the border police were finally brought to trial when the full course of the tragic events came to light.

The recorded testimony of the district court tells, among other events, of the arrival of a lorry at the edge of the village at about half past five. It carried four men and fourteen women aged from twelve to sixty-six years. The dead bodies of nearly two dozen villagers were already scattered by the roadside. Soldiers ordered the driver to pull up and get out. The women had seen the bodies of their fellow villagers and they implored the soldier in command to allow them to stay in the lorry. The soldier ignored their entreaties and their identity cards, and told them to get down. As the men and women lined up beside the lorry the soldier, who had been joined by others, opened fire and continued to shoot until all eighteen persons were dead, or appeared to be dead. A girl of fourteen, Hannah Amer, who had been hit in the head and leg, was the sole survivor.

Almost two years to the day after this incident, the court handed down its judgment. The two chief accused, a major and a lieutenant, were given seventeen and fifteen years respectively. Other sentences ranged from fifteen to seven years, and three men were acquitted. The Kafr Qassim incident shocked the whole nation, although some of the Israeli press, including the right-wing nationalist papers *Herut* and *Lamerhav,* attacked the court for the harshness of the sentences. For the Arabs, the most numbing shock of the affair was the gradual reduction of the terms of imprisonment of the convicted men until the last of them was released just three and a half years after the affair itself. The brigadier who had given the original orders for the curfew and the methods to be used in implementing it was tried by another court and found guilty of a "technical error." He was fined one piastre.

The Kafr Qassim affair impressed upon the Arab minority the extreme precariousness of their position both in terms of security and justice. A young Arab medical student from Haifa explained to me what he believed to be the real significance of Kafr Qassim: "The effect was greatest on the younger generation, people like myself. Our parents could forgive, although they could not forget. We can do neither. We Arabs who were born in Israel, or who can remember nothing else, know no other country but this one. Our defeat in the Palestine War was because of mismanagement by our leaders.

Kafr Qassim happened because there was, at a certain moment, a set of circumstances, an atmosphere which permitted that atrocity to take place. That atmosphere was created by men like one of the defendants at the trial who declared with all frankness that he had always considered us as an enemy within the State. The atmosphere was also created by our own community, because we chose to demonstrate our loyalty to this country through subservience to the masters. As long as we are subservient we will have no real freedom."

He was reflecting on the main characteristic of Arab political life since 1948, which was a kind of paternalistic relationship between Ben Gurion's Mapai party and the Arab community. Mapai did not admit Arabs into its membership, but at election time attempted to reach the Arab electorate indirectly through affiliated Arab lists. The lists were carefully prepared to include rich notables in the large towns, men who had a vested interest in the status quo, who had retained their traditional authority in the local communities and who could dispense patronage through their connections with the government. The strategy was successful and the Arab lists brought considerable support to Mapai in the Knesset. This did not necessarily reflect the real attitudes of Arab voters toward the government, for their support of the Mapai party (traditionally the strongest) was not out of conviction that this would bring changes in the regime, but out of fear that through pressure from the military government the ruling party could make known its favor or displeasure. The Arab Members of the Knesset (MK) affiliated to Mapai were regarded as rubber stamps for the government's policy. The view was justified, if only for the reason that these MKs voted in parliament in 1962 and 1963 for the continuation of the military government.

Mapam is a left of center Zionist party which admitted Arabs to the party after 1954. Mapam tried to foster its image among the Arabs as their friend and champion, although it had shown ambivalent tendencies toward the Arab minority resulting from its Zionist orientation. However, Mapam had contributed a good deal to the material welfare of the Arab community through party-run kibbutzim and other organizations. It had also provided the Arabs with a platform of protest in its magazine *al-Mirsad* which, unlike the Histadrut backed *al-Yaum* (Today), does not attempt to window-dress government policy. Mapam never had the appeal of the Communist Maqi party, however, owing to the greater ideological independence of the latter and the fact that Mapam compromised its image by joining coalitions with Mapai. Maqi's proportion of the popular Arab vote has been second only to Mapai-supported lists, and has been much stronger than Mapam, especially in the towns and villages.

A significant development occurred before the elections to the Sixth Knesset in 1965. Maqi split into two groups, the offshoot Raqah party forming an Arab Communist group, although about 30 percent of its membership was Jewish. The split had been smoldering for several years and was based in part on ideological grounds. Maqi has always held that the Arabs should enjoy absolutely equal rights with the Jews as a national minority within Israel. Raqah, on the other hand, considers the Arabs of Israel to be part of the Palestinian Arab nation and the vanguard in the struggle to win and maintain their rights. Through its party organ, *Unity,* a bi-weekly paper and the best edited Arabic newspaper in Israel, Raqah made its appeal to Arab voters as a non-Zionist Arab party. The party's results were impressive as it outscored Mapai in the towns and virtually wiped Maqi off the map as a political force among the Arabs. Raqah also gained two seats in the Knesset.

An earlier rift within Maqi dating back to 1958, produced in 1960 an all-Arab nationalist group known as al-Ard (The Earth). After long and bitter litigation with Israeli authorities, the movement was outlawed as subversive.

Hence the importance of Raqah becomes even greater, because as Sabri Jiryis, one of the founders of al-Ard concludes pessimistically: "it can be assumed that the official Israeli policy of suppressing any manifestation of the nationalist movement among the Arabs resident in Israel, and of combatting any organization that claims to defend their rights, will continue unchallenged."[19] **There is justification for this apprehension.** The chief of Mapai's Department of Arab Affairs declared in 1966 that the existence of an Arab party which was not allied to a Jewish party was a threat to the State. His reasoning was that Arab nationalist parties eventually throw up extremist elements and it would be a disaster for Israel and her Arab citizens to allow a party to exist which did not identify with the State.

From the Israeli viewpoint, the conflict between Zionist ideology and any modern Arab movement of liberation must be irrevocable.

11

Pax Israelica

Early on the morning of June 5, 1967, Israeli Mirage jets, flying in groups of four, skimmed across the silent waters of the Mediterranean and slipped under the protective beams of Egyptian radar. Within hours every airfield was pockmarked with bomb and rocket craters and scarred by grotesque heaps of metal which, only the night before, had been MiG fighter planes. The June war ended then and there.

The harvest of books produced by the June war far exceeded the output from the two previous Arab-Israeli encounters in 1948 and 1956. The tremendous outpouring of words emphasized the obvious: the overwhelming Israeli victory which left her enemies' armies strewn across the steaming deserts in tattered shreds. Nasser of Egypt had lost half his army; Hussein of Jordan half his kingdom. Brave David, defending embattled Zion, had humbled the giant Goliath. Indeed, David was now, unquestionably, the dominant power in the region. In the euphoric post-war atmosphere, Israelis and their sympathizers hoped and expected that peace was finally possible. Moshe Dayan, Israel's popular one-eyed general, smilingly told reporters, "I'm just waiting for the telephone to ring from Amman and Cairo." Foreign Minister Abba Eban, gesturing to his Arab neighbours, said, "Try us and see how generous we can be."

The prelude to the war and its day to day conduct are not an essential part of our present story. After nearly a decade and another major war, these details have receded in importance within the wider framework of the conflict. Victory was a tangible fact. But the anticipation of peace was an illusion. Almost as soon as the dust settled on the battlefield the moment for optimism had faded. It is important, therefore, to examine the forces which, in the months following the June war, inhibited the emergence of any common ground upon which a lasting solution might be built.

On the international diplomatic front, the hot war gave way to weeks of badgering debate in the United Nations Security Council. Five weary months after hostilities ended a compromise of sorts was reached, embodied in the Council's Resolution 242 of November 22, 1967. The resolution rested on two necessarily related principles. The second paragraph of the introduction stressed (1) "the inadmissibility of the acquisition of territory by war" and (2) "the need to work for a just and lasting peace in which every state in the area can live in security." In accepting the resolution, the Arab governments emphasized part one of the statement and consequently demanded the complete withdrawal of Israeli troops from *all* occupied lands. Israel, on the other hand, stressed her demand for secure frontiers, implying the need for *more* territory. The two sides were therefore deadlocked on matters of principle from which no bargaining positions seemed possible to adopt. As I. F. Stone described the impasse, "If God is dead, he surely died trying to solve the Arab-Israeli conflict."

Time tended to confirm the attitude of seasoned cynics toward the Council's deliberations. There was something in both the spirit and substance of Resolution 242 reminiscent of the British Government's futile efforts during the Mandate to offer the Zionists and the Palestinians alike the whole of the same cake. As we shall see later on, the gravest flaw in the international community's diplomatic exercises in late 1967 was that now the Palestinians were to be offered only the crumbs on the plate. Theirs was still merely a "refugee problem" in search of a "just solution." Nevertheless, before the year was out, events had unfolded both within the occupied territories and beyond—rendering Resolution 242 obsolete—although both Egypt and Israel continued to argue their conflicting interpretations of it like recitations from a sacred text.

Diplomats believed that Egypt's President Nasser was the sole Arab leader capable of effecting a compromise solution. While Israel could afford magnanimity in victory, Egypt was urged to be prudent in defeat. From his perspective, however, Nasser faced the prospect of negotiating only the terms of his country's total surrender. He, too, had a security problem to worry about. The June war had left Israel in full command of the skies and gave her a strike capacity to hit any point inside Egypt with impunity. The Bar Lev line, named after the Israeli chief of staff, marked the forward defense/offense position along the east bank of the Suez canal. When Israel showed no inclination to respond explicitly to the terms of settlement judged by Egypt as acceptable, Nasser attempted to break the diplomatic deadlock by initiating extensive bombardments of the Bar Lev line. This War of Attrition,[1] as it was known, commenced in mid-1969. Israeli retaliatory raids by air were successful in knocking out Egyptian surface-to-air missile sites—a development obliging the Russians to introduce the more sophisticated SAM III missiles designed to bring down warplanes flying below 2500 feet. Meanwhile, Israeli air strikes took their toll of civilian lives. On February 12, 1970, a scrap metal factory at Abu Za'bal near Cairo was hit. Seventy persons were killed and another hundred wounded. On another occasion a school was demolished also with heavy loss of life. The Israeli Defense Ministry called these strikes "accidents," leaving many Israelis incredulous. "We don't make mistakes like that," one young woman told a reporter, "there were probably good military reasons for hitting those targets." Israelis, it seemed, had become victims of their self-image of invincibility.

Military casualties on both sides climbed although the attrition rate was higher than Israel could afford over the long haul. When American Secretary of State William Rogers proposed a new peace initiative in June 1970, Egypt and Israel were prepared to let their diplomats play the next round. In fact there was nothing new in the Roger's Plan at all; it was just as unimaginative as previous efforts. The cessation of fighting along the Suez front in August 1970 was followed by a prolonged "no war, no peace" stalemate. It was only broken three years later (in October, 1973) when Egyptian troops swarmed in swift surprise across the canal, captured and destroyed the multi-million dollar defenses of the Bar Lev line.

The failure of post-1967 diplomacy was due in the main to statesmen's almost total blindness to the dynamics of the past deeply embedded in the current and ongoing aspects of the conflict. Abba Eban once said shortly after the war: "The hands of the clock cannot be turned back." This was, of course, evident. Western diplomats, therefore, tended to accept the literal meaning of their Israeli colleague's words. It was absurd, for example, to imagine a solution in 1967 based upon the 1948 United Nations' partition scheme. On the other hand, how much more dangerous was it to misread or ignore Eban's *intended* meaning to freeze time into one dimension: today's *fait accompli* is tomorrow's reality. The past is irrelevant to both.

One day early in September 1967 my twin-engined craft of Cyprus Airways approached the Israeli coastline and descended for the brief run inland to Lydda airport. By the time I had checked into a small hotel in downtown Tel Aviv night had fallen.

Almost my very first meeting with the victorious Israeli public was the hotel proprietor busily pouring over a mound of paper on the reception desk. Preparing his accounts for the tax people, he explained. From his acid comments I gathered Israelis were, per capita, the most heavily taxed populace in the world. I commiserated saying that victory, however sweet, must always be costly. He smiled and shrugged, "If the price of victory is so high, what then the cost of peace?" The answer to that question lay in the nature of Israeli society itself, in its government and institutions, in the attitudes and expectations of every segment of its people, young and old, rich and poor, European and Oriental. What Israel has become today reflects what it was in infancy under the British Mandate through the youthful years of statehood: aggressive, uncompromising, domineering and expansive.

To the sensitive observer, the cost of peace may be calculated from incidents of daily life where Israelis encounter the Arab population in any number of ways. A cinema in Tel Aviv is playing the feature-length documentary *Six Days to Eternity* to packed houses. It is about the June war and the audience is vocal and enthusiastic. There is a cast of thousands (the whole Israeli army) and the theme is exciting. The heroes on the screen are the heroes of real life: Dayan, Allon and Rabin all receive loud applause and cheers. The Voice of Israel, on the other hand, heavy jowled, bespectacled Abba Eban gets the cat calls; he is not the man of action the moment demands. Israeli warplanes streak out of the sun, descend to deliver their payloads of destruction then sweep back into the cloudless skies. More cheers as the narrator describes the play by play action. Next the camera pans across the wastes of Sinai studded with the burnt out hulks of Egyptian tanks and armoured vehicles. Then a close-up shot of the twisted shellburnt, sunscorched corpses of Arab soldiers, the flies and insects feeding upon their putrid flesh. Here is the true villain of the piece and the audience fills the hall with chilling hisses and angry boos.

In the eastern or Arab half of Jerusalem which Israel annexed immediately after the June war there stands a graceful stone building of pale pink hue, the upper portion of which was damaged during the fighting. This is the YMCA hostel. There are few guests in residence in September 1967. Tourists invading the country avoid staying in the "old" city simply because it is Arab. Early one morning Israeli tanks lined up outside the building, their gun turrets thrust menacingly at it. Soldiers heavily armed moved in attack patterns upon the entrance. The boom of cannon and the chatter of machine guns filled the air. Then, a sudden silence. The tanks trundled off followed by a large truck fitted out with tower crane, movie camera and cameraman perched on top of it all. Another "documentary" was in the making. The soldiers were now milling about in festive fashion. Across the street out of camera vision a group of some fifty persons, young and old, had stood in silence watching the spectacle. Some soldiers approached them waving their machine guns in triumphant gestures and laughed. Mutely, the Arab Jerusalemites stared back. Having lost their city they had to relive the humiliation of their occupation and illegal annexation as their new masters meticulously recorded the event for posterity and, one suspected, for fund raising purposes.

These scenes, spontaneous expressions of deeply ingrained patterns of behaviour toward the Palestinian Arab, say more than the rhetoric of statesmen and their pleas for peace. For the Zionist the Arab was a mere object—to be scorned or ignored; to be excluded or, worse, expelled. During the Mandate years Zionists believed that if Washington or London supported their program Palestinians need never be consulted over their future fate. When approaches were made, and they were few and far between, a spirit of conciliation and cooperation were notably lacking. In November, 1921, a meeting was arranged in London between Zionists and a visiting Arab delegation from Palestine. The Arabs had come to press the British to abandon their scheme for the Jewish national home. The British urged the Zionists to attempt appeasing the Arabs' basic fears concerning the national home idea. Chaim Weizmann who addressed the delegation later claimed that his approach had been conciliatory although futile. A British official, Eric Mills, witnessed the session but saw it in a very different light. "Weizmann's attitude was of the nature of a conqueror handing to beaten foes the terms of peace. Also, I think he despises the members of the delegation as not worthy protagonists—that it is a little derogatory to him to expect him to meet them on the same ground."[2]

These attitudes have persisted among the Israeli political leadership and the general public down to the present day. Jewish statehood and Palestinian self-determination and independence were always two sides of the same coin. In turning the coin face down Zionists blandly assumed that Palestinians were not a part of *their* problem. The Israeli journalist Amos Elon has written that "Israelis still hope, a hope as old as Zionism, that the Arabs will come round to recognizing that their decades-old opposition to the return of the Jews has been a horrible misunderstanding."[3] Elon acknowledges that this perspective is myopic for such hopes "can be self-defeating if they are linked to an ideal that ignores the complicated realities of human life."[4] The celebrated Israeli novelist, Amos Oz, has bitingly pinpricked the hopeless self-righteousness of this posture. "We want not only a settlement with the Arabs, we want them to tell us nicely that they are sorry; we want them to realize their mistake."[5]

As described by Elon, Zionist and Israeli policies are fortified by a deep psychological rationalisation, an awareness of *ain brera*, "there is no other choice." Accordingly, Zionist designs and ambitions in building a Jewish state on Palestinian soil were not the cause of the head-on clash between the alien settlers and the indigenous Palestinian. Rather, it was owing to the force of circumstances and guided by some blind, inexorable fate that the Zionist mystique of redemption became intertwined with the mystique of violence toward the Palestinian. This justification is, of course, profoundly apologetic. It implies the plea "judge us only by our motives, not by our actions regardless of the consequences." Therefore, the creation of Israel founded on the destruction of Palestinian society is neither causally joined nor morally linked in the Israeli mind. Zionist policies were not responsible for creating the Palestinian diaspora. Rather it was Palestinian resistance to their gradual subordination which forced the Zionists to drive them from their lands and homes. There was no other choice. And where there is no choice there is no guilt. It is this cult of innocence which has been the cardinal virtue cultivated in the Zionist military monastery.

In the months and years following the June war Israeli leaders have repeatedly insisted that "all is negotiable" in eventual peace negotiations. Their actions, on the other hand, have been consistently and perversely calculated to sustain the conflict for decades to come. The postwar tactics of the Israeli government in the occupied territories are characterized, in the contemporary euphemism, by the continuous "creation of facts." Among these facts are the expropriation of Arab land, the expulsion of the Arab population and the establishment of Jewish colonies. The overall strategy, again in the popular phrase, is "creeping annexation" of the occupied lands. This strategy is pursued by the dominant military and unique nuclear power in the region; it has been adopted neither from any overpowering force of circumstances nor from a compelling need for greater security. This much has been publicly conceded in Israel by ranking members of the military establishment who claim that at no time before, during or since the June war has Israel been in any danger of defeat.[6] Therefore, with the creation of each new "fact" in the occupied territories the Israeli government makes a clear and decisive choice among the available options depending upon whether her real objective is peace or expansion. The conflict between official statement and design has, in Christopher Sykes' words, given Israel "a not undeserved reputation in the world for chronic mendacity." The unfolding drama in the occupied territories since 1967 has torn a wide hole in the camouflage of confusion arising from official Israeli statement and design regarding the future of the Palestine problem. It may be a mere truism to say that history does not repeat itself. It is true, however, that patterns of thought and behaviour change very slowly over time. Israeli policies in the occupied territories have been witnessed before both prior to and after the creation of the Jewish state. Originating with Zionism itself, the basic impulses are the same: to take the land without the people or with as few of them as possible. If Israel bought its June victory dearly, the cost of her current adventurous strategy will be infinitely greater and the purchase of a final peace perhaps unattainable.

At the outbreak of war in June 1967 Moshe Dayan proclaimed that Israel's intention was not the conquest of Arab territory. On June 7, a few hours after the capture of Arab East Jerusalem, Prime Minister Levi Eshkol stood before the Wailing Wall bordering the Dome of the Rock mosque in the Old City. He addressed the nation speaking from "liberated" Jerusalem, "the eternal capital of Israel." On the same spot four days later bulldozers razed to the ground the houses of some 135 families living in the 700-year-old Moroccan quarter. The purpose of this demolition was to create a plaza for more visitors and worshippers. It was here, next to the site of the ancient Temple Mount that the Israeli army held a massive victory celebration. The 650 evicted inhabitants of the quarter were given a moment's notice to leave before the bulldozers moved in. No compensation was offered for their loss of property and most were forced to seek refuge in nearby villages. On Thursday, June 29 at one o'clock in the morning, East Jerusalem was formally annexed to Israel. That same day Yaacov Salman, the assistant Military Commander of Jerusalem, "had the honour to inform" the Arab mayor, Rouhi al-Khatib, that the East Jerusalem Municipal Council was dissolved. The order concluded on this note: "I thank Mr. al-Khatib and the members of the Council for their services during the transitional period from the entrance of the Israeli Defence Army to Jerusalem to this day." The ex-mayor was later deported from his city and his country for publicly opposing the Israeli act of annexation. On July 4, the General Assembly of the United Nations passed a resolution considering these measures invalid. On July 14 the Assembly deplored Israel's failure to rescind them. Chief Rabbi Untermann retorted: "We cannot believe in international guarantees, only in our possession." Jerusalem was on its way to becoming what Housing Minister Zeev Sharif called "an emphatically Jewish city."

"We take the land and the law comes after" was how one official described Israel's policies in Jerusalem to David Hirst, Middle East correspondent of the *Guardian*.[7] The mentality underlying this candid remark has had far greater impact upon the daily lives of Arab Jerusalemites than all the provisions of the Geneva Convention. In fact, the Israeli government has claimed that for "legal reasons" this convention, to which she is a signatory, does not apply to any of the occupied Arab lands, including Jerusalem.[8] When pressed in various United Nations special committees for an explanation of these "legal reasons," Israeli representatives have maintained a studied silence. At the time of the June war, Israeli Judge Advocate General, Meir Shamgar, coined the phrase "Controlled Territories" mainly to avoid the internationally recognized responsibilities incumbent upon Israel as an occupying power.

Every aspect of the Arabs' life in Jerusalem has been affected by Israeli rule. Thousands of acres of land have been expropriated and hundreds of Arab homes have been demolished to make room for new Jewish immigrants in extensive housing projects such as Ramat Eshkol and French Hill. A Master Plan for Greater Jerusalem, conceived even before the annexation, has been pushed ahead at a rapid pace despite scathing criticism of it from world-renowned architects and town planners. Individual deportations and mass expulsion of the Arab residents have helped "thin out" the original population. One example was the eviction of over 4000 residents of the Jewish Quarter, an area in which Jewish property owners did not exceed 20% of the total. The exiled mayor of Arab Jerusalem, Rouhi al-Khatib, estimated that nearly 100,000 Jerusalemites by birth, background and property rights are absolutely denied access to the city. A painful problem for many Jerusalemites, as for many in the occupied territories as a whole, is the reuniting of families separated by war or other causes. According to Professor Shahak, Chairman of the Israeli League for Civil and Human Rights, male Palestinians between the ages of 15 and 50 have no right to reunion with their families.[9] All East Jerusalem schools have been placed under the control of the Israeli Ministry of Education. Christian and Muslim students now pursue an almost exclusive study of Jewish culture and the Zionist version of contemporary history, while there is virtually no treatment of their own traditions. Teachers, too, of course, must submit to the Israeli curriculum or lose their jobs. All professions, companies and co-operatives are obliged to be licenced under Israeli law. Failure to comply with the law could lead to deprivation of livelihood; hence the alternatives for Arab Jerusalemites are either complete collaboration or exile.

Shortly after the war I spent an evening with Dr. Antoun Atallah, a former Foreign Minister in the Jordanian government. He was a soft-spoken, elegant gentleman with an intense love for his city, *his* Jerusalem. He expressed strong doubt that religious or historical sentiment were the primary motives for the Israeli conquest of the Old City. Jerusalem, he said, was the commercial center of the West Bank. Businessmen, merchants, tradesmen and farmers from all the towns of the West Bank had dealings in Jerusalem. By cutting Jerusalem off from its hinterland, not only West Bank business suffered but the cost of living of Jerusalemites suddenly soared to the Israeli level. "Whatever the hardships," said Dr. Atallah, "it is important for us to remain in Jerusalem for the duration of the occupation."

Resistance to Israeli rule was difficult. The security forces kept a close and constant vigil for the slightest hint or act of subversion. On the other hand, with world concern focused upon the Holy City, Israeli authorities were anxious to demonstrate the Arabs' peaceful, if reluctant, acceptance of their new status. Individual acts of defiance were often dealt with by imprisonment or expulsion. Small groups, however, could evoke considerable sympathy. In January, 1969, the Church of the Holy Sepulchre suddenly became a rallying point for Palestinian discontent. Twenty-five women, Christian and Muslim, began a hunger strike in protest against the occupation. At the entrance of the church, a mother and her daughter handed out leaflets to visitors and passers-by explaining the reasons for the strike. The two were arrested, which only reinforced the strike when a number of other women, some of them quite elderly, joined those already inside. The strike embarrassed considerably the Israeli authorities; the matter was settled only upon the intervention of an

Orthodox priest, who arranged for the strikers to leave the church on condition that the arrested couple be released.

In October of that year Israel decided to extend her brand of democracy to the Jerusalem Arabs. Municipal elections were set for the end of the month. The Palestinians were urged to take an active part in nominating representatives and in voting. To encourage their participation, on the morning of the election rumors were deliberately spread abroad "that anyone who did not have his identity card stamped indicating his having gone to the polls would be dismissed from his work, refused permission to visit relatives in Jordan and not allowed to run his business."[10] In the afternoon Arabs were dragged from coffee shops and off the streets, bundled into buses and lorries and driven to the polls. The Arabs' consequent enthusiasm to exercise their democratic privilege of voting turned out to be inspired by the violent tactics of Mayor Teddy Kollek's own supporters, tactics which were observed in the Hebrew press to be somewhat deviant from accepted electoral practices. Nevertheless, only 4000 out of a total of 37,000 registered voters actually went to the polls.

Time passed and Palestinians became more resigned to the prospects of a long occupation, but Israel had no greater success in winning either their hearts or minds. In the municipal elections of January, 1974, there were practically no queues at the ballot boxes in East Jerusalem. Graffiti appeared overnight on the walls near polling stations vehemently denouncing the elections and Israeli rule. As in 1969, there were no Arab candidates and only 10% of the eligible voters took part. A correspondent of the Hebrew daily *Haaretz* gloomily observed: "the elections have clearly proved that alienation and separateness between the two parts of the city are increasing."[11]

In Israeli eyes the future of Jerusalem is unambiguous. The official stance backed by unanimous public support is that a reunited Jerusalem will remain the capital of the Jewish state. Yet the perennial dilemma confronting Israel persists: Having seized the land of the Old City, what is to be done with its people? How might Jerusalem be made emphatically Jewish while a large proportion of its population is non-Jewish Palestinian? The increasing distance between Jew and Arab in the "liberated" city is put down simply to Arab hostility. Few have explored the fundamental cause of alienation in the very nature of Israeli rule. True, and it is a painfully hopeful sign, some intellectuals have spoken out (especially after the October war of 1973) against the sterility of Israeli policies since the creation of the state. Professor Ephraim Urbach, for example, has stated that "we did on occasion at least declare our desire for peace, but our actions and policies were not in harmony with our statements."[12] Another professor at the Hebrew University, Yeshayahu Leibovitch, argues that "the guideline of our policy has always been that a permanent situation of no peace and of a latent war is the best situation for us and that it must be maintained by all means. This situation puts the whole problem of security at the center of all our thinking; it is the crux of all political, economic, social and even cultural activity."[13] There is an inevitability about this security obsession even when it is unrelated to actual, objective circumstances. It is closely linked to the settler colonialist mentality of the Zionist and is espoused by Israeli experts of Arab affairs who claim, among other things, that Arabs only understand the language of force.[14] By putting this proposition constantly to the test in the occupied territories Israel should have by now built indestructible bridges of understanding between themselves and the subject Palestinian population. That this has not occured, however, does not suggest to the official Israeli mind that the wrong language is being used. Rather, the primary obstacle of communication is always described as inherent Arab enmity. The drive to possess the Palestinians' land void of its occupants is central to Zionist strategic thinking: the Zionist will not embrace his neighbour if he is not a fellow Jew. As Noam Chomsky has succinctly put it, "if a state is Jewish in certain respects, then in these respects it is not democratic."[15]

Israel conquered in June 1967 the remaining territory of Mandated Palestine. Six years later, in the wake of the October war, 1973, the Israeli Labour Party, the dominant faction in the coalition government, issued a statement on its future peace perspectives. Again stressing the "requirements of security" the document defines the goals Israel would strive for concerning the occupied Palestinian lands:

The peace agreement shall be on the basis of there being two independent states: Israel, with its capital in unified Jerusalem, and an Arab state to the east of it. In the neighbouring Jordanian-Palestinian state it will be possible for the identity of the Palestinian and Jordanian Arabs to express itself through peace and neighbourly relations with Israel. Israel does not agree to the establishment of an additional separate Palestinian state west of the River Jordan.[16]

The statement is revealing for what it says as well as for what it omits. First, it denies any expression of Palestinian self-determination and independence *on its own soil,* that is west of the Jordan River. Palestinian identity can only be fulfilled, the argument goes, in conjunction with a Jordanian entity. Israel itself, however, will continue to strive for "the preservation of the Jewish character of the state of Israel so that it may achieve its Zionist goals." In this *Pax Israelica* the complete separation of the Arab and Jewish states is envisaged. It would furthermore dissolve the Palestine problem and consolidate the settler character of the state which necessarily discriminates against its own citizens of non-Jewish faith. Second, the Arab state would lie somewhere east of Jerusalem. The statement does not explicitly include the occupied West Bank in the territories of the Arab state. "East of Jerusalem" could also mean "east of the River Jordan," the present rump of the Hashemite kingdom. This ambiguity regarding the West Bank, in contrast to the specific claim to Jerusalem, is striking. In light of the pragmatic Zionist approach to situations as they arise through the ongoing creation of new facts, and in light of what these have entailed for the Palestinians in the past, such ambiguity can be viewed only as the temporary political unwillingness to be committed publicly to a course of action and objective which is, at the same time, an unfolding reality— namely, the gradual de facto annexation of the West Bank. In an interview on Israeli television just before this official statement was published, Moshe Dayan made the following comment: "The West Bank is not a 'bank' but Judea and Samaria, which must be open to Jewish settlement. Any agreement must be such that allows Jewish settlement everywhere. What is needed is an entirely different, much closer tie between Israel and the

West Bank, if the West Bank areas do not remain in our possession. I say 'if' for I do not think it likely that we'll have to part with them." Dayan's confidence was shared by other cabinet colleagues including Prime Minister Golda Meir who told a group of Russian immigrants settling in the Golan Heights, "the border is here where Jews are living; it's not just a line on the map."[17]

A joke which caught Israeli fancy at the time ran like this: "Certainly Israel wants peace, a piece of Jordan, a piece of Syria, a piece of Egypt . . ." The joke was the more amusing, an Israeli friend told me, when the Foreign Minister Abba Eban was then trotting about the world persuading all and sundry that everything was still negotiable. Humour, however, wore a tragic mask as well. Added my friend, "those of us who do not believe in Zionist dogmatics find ourselves in the twentieth century being transformed into a classical nineteenth century colonialist power." His concern was over the dual processes of economic integration of the occupied territories and Jewish settlement in them.

These developments commenced right after the war and will be discussed presently. The initial preoccupation of the Israeli military was the firm maintenance of 'law and order,' a firmness which frequently went to excess. In the Gaza Strip, for example, Israelis "persuaded" Arabs to leave by various methods of intimidation and collective punishment. The Strip contained eleven refugee camps and over 250,000 refugees who greatly outnumbered the original population. For twenty years before the June war, these Palestinians lived just above subsistence level—through international charity doled out by the United Nations. A day-by-day existence corroded their hope but intensified their longing to return to their homeland, turning them into bitter Palestinian nationalists.

During the June war the Israeli army encountered stiff resistance from untrained, ill-equipped but desperate Palestinians in the Strip. The occupying troops quickly sensed the depth of bitterness among these Arabs, but the Israelis' outspoken contempt for them did not make for comprehension of such emotion. The contempt was returned by bitter hatred until the tension broke all bonds of restraint and the military government freely wielded the iron fist of repression.

A minor incident in January 1968 brought matters to a head. One day a small homemade bomb went off in the Gaza fish market. No one was hurt. The culprit was said to have made his escape along the beach in the direction of a refugee camp. There his fellow Arabs closed about him like a silent, anonymous sea. In reprisal, the Israelis blew up several fishermen's storehouses and destroyed some fishing boats. Total curfew was imposed on the camp for five days and nights. For twenty-eight hours no one was allowed to leave his house on any pretext. This was a particularly trying punishment, for none of the houses contained a latrine. A British observer, Michael Adams, reported that "on the second day the curfew was lifted for an hour at UNRWA's urging to allow refugees to collect water. They were still forbidden to leave camp and no distribution of food was allowed; not many managed to get water. During the break all men between sixteen and sixty were ordered onto the compound on the seashore where they were held for seven hours during one of the winter's severest storms while Israeli guards repeatedly fired small arms over their heads."

In other camps similar punishment was meted out for similar incidents. At the Jabiliyeh camp the male population was gathered and held outdoors for twenty-five hours without food or water. This was in reprisal for the mining of a civilian car, causing injury to its three occupants who, it was later revealed, were Israeli smugglers transporting contraband cigarettes.

The Gaza populace was also placed under a particularly brutal form of oppression. Concentration camps were established in the Sinai desert, in the Qusseima region and near Abu Rudeis, for the families of individuals "wanted" by the Israeli authorities. One camp was for women and children, the other for male relatives of the wanted persons. The existence of these camps was at first denied by the Israeli government. When they were confirmed, the official acknowledgment stated that with each group of mother and children at least one man must accompany them "so that no one will say that we do not respect the honour of the Arab woman."[18]

For four years the Gaza Strip remained a hotbed of intense resistance to the occupation. Guerillas, especially those of George

Habash's Popular Front for the Liberation of Palestine, were active in the Strip as they had been since the late 1950's when the Arab Nationalist Movement was formed. Militant schoolchildren also gave headaches to the military authorities. A few days after the affair of the Holy Sepulchre in Jerusalem, a crowd of some 3,000 schoolgirls demonstrated for the release of three schoolmates who had been arrested for allegedly harbouring a Palestinian commando. The demonstration got out of hand when the girls mobbed Israeli armoured vehicles and the soldiers turned upon them with their guns and batons. Ninety-three girls were wounded, forty of whom were detained in hospital with broken limbs and other injuries. In an effort to cool the situation the Israelis released the three girls from confinement. A week later the troops were at it again, this time breaking up a demonstration of stone-throwing schoolboys. In October 1969 a graduation ceremony at the Palestine High School erupted into an anti-Israeli demonstration and several attending Israeli journalists were caught by flying rocks. The school was immediately commandeered by the army for "military purposes." As a result of almost constant disturbances military officials deported nearly sixty teachers from Gaza for alleged incitement to violence. Six other prominent Palestinians were banished to a desert camp on similar charges.

Another form of Israeli retaliation at this time was the so-called "surrounding punishment," the indiscriminate destruction of houses and shops surrounding or near a center of resistance. The results of all these forms of repression were generally unsuccessful until finally, in 1971, an entirely new approach was devised. Wide security roads were built around and inside the refugee camps permitting quick and easy armoured vehicle control of them. About fifteen kilometers of roads were constructed entailing the destruction of nearly 2,000 houses and the expulsion of some 10,000 persons, over 80% of whom were left to find shelter wherever they could. Many went to the West Bank and crossed over into Jordan. Following this opening move a systematic "purge of terrorists" took place and hundreds of other Palestinians were arrested, imprisoned and deported. The pacification of Gaza was complete.

The West Bank after the June war was only marginally less

explosive than the Gaza Strip. In the Strip, with its smaller number of inhabitants, around 100,000 Palestinians had been "thinned-out" of the pre-war population by 1970. None has returned. Of the 200,000 persons who fled the West Bank during the war, only 14,000 of 170,000 who applied had been permitted to return up to 1970. Since then deportations have swollen the numbers by several hundreds of those making the no-return journey across the Jordan River.

When the cease-fire had gone into effect the inhabitants of several villages located along the 1949 armistice lines resumed their normal lives, albeit now under Israeli occupation. Suddenly, some weeks later, the Israeli army descended upon Zeita, Beit Nuba, Yalu, Amwas, Beit Jala and Emmuas, totally destroying the villages and dispersing the more than 5,000 villagers. At Zeita, for example, the villagers were assembled at half past six one morning and kept all day under the blistering 100 degree June sun while soldiers demolished sixty-seven homes plus a school and a clinic run by the International Council of Churches. That evening the commander appeared with a loudspeaker and told the villagers they could "return to their homes." Amos Kenon, the Israeli journalist, was an army reservist whose unit was involved in the destruction of Yalu and Beit Nuba.[19] He later recounted his sense of outrage at this incident, "I could not understand how Jews could behave this way." An Israeli settlement was built on the site of Beit Nuba. At Emmuas the area was zoned, planted with forest trees and called Canada Park.

Strikes and demonstrations against the occupation were common throughout the West Bank, especially in Nablus, the largest city and the pulse of Palestinian nationalist feeling. The then mayor, Hamdi Kan'an welcomed me to his office one day in the late summer of 1967. He was a large avuncular man with a small grey moustache and kindly enquiring eyes. His office was full of citizens bearing requests for assistance and complaints against the Israeli authorities. One elderly man had a son who was preparing to leave for university in Europe. In order to secure his travel papers from the military governor, he was forced to sign a document renouncing his right to return to his homeland. I was to encounter more cases like this in other towns on the

West Bank. The father asked the mayor if there were no appeal against this illegal act. Kan'an replied sadly that he feared any appeal would only fall on deaf ears. Turning to me he said, "Our military governor (Lieutenant-Colonel Zvi Ofer) is not even aware of such common courtesies as a hand shake. How would he admit this act was illegal and inhuman?" In further conversation Kan'an said that all indications of the occupation pointed to a permanent relationship with the Israelis in which Palestinians would not have real or substantial control over their own affairs.

The mayor of al-Bireh town, Abdel Jawad Saleh, was a tall ruggedly handsome man in his forties. His deep tanned complexion and greying hair made him very distinguished in appearance. Unlike Kan'an, his dress was casual, matching his manner of speaking. He talked about the occupation and its impact upon his people. "We're being Judaized," he said. "Nablus is now called Shechem, the ancient Biblical name." He laughed, "As yet, they haven't found al-Bireh in the Bible."

We discussed a situation which was just then causing great anxiety among the West Bank population. The Israeli educational authorities had withdrawn many texts from the school curriculum on the grounds that they contained anti-Israeli, anti-Zionist or anti-Jewish references. The proscribed texts were either rewritten or replaced by books used in Arab schools in Israel. The censors were obviously overzealous and hypersensitive. I was able to examine one forbidden book called *The Problem of Palestine* used in Jordan's secondary schools. Here, in a book dealing with the very problem with which Palestinians live day by day, was the place to find anti-Israeli sentiment. The book recounted the illegality of the Mandate based upon the Balfour Declaration and the fact that the Mandate was imposed upon an unwilling people. There was no attempt to justify the Zionist position or to describe the movement in anything but political terms. There were no derogatory references to Jews as people. The causes of the 1948 defeat were put down to lack of preparation, weakness and division among the Arabs of Palestine. The historical, legal and moral rights of the Palestinians to their homeland were emphasized; it was *these* points which a Zionist expert in education would be most anxious to suppress. As Mayor Saleh pointed out, "Just as they deny our existence as a community, they nevertheless want to eradicate our consciousness of being a people."

The mayor went on to describe Israeli treatment of the civilian population. Administrative detention and torture in prisons were two of the harshest features of the occupation. Administrative detention is similar to the policy of internment employed until recently by the British in Northern Ireland. Any person, on the merest suspicion that he might be *thinking* of committing some subversive act, may be held by law for up to 90 days without charge or trial. According to Israeli lawyer, Felicia Langer, many Palestinians have been held for three years without being charged or tried. For example, a physics instructor of Birzeit University near Ramallah, Mr. Tayseer Aruri, has been in detention since April 1974. Prison conditions and the general treatment of inmates was so bad that in April, 1970, strikes broke out in every major prison on the West Bank. The strikers were supported on the outside by Jewish and Arab intellectuals who demonstrated against the extreme cruelty of the detention measures.

Loutfiya Hawari, a mathematics teacher in al-Bireh, was first arrested in late 1967. She was 22 years old. This was the first of six arrests and she spent a total of seven years in various prisons on the West Bank and in Israel. On one occasion, during her fifth incarceration in the Muskoviya prison in Jerusalem, she was physically abused in the presence of her husband, also a prisoner. I met Loutfiya in Europe a few months after she and her husband had been deported from their country. She was a bitter but unbroken young woman who told me simply, "I have a mission here in Europe to tell others how my people are suffering under occupation." Then, with a quick smile, she added, "One day I'll teach our children mathematics again, but first there are a few things I must attend to."

When an occupying power exceeds recognized international norms of behaviour towards civilians, the finger of censure is bound to be pointed at it. Israeli practices in the occupied territories have been closely examined and condemned by several United Nations committees and commissions, most recently in November 1974. Despite Israel's persistent refusal to cooperate with any of these investigations, testimonials were received from both Israeli lawyers and Palestinian witnesses. Despite Israel's claim that the Geneva Convention does not apply to the occupied territories, international commissions have judged the following articles of the Convention to have been patently violated: article 27 on the special protection for women; article 32 on torture; article 33 on collective punishment and the punishment of an individual who has not personally committed a crime; article 47 on annexation; article 49 on the transportation or deportation of protected persons, "regardless of motive," from occupied territories. This article also prohibits the occupying power from transferring its own population into the areas it occupies.[20]

Of necessity there exist degrees of cooperation between the West Bank municipalities and the Israeli military authorities. The feeling of the mass of the Palestinian population is nevertheless unmistakable. No one wants to live under occupation no matter how sincere the efforts of individual Israelis might be. The mere existence of the military regime is a source of tension. The occupied population is faced with a no-option situation which can set in motion an upward spiral of violence. Following a guerilla grenade attack in Hebron on November 4, 1969, in which two Arabs were wounded, Israeli troops confiscated twenty-six shops on the town's main street. A military spokesman said that unless the Arabs in the Hebron area cooperated life would be made unbearable for them. Arabs had three alternatives, the spokesman said: fight the terrorists themselves; assist the Israeli army to do the job for them by supplying information on terrorist activities; or accept neither of these alternatives and take the consequences. In effect, therefore, the military regime would tolerate neither passive resistance nor non-cooperation, but rather would demand the active assistance of Palestinians in subduing their own people.

Under these conditions there is a fine line of distinction between cooperation and collaboration. It is not an easy task for committed Palestinian nationalists in responsible positions to cope successfully under an oppressive military regime and remain uncompromised in the eyes of their people. For others, on the other hand, loyalty is merely a marketable commodity. The ageing mayor of Hebron, Sheikh Ali Ja'bari, was one such official who collaborated with the Israelis from the first day of the occupation. He became known as a personal friend of Moshe Dayan. The Israelis had secured a pliable tool, and the Sheikh a powerful patron. The people of Hebron, however, were left without a representative they could trust. Finally, during the municipal election campaign in April 1976 a middle-aged, French-educated dental surgeon and hospital director decided to challenge the Sheikh's position. Fed up with both the Sheikh and his corrupt sons, Hebronites warmly supported the soft spoken, rotund little figure of Dr. Ahmad Hamzeh and his National Bloc list. The Israelis lost no time in reacting to this defiant gesture. Early in the morning of March 27, 1976, security forces seized the doctor from his home and kept him incommunicado for nearly eight hours. After a summary hearing Dr. Hamzeh and another medical colleague from al-Bireh were deported to Lebanon. The time elapsed between arrest and expulsion was just twelve hours. Even the Sheikh realized the Israelis had blundered. He withdrew from the elections, allowing the National Bloc's number two candidate to sweep in unopposed.

I did not see Mayor Abdel Jawad Saleh for several years after my visit to al-Bireh. The hand I shook on our second meeting bore the ugly scars of a bayonet wound inflicted by an Israeli soldier. He had been arrested and banished from the West Bank on December 10, 1973, along with seven other well-known and respected Palestinians. "The October war unnerved the Israelis," he said. "They started hitting at us with more than their customary severity. It was only a matter of time before they got rid of me and the others. We were local community leaders trying our best to protect the basic interests of the people; this is apparently an offense under some mysterious law of theirs." The eight were expelled through the favorite Israeli exit route for deportees, through Wadi Araba. The prisoners, blindfolded and manacled, were taken first by truck to Beersheba, and from there several hours drive into the middle of the desert. They were dropped and ordered to "walk East. Return and you will be shot." Somewhere to the east through the sands of Wadi Araba lay the Jordanian frontier. The eight had been given a little water and no food. When a Jordanian border patrol picked them up four hours later two of the eight had nearly collapsed from exhaustion. Abdel Jawad Saleh is now a member of the Executive Committee of the Palestine Liberation Organization.

The suppression of any form of resistance, peaceful or otherwise; the mass expulsion of population; the elimination of local leaders through deportation; administrative detention and torture; mass destruction of property and the buying of collaborators—all are found in the catalogue of coercive instruments employed by Israel in the occupied territories.

None has served as a simple end in itself since there is no long-run rationale in the use of terror for its own sake. Yet oppression can instill in the occupied population a sense of the inevitability of its fate, and acceptance of the imposed status quo.

Nor has Israeli coercion been a defensive reflex defined by a sense of insecurity and out of fear for the state's existence. On the contrary, after 1967 Israeli leaders were fully conscious of their unassailable military strength. Israel, they believed, rightly or wrongly, was master of her own destiny.

Nor have the politics of force been adopted from a feeling that there existed no other alternative in the pursuit of peace and the preservation of the Jewish state. Liberal critics (and there are some) inside Israel have increasingly and bitterly attacked successive governments and their policies pointing to other, saner options to achieve the same goals.

A degree or two above the absurd and crude rationalisation mentioned earlier that Arabs only understand the language of force, another justification for Israel's exercise of coercion can be unearthed. In the view of the Israeli military and political elite oppression is a sad and unfortunate necessity. It is, nevertheless, a small price to pay for bringing peace, security and prosperity to the Arabs of the occupied lands. The Israeli leadership has soothingly addressed a convinced majority of its public that a *de facto pax Israelica* has been established in the occupied lands, notwithstanding the continuing state of "no war, no peace" with her other Arab neighbours. But beneath this assertion of "peaceful coexistence" a far cruder reality has slowly emerged in the years after 1967. This reality, in the words of Amnon Kapeliouk, the chief Israeli authority on the subject of the occupied territories, is nothing less than "the creation of a classical colonial structure, exploiting cheap Arab labour to develop its own economic power without even giving these workers the right to spend a night in the locale of their work. The fact that these occupied territories represent a major market for the Israeli economy (90% of production sold in the territories is of Israeli origin) and the existence of a million souls stripped of all political rights does of course cause some inconvenience but does not prevent the majority of Israelis from sleeping at night."[21]

Colonial relationships are not new in the Palestinian experience. Throughout the British Mandate and following the inception of the Jewish state either all or a portion of the Palestinian people have known some form of colonial rule. Today, the Star of David has replaced the Union Jack and Israel rules one and a half million Palestinians, fully half of its dispersed people in *all* of its land.

These numbers haunt Zionist purists. They may desire retaining the territories of historic Eretz Israel but fear loosing the exclusive Jewish character of the state. Zionist annexationists are less inhibited about their solution. Shraga Gafni, writing in the official magazine of the Israeli army rabbinate, states: "The Arabs who inhabit this country today are an essentially alien element to it and to its fate and should be dealt with according to the rules which applied to the aliens in antiquity." The ancient rule, according to Gafni (citing Exodus as his authority), was expulsion—whose modern, more civilized equivalent, is Population Exchange and Transfer. Concludes Gafni menacingly, "those who will disturb shall be expelled."[22] For the pragmatic Zionist, of whom Moshe Dayan is a glowing example, the problem is resolved in the following terms: keep the territories and create extensive Jewish settlements in them linking the territories as a whole closely to Israel's economy. The Palestinian population will be necessarily kept under military rule while the burgeoning Jewish colonies shall benefit from Israeli law and the protection of its security forces. The Jewish character of Israel is thus preserved by these hermetically sealed satellites on Palestinian soil. "Mutual love is not required," Dayan once commented piously, "only the prevention of mutual hatred." The racist implications of Dayan's position have not been lost on some

Israelis, including the maverick member of the Labour Party, Mrs. Shulamit Aloni. Nevertheless, Dayan has been the chief architect of Israel's designs in the occupied lands.

Economic integration is one pillar of Dayan's programme.[23] This means redirecting the economic ties of the more underdeveloped occupied areas towards dependency upon the stronger Israeli economy. One direct method, employed by all colonial systems, is the exploitation of labour from the conquered lands. Since the June war the numbers of Palestinian workers employed in Israel have shot up dramatically: from 5,800 in 1968 to 20,600 in 1970; 50,000 in 1972 to over 100,000 at the present time. Roughly 60% of the imported labour is used in the construction industry, particularly in the Jerusalem area where apartment blocks for Jewish residents are rising on captured Arab land.

Apologists for this labour policy are quick to point out that wages earned by Arabs in Israel are as much as 70% higher than wages paid in Gaza or the West Bank. Certainly, wages of Arab labour employed in Israel account for at least a third of the gross product of the occupied territories. Moreover, it is argued that vocational training programmes are provided for Arab labour which thereby "raises their standard of efficiency and skill." Colonialist policies always find their defenders but the mere assertion that they are good cannot replace the demonstration that they are, in fact, exceedingly bad.

In the first place Arab labour in Israel is paid at a rate of between 40% to 50% less than Jewish labour for the same work. This patent discrimination is more important to the workers themselves than the fact that their money wages may be higher than before. Arab workers have no rights except the right to work. They can be fired without notice, they are not allowed to join trade unions, they have no medical protection and no social security services. Indeed, a small portion of workers' wages is withheld for a general benefits fund the purposes of which have never been spelled out. Workers, too, must often travel considerable distances to and from their place of work the same day as they are forbidden to stay overnight in Israel. One labourer from Gaza, for example, reported that for every hour he spent at work he spent another hour travelling either to or from it. His case is not exceptional. Many who break the law to preserve their physical strength must sleep in the most miserable conditions, in packing houses, sheds or in the gutter. In these cases workers pay an additional price of passing only one day a week with their families. Workers must also pay for their transportation and food while away from home, expenses which cut sharply into their earnings. Owing to the much higher cost of living in Israel, such expenses mean that Arab workers' *real* incomes, their actual buying power, is not as high as their money wages would suggest.

In the second place, Arab workers are channeled into the most menial tasks, unskilled or at best semi-skilled jobs and they are denied any job for which an unemployed Israeli might be suited. This trend of the hired Arab hand has grown to such an extent that one commonly hears the expression in Israel 'Let Muhammad do it." This, of course, is a far cry from the traditional Zionist insistence on the ethic of Jewish labour. The so-called vocational training centers actually only change already acquired skills of Arab labour rather than raising those skills to a higher level. This is due to the fact that the training programmes heavily emphasize the needs of the construction industry in Israel rather than the needs of the occupied territories' economy. For example, West Bank farmers and farm workers are being redeployed for their jobs in Israel with the consequence that agriculture on the West Bank is suffering from labour shortages in certain areas. The growing pool of cheap Arab labour has, moreover, helped Israeli employers avoid wage inflation. Another aspect of labour exploitation is the attempt to recruit women and young girls as seamstresses for the Israeli clothing industry, as crop pickers in the citrus groves or as workers in canning and packing industries.

Is Arab labour "attracted" to Israel simply because of the higher wages? Or rather, are workers "induced" by circumstance to follow this option? Certain dynamics of Israeli colonial policy may be illustrated by the following examples. The villagers of Aqraba in the Nablus district had stubbornly refused to relinquish their lands which, if vacant, would have ultimately drawn an influx of Jewish settlers. In April 1972 the Israeli military sprayed five hundred acres of wheat with a chemical defoliant which destroyed the entire crop at harvest time. The suddenly impoverished and dispossessed villagers were left overnight with the choice of becoming wage labourers in Israel or refugees in Jordan.[24]

The Rafah Heights are situated at the southern end of the Gaza Strip adjacent to the Sinai peninsula. Semi-nomadic Beduin inhabited the area as stock breeders and cultivators of fields and orchards. Early in 1972 the Israeli government began implementing its unofficial decision to create closed areas in the Heights for future Jewish colonies. Initially, about 6,000 Beduin were forcibly evicted, their homes destroyed, wells filled in and their property confiscated. Fifteen thousand acres of land were fenced off. This act, unlike the Aqraba incident, created a public controversy in the Israeli press. Finally, the persons responsible for these measures were "reprimanded" although neither their names nor their punishment were ever disclosed. The reprimand did nothing for the Beduin either. By mid-1975 some 20,000 Beduin had been evicted and 40,000 acres of their lands confiscated. Enquiries into the treatment of the Beduin revealed the authorities' methods to persuade them to give up their lands. One offer was that whoever freely relinquished his property rights would receive a permit to enter the land and cultivate it. Another method was to stop distribution of food rations from the American CARE organization; yet another method was imprisonment for any offense whatever, parole being granted only to those who signed away title to their land. The most stubborn holdouts had their lands confiscated for security reasons.

Two forms of compensation were offered which made these measures in appearance at least something less than outright robbery. One was a meagre lump sum of money, fixed regardless of the size of the property. The other was an alternative piece of land of five dunums for each Beduin. This was in contrast to an incoming Jewish settler who could be granted between 25-35 dunums of land. One investigation concluded that "such staggering disparity will force the Beduin to work as hired labour for the Jew, thus providing a firm foundation for the rise of a situation similar to that in South Africa."[25] Another commentator who visited the Heights said that "the lands from which the Beduin had been expelled and handed over to Israeli settlers were being cultivated by the very Beduin from whom they had been taken away."[26]

Israeli policy has also substantially affected Palestinian agriculture, especially on the West Bank. Certain crops are discouraged such as water melon which formerly had been exported to the Arab countries. The production of other crops required by Israel (such as sesame and tobacco) has increased while vegetables such as peppers and eggplant are encouraged for export to Europe.

In short, the occupied territories serve a dual purpose common to all colonial regimes, as "a supplementary market for Israeli goods and services on the one hand, and a source of factors of production, especially unskilled labour for the Israeli economy on the other." Thus the Israeli Ministry of Defence in a report on the development and economic situation of the occupied areas. In this context, of course, "economic development" refers to the current rate and future prospects of Israeli exploitation in the territories, not to any benefits the regime may have bestowed upon them. Israel has been able to breech the encircling Arab economic boycott imposed against her since 1948. For the first time Israeli products have reached an Arab market in the territories which have become the second best customer (if diamonds are excluded) behind the United States. If "progress" is measured by the increased buying power of a population then the 1300% increase in television sets on the West Bank would indicate a dramatic step forward. The actual situation, however, is quite different. As Mordechai Nahumi has conceded, there has been "no significant economic development in the territories for lack of capital and a labour force."[27] The reasons for this are clear enough. Israeli colonial policy drains off Palestinian labour to help meet its own needs, and provides capital for those enterprises which will contribute to Israel's economic welfare first and foremost. Israeli control over the deployment of capital and labour is complemented by its domination of the third factor of production, the land which, through the instrument of the Jewish colony, is being systematically transformed to Jewish ownership.

In the nine years since the occupation commenced the Israelis have constructed sixty-eight settlements throughout the Golan

Heights, the West Bank and the Gaza Strip. Their originally stated purpose was for security reasons, an argument as old as Zionism itself. It was evident that only a small proportion of the new Jewish colonies were founded by the military (Nahal) and many were quickly converted to civilian settlements. Security matters were handled by the occupation army. Hence the real purpose of the colonies is political and economic. Their life expectancy is eternal.

The Jewish colonies range in size from small frontier outposts, to the nucleus of a major town such as Kiryat Arba neighbouring Hebron, to the grandiose vision contained in the Yamit project.[28] This latter scheme calls for a new city of a quarter of a million inhabitants to be situated between al-Arish and the Gaza Strip on presently occupied Egyptian soil. Its future attractions will include everything from a nuclear power station to bikini-clad beaches. Moshe Dayan's explanation for the establishment of Yamit was that it may "serve as one of the factors enabling us to move the border further to the West." The groundwork for the Yamit project was the mass expulsion of Beduin mentioned above. On the ruined fields of Aqraba, Nahal Gatit was created in a single day. And so colonization proceeds, like Dr. Kissinger's diplomacy, step by step.

Israeli governments tend to transmit an impression of vagueness in the international community whenever the question of frontiers is discussed in the framework of a peace settlement. By 1970 only one specific plan was being openly discussed, namely, that of the then Deputy Prime Minister, Yigal Allon. His plan inspired the creation of a "security line" of military settlements (Nahal) along the west bank of the Jordan River. A small gap in the center, a kind of open corridor, would link the West Bank to Jordan. According to this formula, Jordan's sovereignty over the West Bank would be, at best, tenuous. Hence King Hussein denounced it. However, the plan also meant that over one third of the West Bank would be effectively annexed by the construction of the "security line." By September 1973 the so-called Galili document had been quietly adopted by Golda Meir's government; this instrument was more radically annexationist, providing for more intensive colonization and including among its schemes the Yamit project. At the present time if one were to draw a line on the map through the existing Jewish colonies the frontiers which Israel has unilaterally decided she will accept would comprise all the occupied territories with the exception of the western half of the Sinai peninsula.

Thus between the June war of 1967 and the October war of 1973, the Israeli government through its settlement schemes systematically drew the outline of the new Israel. At the second stage, in the months following the October war, the government began to yield with only apparent reluctance to extreme right wing pressure to fill in the picture, that is, to approve settlement of *all* the "liberated" areas.

This openly expansionist policy excited little adverse criticism from western capitals and the Israeli government concluded, rightly it would seem, that no opposition meant tacit approval of its designs. At best, western reaction could be construed as indifference to the problem of Palestine. Ignorance, however, is inexcusable. And yet no less a figure than the British Foreign Secretary (now the Prime Minister) James Callaghan, when asked to comment whether he thought the Israeli settlements might be an obstacle to peace, replied: "I have no particular knowledge of the settlements."[29] To such a response cynicism is justifiable. A leading Palestinian educator who had been deported in 1974 summed up for me the way he viewed western attitudes of Israel's policies. "Imagine the following situation. Kissinger is holding a press conference after a meeting with (Prime Minister) Rabin. Solemnly Kissinger announces, 'In reply to those critics who claim that Israel's settlement policy is a barrier to peace, I wish to make clear that the Israeli government has given me its full assurances that it intends no further confiscations of non-Jewish lands nor the construction of further colonies until formal annexation of all occupied lands has been executed.' Everyone would nod approvingly at Israel's sincere efforts to work towards peace." Later he added with just a touch of the Irish, "You have to hand it to them. For decades Zionists have struggled to build up Eretz Israel. Look at what they have accomplished today: Ersatz Israel." This was his way of saying that Israel was not quite the real thing—the purely Jewish state of the Zionist Utopians.

Indeed, perennially confronted by a Palestinian presence of

some kind, Israel has proven incapable of formulating an Arab policy in anything other than racist terms. The Zionist struggle to create the free Jew was premised upon the destruction of the free Palestinian. This proposition is illustrated by a public debate which centered around the conflicting views of Pinhas Sapir and Moshe Dayan after the June war. Dayan, as we have seen, was the chief architect of economic integration of the occupied territories. His policy was based upon the working principle that a *de facto* "peace" existed so long as the Palestinians under occupation had no chance of overthrowing the military government. Thus if, in addition to "peace," economic integration benefited Israel, what better arrangement was there than this? Dayan often spoke in terms of "good neighbourliness" which seemed to mean in practice that he felt free to invite himself into a Palestinian's house without the obligation of returning the enforced hospitality.

On the other hand, Pinhas Sapir, who was then Minister of Finance, viewed the occupied territories quite differently. He would be content to return most of the Arab land (Golan and East Jerusalem excepted) for minor border adjustments. His fears were twofold. First, he believed that the employment of Arab labour in Israel would change the image of the Jewish state and Israeli Jews would no longer be "working people." Second, as he said at a meeting of Labour Party workers on November 11, 1968, "I am opposed to the addition of a million Arabs to the 400,000 Israeli Arabs who will then constitute a minority of forty percent of the Israeli population and especially if their birth rate continues to be three times that of the Jewish population it won't be difficult to calculate when the Arabs will become a majority in Israel."

Israeli journalist, Shabtai Teveth, an enthusiastic admirer of Dayan, describes the former Defence Minister's vision of Israel:[30]

> Dayan regarded *Palestine* as a *Jewish State* whose citizens were Israeli citizens, but which also contained *an area with an Arab majority* (i.e. the occupied West Bank and Gaza. D.W.) whose inhabitants were not Israeli citizens; two nations in close proximity, functioning as a singel economic unit in spite of belonging to different cultures and *different sovereignties*. (Emphasis added)

Translated into English this passage seems to say: Israel is a Jewish State comprising *all* of British Mandated Palestine parts of which contain a hundred percent majority of Arabs who are really citizens of Jordan and not Palestinians at all. As a single economic unity this Jewish State of Israel would afford full citizenship rights under its own law to its Jewish citizens but would enforce all the restrictions of military law upon its non-Jewish non-Israeli citizens, whose labour could then be exploited and whose land could be expropriated for the benefit in perpetuity of the Jewish people. Dayan the pragmatist had kicked over the traces of the Zionist Utopian chariot and opted for the vehicle of classical colonialism. By way of qualifying Dayan's vision, Teveth concludes with this remark: "Dayan had not yet decided whether it (the occupied areas) were to be an independent state, or a section of the State of Jordan whose inhabitants lived in Israel." Such argument would do proud the tortuous mental perambulations of a medieval Talmudic scholar.

Nonetheless, Sapir's fear of eventually being swamped in a sea of Arabs is widely shared in Israel. Some fear that within a generation the Arab population would outnumber the Jewish. It may be recalled that during the British Mandate it was the Palestinians who feared *they* would be submerged if Jewish immigration were not stopped. Other Israelis argue that their predicament may not be so dangerous. An article appearing in the Israeli newspaper *Maariv* suggested, for example, that a Jewish majority and political control of the country could be maintained even in an "enlarged" Israel containing the conquered lands. The real danger of a high Arab birthrate in the short run lies not in the threat to the Jewish majority, but rather in the threat to the "material basis" of Israel. As the Arab population, the article continued, outgrows the limited agricultural land, "the Arab village will be unable to support its inhabitants, while the Jewish town will not happily adopt them." Jews will not willingly bear the financial burden created by rising Arab unemployment as the Arab contributes less to the State's income while enjoying its benefits. The author's solution is that it is "the duty of the parliament to fight the unnaturally high birthrate among the Arabs."

There is nothing immoral about this, the writer continues,

for if the governments of India or Egypt are free to initiate birth-control campaigns among their citizens, then Israel can do what it will with her Arab population by fighting "with all the means of legislation, propaganda, and coercion, against the population explosion which endangers the future of both Arabs and Jews." The author looks to the future: "In the longer run we must act, by appealing to the loyalty and economic sense of the Jews of Israel, to convince them that big families are a prerequisite to their existence. At the same time it must be made clear to the Arabs that they cannot be free to maintain the world's highest birthrate in our small and poor country."

In the light of the above arguments, both official and private, and by a careful judgment of key laws of the Zionist Israeli state like the Law of Return, it should excite no surprise that the United Nations General Assembly on November 10, 1975, determined that "Zionism is a form of racism and racial discrimination."

12

Whither Palestine?

The six explosive days in June 1967 altered more than the political map of the region. The war unleashed forces which caught most observers by surprise. Defeat and humiliation had paralyzed the Arab nation and trapped it in a political, military and moral vacuum. It was into this vacuum that the Palestinians stepped. The rapid rise of the Palestinian resistance movement marked the resumption of their struggle for national liberation, a struggle waged in vain during the years of the British Mandate. The Palestinian dimension of the Arab-Israeli conflict was restored.

Nearly twenty years had elapsed since the calamity of forty-eight. The international community had paid scant attention to the political aspects of the Palestine problem. It is true that the General Assembly of the United Nations each year reiterated the principle that Palestinian refugees should be allowed to return to their homes or be granted compensation for their losses. No one really believed that the principle could be enforced. Except perhaps the Palestinians themselves. To make up for their weakness as an uprooted, scattered and leaderless people, Palestinians clung passionately to the simple human justice of their cause. It fell upon others, the Arab League, the United Nations, the conscience of mankind, to recognize and restore their basic rights as the victims of aggression.

Meanwhile, many drifted from shock into apathy. Some of the once-famous figures like Hajj Amin Husseini retreated into obscurity, discredited. Still others set about with a puritan fanaticism for work and began to piece together the shattered fragments of their lives. But wherever the Palestinian's place of exile, intangible realities of the past became petrified deep within his consciousness. The older generations recalled birthplaces abandoned in war while the young spoke of ancestral villages they had never seen. Such memories and longings impelled people to defy history and thwart the perversely short memory of man. And even if, in the end, a father raised the flag of surrender it was in expectation that his son would raise the flag of rebellion. Thus, for two decades following the forty-eight disaster the international community succeeded only in buying time to prevent a lit fuse from igniting the powder keg.

The first blow struck "for the cause" was the pathetic gesture of a youth called Mustafa. King Abdallah of Jordan who had annexed the West Bank to his Hashemite kingdom was known to have undertaken secret negotiations with the Israelis. One Friday in June 1951 as the aging monarch entered a mosque in Jerusalem to perform the sabbath prayers he was struck down mortally wounded. As the king fell, he cried out to his assailant, "You have killed me. May God kill you!" The king's wish was not fulfilled; would God be likely to punish a boy whose name in Arabic meant The Chosen One!

Individual acts directed against Israel grew more common. From Jordan and the Gaza Strip, Palestinians infiltrated into what was referred to as "Israeli occupied territory." The temptation was irresistible as boundaries were often marked by little more than a shallow furrow in the ground or by an iron post. Former land and property were within sight and easy reach. It was simple to venture into a nearby village to see a friend or relative. Some returned unobtrusively to cultivate a patch of land, to steal tools or machinery or rustle livestock to which they felt entitled. Frustration and bitterness drove others to kill Israelis, blind vengeance bringing its own price which was often high.

Israel's policy of retaliation for these raids was directed first against Jordan. Infiltration and repatriation set in motion a rising spiral of violence until the night of October 15, 1953, when Israeli regular forces attacked and destroyed the village of Qibya, killing sixty-six persons, mostly civilians. This was the culmination of a long series of isolated acts by Palestinians—and in direct response to the killing of a woman and child only ten miles from Tel Aviv the day before the Qibya raid.

Retaliation on this massive scale was aimed at forcing the

Jordanian government to police its own territory more effectively against Palestinian infiltration. In the year and a half following the destruction of Qibya, Jordanian authorities cracked down severely: more than one thousand Palestinians were imprisoned either for attempting to cross the armistice lines or for any reason judged to affect Jordan's internal security.

A second major attack, this time against Egyptian administered Gaza on February 28, 1955, resulted in seventy-six casualties. The underlying rationale of Israel's retaliation policy was to prod the Arabs towards a final peace settlement through the demonstration of her superior military strength. The Gaza raid, however, did not have the desired effect. Egypt's President Nasser turned to the Eastern bloc for military supplies which resulted in the Czech arms deal of September 1955. Moreover, the Gaza incident led to the rapid increase of Egyptian trained commandos who were selected from among the Gaza refugees for their intimate knowledge of the Israeli countryside.

These developments pointed to the shape of things to come. Driven by the abrasive efforts of Secretary of State Dulles to bring Egypt under the American eagle's wing, President Nasser defiantly nationalized the Suez Canal to provide revenue for the Aswan Dam project. The Suez Crisis erupted into full-scale war in October 1956 as Britain, France and Israel coordinated their aggression against Egypt. Nasser was not only able to wrest political victory from military defeat; he also needled an infuriated Israeli government for its attempt to goad him into submission by force. From this triumph Nasser soon scored another with the formation of the United Arab Republic with Syria in 1958. This experiment, hailed throughout the Arab world as step one to the complete unity of the nation, crumbled in bitter recriminations three frustrating years later.

Small, widely separated groups of politically aware Palestinians took careful note of these events throughout the fifties as they tried to assess their implications for the future of the Palestine problem.

The American University in Beirut has been justly famous for many things, its elegant sandstone buildings, the splendid palm shaded campus overlooking the rocky shore of the Mediterranean, an ageless banyan tree and a highly politicized student body. Across the street from the campus walls Feisal's restaurant served excellent and inexpensive food to suit any revolutionary's palate. Among its clientele was a young medical student born in Lydda, Palestine, of a well-to-do Christian family. The world of George Habash was turned upside down by the Palestine war. With his family he joined the hundreds of families which fled the Lydda district driven forth by the onslaught of the Haganah. From his own experiences of that nightmare flight to Jerusalem young Habash determined to combine his studies with a political commitment to his people.

In the early fifties Habash and his circle were aware that no contemporary post World War II regime or party served the real interests of the mass of the Arab people. Moreover, in striving to protect and preserve their privileges these same regimes might submit to big power pressure and reach accomodation with Israel. To combat this possibility Habash's small student study group secretly published a weekly bulletin for distribution in the refugee camps aimed at rallying resistance to any proposal which threatened a sell out to Palestinian rights. From these modest beginnings, the Arab Nationalist Movement (ANM) was formed with Habash as its leading figure [1]. ANM cells eventually sprang up as far afield as Libya and Kuwait. Habash exemplified the Movement's efforts to build grass roots support by setting up a people's clinic in Amman, which he operated until 1957. That year he hastily vacated the city to avoid arrest for his active backing of the radical nationalist government of Sulaiman Nabulsi against King Hussein. Their intense concern to protect the Palestine problem from liquidation brought the ANM into close association with the rise and spread of Nasserism in the period between the Suez Crisis and the June war of 1967. The ANM believed that a unified Arab state encircling Israel could, with a conventional army and a Palestinian vanguard, force a favorable solution to the presence of this western backed colonialist Zionist enclave in the region. Hence the collapse of the United Arab Republic in 1961 was the first stage of disillusion and the collapse of the Arab armies in 1967 was the finale. In the interim between these two events the Movement shifted perceptibly to the left, criticism of Nasser was more vocal (especially over his adventure in the Yemen), and a commando group was formed to run operations into Israel and establish intelligence channels with Israeli Arabs. Each of these developments prepared for the emergence of the Popular Front for the Liberation of Palestine (PFLP) after the June war, with Habash still as leader. The PFLP frequently chose to remain on the margin of the Palestine resistance just as the ANM had been a marginal force to the Nasserist-Baathist mainstream of Arab politics since the early fifties. Nevertheless, in George Habash Palestinians had a shrewd and able organizer; the PFLP was an important wing of the resistance acting as watchdog and critic of the programmes and policies of the more popular and stronger groups like Fateh.

In Gaza, during the Israeli occupation of 1956, another group of young Palestinians met and agreed to form a clandestine organization which would eventually allow Palestinians to take their cause into their own hands. At its head was a swarthy young man of twenty-seven, three years junior to George Habash. Like the latter, Yasir Arafat's life took a decisive turn in 1948. Of middle class background, Arafat spent his childhood and youth in Jerusalem within a stone's throw of the Wailing Wall. The Palestine war caused his family to move to Gaza where Arafat saw the results of the sudden and degrading transformation of his people in the camps of the Strip. His reaction, again like that of Habash, was to combine higher education with political activism. In Cairo he entered the faculty of engineering at King Fuad I University (now Cairo University) during the twilight years of the decaying monarchy. He organized Palestinian students and later engaged in commando training and demolition work against the remaining British bases in the Suez Canal zone. Following the Gaza conversations in 1956, Arafat moved his operations to Kuwait where the real nucleus of Fateh was formed. The foundation stones were slowly and carefully laid. Political work was carried out mainly among Palestinian students in the Arab world although Stuttgart University in Germany also boasted a Fateh cell. By 1959 a small circulation monthly called *Our Palestine* began to appear in Beirut. Its main message was that the Arab government should allow and encourage Palestinians to work with a free hand towards the liberation of their country. The message was audaciously simple, the solution formidably complex. Where amid the wreckage of a torn and battered people was the stuff of which liberation movements are made? Yet there was an urgently pragmatic thrust to this argument. As one commando leader, Abu Saleh, explained, "In those days, each of us was a prisoner of his past. We dreamed romantically of returning to our homeland, but no one was able to take the first step. Servitude is a state of mind; only *we* could break our chains and set ourselves free to *plan* the future rather than just *dream* about it."

The year 1964 brought matters a step closer to a breaking of the chains. Israel had declared its intention of diverting the headwaters of the Jordan for its own irrigation uses and defied the Arab countries to try and stop the project. The Arab governments acknowledged their impotence by convening a summit conference in Cairo under the patronage of President Nasser. The Egyptian president bluntly told the conference that the Arabs were in no position for an open confrontation with Israel. Hence the problem of the Jordan waters was shelved. Instead, the summit meeting acted upon an earlier Arab League council decision to create an official Palestinian entity, the Palestine Liberation Organization. Ahmad Shukayri was appointed its first leader.

In January of the next year, 1965, Fateh commenced its campaign of sabotage inside Israel. Operationally, the beginnings were modest, even inauspicious. During the thirty months prior to the June war Israeli sources reported only 122 commando operations. Israeli casualties were low, those of Fateh relatively high. Nevertheless, as the old chains were being broken Palestinians were collectively asserting a new state of being.

Between 1964 and 1967 the Palestine Liberation Organization was properly an instrument of the Arab governments although forged, perforce, in the fires of a passionate Palestinian longing to return to The Land. For their part, the Arab governments hoped their patronage of the PLO would serve two interrelated purposes: containment of the more militant underground elements like the PFLP and Fateh which could strike out independently and thereby disrupt the region's delicate balance of stability; and to insure that the PLO leadership would be acceptable within the general ideological framework of the contemporary Arab state system.

Palestinians, on the other hand, needed some national agency as an institutional focus for the energies of their dispersed people in order to preserve their identity and consciousness. Through the PLO, a National Council (which elected the executive committee of the PLO) met each year to debate openly the problems and progress of the proliferating Palestinian civil institutions (such as trade unions, student unions, and writers and journalist unions) and their military organization, the Palestine Liberation Army. On the eve of the June war, therefore, the Palestinian resistance, as one writer has aptly expressed it, had "two faces." One of these was "public and official represented by the PLO which was more but not completely acceptable to the Arab states, the other secret which was represented by the underground and militant organizations. For the most part they acted independently of each other though pressure was constant for a certain degree of fusion."[2]

Whatever the motives behind its creation, the PLO was a first step in restoring to the Palestinian people a sense of cohesiveness and purpose which had been wrecked by the debacle of 1948. Moreover, it was an important first step towards international recognition and legitimation of the Palestinians' right to pursue the thorny path of national liberation. Only a prophet might have foreseen that a decade later the PLO would be admitted to the deliberations of the United Nations with full observer status.

The collapse of the Arab armies in 1967 compromised the "public" face of Palestinian resistance owing to the PLO's association with the ideology and strategy of the Arab governments which supported its foundation. The PLO's bombastic leader, Ahmad Shukayri, had not helped matters either. His horrendous declarations before the June war about exterminating Israelis or shipping them back to their countries of origin endeared him to no one except perhaps Zionist propaganda agents and other sympathetic media writers who cheerfully made out all Arabs to be little better than vultures.

In Beirut after the war I secured an introduction through a lawyer acquaintance to members of the political executive of the PLO. The first thing I wanted to know was where they stood on the question of Shukayri who at that moment was in retreat in his magnificent villa atop a forested hill overlooking Beirut and the sea. Shukayri's life style, in stark contrast to that of his successors in the commando leadership, had been subject to criticism even before the war. "Is Shukayri representative of what Palestinians want and think?" I asked. There was an embarrassed silence. Their answers were non-committal and we shifted to other topics. Afterward, as the lawyer accompanied me from his office to the elevator, he said, "You put them on the spot about Shukayri. The PLO is undecided over how to deal with him. I personally think the man is a dangerous fanatic. He has harmed the cause enough and he won't last long." He was right. Shukayri was ousted a few weeks later, abandoned to write his voluminous memoirs.

Shukayri's departure, however, did not mean simply the replacement of a discredited leader by totally new and untried actors. The effect of the June war was "to allow a generation of relatively obscure Palestinian activists to emerge as visible spokesmen for a cause they had been pursuing during much of the previous two decades."[3] One member of this generation is Zuhayr Alami. The Alami family story is a tale of success, not untypical of its kind, of Palestinian response to adversity and subsequent contribution to Arab society and their own national cause. As a result of the Palestine war the family left Gaza and moved to Lebanon. The determination and affectionate bullying of Zuhayr's eldest brother were in large measure responsible for his brothers' acquiring higher professional education. The results were impressive: a banker, two surgeons, a pathologist and a businessman. Zuhayr, now in his early forties, became an engineer, built up his own consulting office and taught at the American University of Beirut. His political preoccupations go back at least to 1956 when he accompanied Yasir Arafat to Prague as the official delegation sent by the General Union of Palestine Students to the International Union of Students Conference. In 1970 he became a member of the central committee of the PLO as head of the Palestine National Fund. To my surprise Zuhayr was in a mood of buoyant optimism over the Arab defeat in 1967. "For us, the fifth of June is not a day of mourning, but a day of hope. Now, after twenty years, we are free to take a hand in guiding our own destiny. The time

WHITHER PALESTINE?

has come for the Palestinian masses to organize and take the struggle into their own hands. Then our voices will be heard. Until today, we have been regarded as refugees or simply United Nations statistics. The word refugee no longer exists for us. We are a nation of men, women and children who join the struggle to regain our roots in our homeland." For all that, he was under no illusion that the obstacles would not be formidable or even that liberation may not be achieved. As he said with a shrug, "For us, the Palestine revolution is an imperative."

What Alami's generation of Palestinian stood for, regardless of the political leaning of any particular individual, was a clear alternative to the prevalent hollow ideologies and strategies of the Arab governments regarding the Arab-Israeli conflict. This previously 'silent' generation of young Palestinian activists turned their backs on the struggle guided along the lines of past experience. They rejected the old slogan that Arab unity was the road to the liberation of Palestine. Now, consciously they accepted the fragmentation of the Arab world as reality. True, the modern Arab states were artificial creations reflecting the legacy of the recent colonial past. Was not even the Arab League a British inspiration? With the end of colonial rule the Arab states, or at least their ruling elites, had quite naturally assumed national responsibilities and thus developed a sense of national "self-interest." Their commitment to the Palestine problem, therefore, came to be seen by many Palestinians as merely one means for advancing their national interests. For, as long as Israel did not appear to threaten them directly, a showdown could be postponed indefinitely or ignored altogether. And so the new generation of Palestinians, the Generation of the Exile, reversed the old slogan: Palestinian liberation is the path to Arab unity. In this slogan Palestinians expressed their need to seek a specifically Palestinian solution to their conflict with Israel while at the same time appealing to the deeper but inarticulate instincts of the Arab masses. The post-1967 Palestine resistance put forward the concepts of popular armed struggle and self-reliance, neither of which had been envisaged by the founders of the PLO. The imperative of this strategy was to arouse Palestinian consciousness, subordinating the interests of the Arab regimes to the struggle for their own liberation.

The first Christmas of the occupation came with lead-grey skies settling over the country. The drizzle, icy winds in the hill districts and near-freezing temperatures harmonized with the sullen mood of the occupied Palestinian population. A first snow in Galilee brightened an otherwise somber landscape. On the heights of Golan Israeli soldiers built snowmen and, armed from their arsenals of snowballs, fought pitched battles among themselves. For them at that moment the Palestinian resistance was the farthest thing from their minds. At the pilgrimage sites, however, other security forces waited tensely for the season's celebrations to end. The threatened disturbances had not broken out and the days passed without incident. On Cyprus that Christmas a lonely man prepared to leave for Jerusalem on a peace mission for the United Nations. Gunnar Jarring's was a hopeless and thankless task, traveling to and fro between Arab capitals and Israel, striving patiently to find some way out of the political impasse. Six years later Henry Kissinger took up Jarring's original efforts at shuttle diplomacy; the difference was that Jarring carried neither a carrot nor a stick in his attaché case. Six months after the June war the prospects for peace were washed away with the winter rains.

While Israeli authorities tried to reach some modus vivendi with the political leaders on the West Bank, the Hebrew press reported the first stirrings of Palestinian resistance to the occupation. Press items included "Incidents in Gaza" . . . "General strike called in East Jerusalem" . . . Arab terrorists strike kibbutz." Hypersensitive to real or imagined dangers, over-reaction was common: "Arab in Hebron sentenced to ten years for possession of rifle and sword." Or, in the following incident at Ramallah, a beautiful little town a few kilometers north of Jerusalem. In October, 1967, a crowd of three hundred girls sat in their school compound chanting slogans such as "Palestine is our country," and "Long Live Fateh." Steel helmeted soldiers, armed with guns and clubs stormed into the compound swinging their weapons in every direction. According to the school's headmistress "the soldiers came tearing into the buildings. They clubbed anyone they saw. I saw my teachers being held by two soldiers and beaten by a third. Some of them had not been demonstrating but were attending classes peacefully with their students." The *London Observer's* Gavin Young reported the incident at the time. "I saw girls of fifteen or less who had evidently been struck several times. One young teacher, covered with bruises and with a severe swelling on her forehead, was in bed unable to move. Other girls had multiple bruises. All told the same story of a wild charge by Israeli soldiers."

The clash at Ramallah became part of a pattern of conflict between Israeli and Palestinian. The school-age population, armed with little more than slogans and fists, was the catalyst of much civilian unrest and opposition to the occupation. After nearly a decade of Israeli rule the younger generation continues to galvanize its elders into open challenge of Israel's colonial policies. The major civil disturbances of the first quarter of 1976 were again led by Palestinian youth confronting the batons and bullets in the streets and alleyways of the occupied lands.

However, in the early months after the June war, it was activity in areas outside of Israel's control which captured much of the attention of the world's press. In January of the new year, 1968, Fateh issued its first communique. "The Palestine problem," it stated, "is essentially the problem of an entire people, the Arabs of Palestine uprooted and expelled from their homeland in order to permit the establishment of Israel." Fateh acknowledged the failure of the United Nations as well as the failure of their own people through the PLO to further the cause of liberation of the homeland. Circumstances had now changed. Face to face with the occupier the Palestinian was entering a new phase of popular resistance of the masses. Arab citizens of Israel, inhabitants of the occupied territories, the refugees and Palestinians throughout the Arab world would join the struggle since it involved the fate of the nation as a whole. The first stage of the revolution was the mobilization of Palestinians everywhere to the cause of liberation.

The ultimate goal of the Palestinian revolution was the establishment of a new secular order. Its vision of the future was the day when "the flag of Palestine is hoisted over their freed, democratic, peaceful land, and a new era will begin in which the Palestinian Jews will again live in harmony side by side with the original owners of the land, the Arab Palestinians."

This vision of a democratic, non-sectarian state of Palestine has given rise to bitter controversy despite the fact that its realization is decades, even generations away. Israelis have violently impugned the sincerity of Palestinians who espouse it while Palestinians hold with equal fervour that they view their conflict with Israel in far more humane terms than before.

The center of the controversy is Article Six of the PLO's National Charter, drawn up in 1964. The article implied that the citizens of a future Palestinian state would include only those Jews (now Israelis) who had come to Palestine before 1948. The same article was revised in 1968 to read, "Jews living in Palestine until the beginning of the Zionist invasion are considered Palestinians." The Zionist invasion was interpreted to date from 1917. Israeli writers have had a field day with this article, claiming it exposes the concept of the secular Palestine state as a patent fraud which would in reality rid it of all Jews—an act of national suicide if Israelis ever embraced the plan. However, as one neutral scholar has pointed out, "In the rapidly changing Palestinian context, a document drafted in 1968 by PLO leaders chosen in 1964 is unlikely to reflect the opinions of the leaders of the 1970s, even if the charter is supposedly still in force."[4]

A recent public exchange between an Israeli and a Palestinian is more revealing of the state of the debate today. At a colloquium on Palestine held in Brussels, May 1976, Dr. Uri Davis, an Israeli scholar, told the packed auditorium at the Free University that if Palestinians expected any support and sympathy from anti-Zionist Israelis then Article Six of the Charter would have to go. "It is morally unacceptable to us," he said. Dr. Nabil Shaath, a former professor at the American University in Beirut and head of the PLO's Planning Center, took up Davis' challenge. The present PLO leadership, he said, had long recognized the need for a complete revision of the National Charter, not only Article Six. Work on it had in fact already commenced. Shaath conceded that the question of a democratic secular state had in the past been a somewhat remote and abstract topic. There were two reasons for this. Since 1967 the Palestinian resistance had been dealing with the more immediate problems of mere survival and warding off attempts to liquidate it entirely. In addition, it seemed premature to work out a detailed blueprint for future Jewish-Palestinian relations so long as Israelis and

Zionists refused to acknowledge Palestinians as the main party to the conflict. Nevertheless, Shaath continued, Palestinians have moved a long way from the days of desiring simple revenge. The Palestinian revolution had matured beyond such primitive objectives. "For the resistance Article Six, which has been forced to mean many things, is a dead letter," he said, "and it has been superceded by the political program of the PLO in force today." That program was clearly spelled out by the Chairman of the PLO, Yasir Arafat, in his address to the United Nations General Assembly, November 13, 1974,

> . . . our revolution has not been motivated by racial or religious factors. Its target has never been the Jew as a person, but racist Zionism and aggression. In this sense ours is also a revolution for the Jew, as a human being. We are struggling so that Jews, Christians and Muslims may live in equality, enjoying the same rights and assuming the same duties, free from racial or religious discrimination.

Looking at Davis, Shaath concluded his remarks, "I trust the day will come when my Jewish Palestinian brother Uri Davis and I will walk the soil of a free Palestine which is free for us both equally." To which Davis responded, "I thank my Arab Palestinian brother for his forthright and honest statement, as an official of the PLO, concerning their position on the question of Jewish Palestinians."[5] Times have changed, as this encounter indicates. Further changes are in store: for example, it has been proposed by the PLO that two Israeli Jews be elected as full members to the Palestine National Council at the next annual conference. It is a small step forward but a positive one nonetheless.

Still, a Brussels spring was a long way from winter in Jordan that first year of the post-war period. Popular armed struggle had captured the popular imagination. It was like an antidote to the numbing poison of defeat. The various groups of the burgeoning resistance, of which Fateh was swiftly becoming the largest and best known, were busy training recruits and setting up auxilliary services like clinics, schools and information centers. A scene in one fidayeen camp was much like another: early morning physical training and mastery of the art of unarmed combat; despite the bitter cold of the winter nights, long marches over unfamiliar terrain; training in the use of rifle, mortar, machine gun, bazooka, rocket and the techniques of dynamiting.

Most commando groups established their contingents of *ashbal* or "lion cubs," boys ranging in age from seven to fourteen. They, too, received intensive training in unarmed combat and in the use of more sophisticated weapons and explosives—as well as their regular schooling and political education. At age fifteen they would graduate to full-fledged fidayeen. Gerard Chaliand, the French journalist, became familiar with their camps during an extensive tour in early 1969. "I noticed that the fidayeen in no way consider themselves as an elite, nor do they disdain the refugee population. They do not have a commando mentality, but a very clear awareness and feeling that they are fighting *for* the refugees, of whom they themselves form an organic part. This feeling is a guarantee for the continuation of a close relationship with the mass of the refugees."[6]

Young girls, and women too, began to play an increasingly important role in the resistance. As teachers, nurses, welfare workers and couriers, almost all received some training in handling automatic weapons. There remain many traditional values which hinder a woman's full participation in armed struggle but changes are occuring even in the older generation. One commando leader, Abu Marwan, recounted an incident from his own experience. "The Arabs," he said, "take death very seriously. Women cry and weep and moan for days after a death in the family. You can imagine my apprehension when I had to break the news to a mother that her son had been killed in action. I tried to introduce the subject gently, and then I just blurted out the news. I waited for the outburst. Nothing. Not a tear, not even a wrinkle on her poor face. 'It is for our country,' she said to me. 'I know that we must sacrifice for our country to be free.' Our mothers are very possessive about their children, you know. I was deeply touched by her words."

By both direct and subtle means the Palestinian community was undergoing a gradual transformation while at the same time the surrounding environment, locally and internationally, was being affected in turn by the emergence of Palestine-in-arms. Once the old-guard leadership had been dispensed with, the PLO (since February 1969 under the chairmanship of Yasir Arafat,

WHITHER PALESTINE?

leader of the dominant Fateh group) pressed their claim to Palestine on all fronts.

On the Palestine front, they mobilized their own consituency, which meant, on its outer boundaries, reaching half-way around the world. The educated and the well-to-do contributed their money and a wide range of organizational capacities and expertise. Some left comfortable professions in America or Europe and turned their skills to the day to day and long range planning of the resistance. Students from abroad also returned to the home front while others organized seminars and teach-ins on their campuses. Few, in fact, were left totally untouched or indifferent by the June war and its aftermath even if it only meant reassessing long-suppressed feelings of Palestinian identity.

Palestinians in the refugee camps were perhaps the most dramatically affected. The ideas of a secular nationalism, equality between the sexes and self-reliance were being instilled in the very young, the consequences of which will become more obvious as this youngest generation reaches political consciousness in the 1980's. Certain changes, however, became quickly apparent. In the camps the inhabitants had since 1948 grouped around the Palestinian villages from which they originated. "In this way," states one investigator of the refugees' life, "many villages which the Israelis occupied by force, evacuated and demolished in Palestine are still, socially speaking, alive and coherent units."[7] That Palestinians should evince such extraordinary tenacity in the face of the destruction of their country was also a potent factor in the re-emergence and strengthening of their national consciousness. Old patterns of village leadership and conflict slowly dissolved to allow new leaders with a radically different orientation to secure the refugees' loyalty and to guide their fate.

On the Arab front, the aim was to draw recruits from among the Arab people and money from the surpluses of the oil-rich countries. Weapons and ammunition were supplied by friendly Arab and foreign governments. However, there was another dimension to the Arab front which went largely unnoticed; its implications, at least, were ignored. Palestinian refugee camps anywhere are not pleasant places of human habitation. Those in and around Beirut seem several degrees more degraded than the average—if only because they contrast so starkly with the surrounding affluence and dolce vita insensitivity of the Lebanese capital. It is true that certain improvements and amenities have raised the camps' standards since their extremely primitive beginnings in the 1950s. On the other hand organizers wage a losing battle with the problem of overcrowding; the Karameh camp near Beirut was established to accomodate 5,000 people while today it contains over 17,000 inhabitants. Very few refugees have the opportunity to leave the camps permanently. Indeed, the very opposite process occurs. There has been a continual movement *into* the camps, *not* by Palestinians, but by poor Lebanese and Syrians unable to afford other kinds of housing. According to a Lebanese survey made in 1971, there were 11,500 Lebanese (of whom 5,000 were from southern Lebanon) and 3,300 Syrians living in Palestinian camps! Regardless of the appeal that the Palestine revolution was designed to solve only the problem of Palestine, the social implications of this revolution would inevitably draw into its orbit the disinherited and dispossessed of other communities as well. In this dimension of the Arab front the Palestinian presence is the mirror image of the Arab regimes' bankrupt policies for the social and economic justice of their own masses.

On the Israeli front, the Palestinian resistance conducted its war of national liberation. The military capabilities of the resistance were hampered by a number of factors. With the exception of southern Lebanon, guerillas had to operate over fairly barren and open terrain which afforded them insufficient cover. Moreover, Palestinians were dependent for the security of their bases and training camps upon the continued goodwill of the Arab 'host' countries. In addition, Israeli security measures, including an electronic fence along the Jordan River and the harsh military regime of occupation, complicated operational difficulties considerably. Between 1967 and the Jordanian civil war in 1970 Israeli sources (which tended to undercount) reported over 300 dead and over 1500 wounded as a result of fidayeen attacks. Military casualties exceeded civilian by a ratio of one to four. During the same period Palestinian losses were much heavier, 1800 dead and 2500 held in Israeli prisons. While the cost was high and the strictly military effectiveness of the guerilla operations was low, another desired effect was achieved. The raids were important for their psychological effect. General Narkis, writing in the Israeli daily *Maariv*, stated, "Things have reached such a point by now (June, 1969) that people have to be continually injected with morale boosters in order to preserve their confidence in our military strength and prevent them from losing it altogether." Another Israeli military analyst, Elie Landau, observed: "The fighting with Fateh goes on violently every day. This is never mentioned in the news. Despite severe casualties the guerillas keep mounting operations as though nothing has happened."

Another objective of the attacks was, in the words of one Palestinian writer, "to bring to the surface the moral contradictions within Israeli society."[8] One symptom of these contradictions was the uncovering of a major espionage ring in 1972 which comprised both Arab Israelis and Jews. The revelations at the trial shocked the Israeli public. Writing in *Davar*, Daniel Bloch noted that the importance of Jews in the network was that it marked the appearance of an wholly new phenomenon: ideological treachery. "Its incentive was not a money deal, fear or danger; it was the result of a free choice to cooperate with mortal enemies, to the extent of readiness to assist in sabotage operations."[9] The failure of Israel's policies toward her Arab Palestinian minority was indirectly acknowledged at this time by Shmuel Toledano, the Prime Minister's advisor on Arab affairs: "Anyone who studies the cases of the 370 Arab detainees who have joined terrorist organizations since 1967 must reach the conclusion that most of them enjoy economic prosperity, education and culture."[10] These qualities had not compensated for the sense of loss of human dignity which life in the Zionist state had brought.

Finally, on the international front, Palestinians strove to emphasize the central position of the Palestine problem in the Middle East conflict; to identify their struggle with the worldwide war against oppression; and to secure international recognition of the legitimacy of their cause. The PLO has also recently taken steps to provide assistance for Russian Jewish emigrants who wish to establish new lives other than in Israel. The PLO was instrumental, too, in pressuring certain Arab countries like Iraq and Morocco into issuing decrees which would permit Jews in Israel originally of those nationalities to return.

The main components of the Palestine revolution's ideological base—forming a general consensus among the various groups within the Palestine Liberation Organization—may be summed up as follows: The revolution's chief weapon is popular armed struggle, the end objective of which is the liberation of both Arab and Jew from a nationally and racially oppressive regime, the Zionist state of Israel. The Palestinian struggle, therefore, is viewed as part of the more universal struggle against all colonial and settler regimes (such as those of Rhodesia and South Africa) which are linked to and which enjoy the protection of the imperialist system dominated at present by the United States.

On one issue, however, there were sharp differences within the resistance. Fateh, whose revolutionary strategy prevailed within the PLO ranks down to 1970, argued that armed struggle should be directed solely at Palestinian national objectives. Initially, this moderate revolutionary line gave the resistance a certain flexibility in its relations with the Arab governments. Fateh insisted that Palestinians should not be diverted by "side issues" such as the internal affairs of the host countries. On any number of occasions Yasir Arafat reiterated this theme. "Since we don't interfere," he said, "in the internal affairs of the Arab countries, where we have no ambitions, since we have in common with them and the Arab people the objective of ending the Israeli occupation, we see no reason for a conflict between us." Fateh made strenuous efforts to avoid clashes with the Arab regimes; in return it demanded full autonomy in its operations while at the same time seeking their aid and support. And there, cried the critics, was the rub. Independence of action and support without strings was a desperate and dangerous illusion.

The quarrel was joined on ideological grounds just where Fateh had sought to elaborate a non-ideological revolutionary philosophy. George Habash's Popular Front for the Liberation of Palestine and the Democratic Popular Front led by Jordanian-born Nayif Hawatmeh were both sensitive to the limitations of armed struggle conducted against Israel by Palestinians alone.

Their criticism of Fatah, therefore, was that the revolution should not be confined exlusively to Palestine but should engulf all of Arab society. The struggle was not only against Zionism but also against American imperialism and all reactionary Arab regimes. Palestinian objectives would not be achieved, they maintained, until social and political revolutions occured in most of the Arab world with the active participation of the peasants, urban workers and the Palestinian masses. From his analysis, Habash drew quite the opposite conclusion to that of Arafat; in an interview in 1969 he remarked, "The relation of the armed struggle—Palestine at the moment and Arab in the future—is one of conflict with the reactionary Arab regimes in spite of any temporary tactical positions that may be forced on both." No matter that the predictions of Fateh's critics were borne out in practice; Palestinians have always faced cruel dilemmas. This was no truer than in the brief period between the battle of Karameh and the civil war in Jordan—Green March 1968 to Black September 1970—when the main weakness of resistance strategy came to the fore.

It began with an incident on March 18, 1968, when a bus carrying vacationers struck a mine in the southern Negev near Beer-Ora on the road to Eilat. A doctor and a young man accompanying him were killed and twenty-eight persons injured, most of them children. The Popular Front claimed responsibility while Fateh actually condemned the incident. A deep sense of outrage ran through Israel and there were loud cries for immediate reprisal. In the early morning of the 21st, tanks and other armour, aircraft and helicopters and a reported 10,000 troops of the Israeli Defense Forces moved across the Jordan River in a two-pronged attack. The major assault was against the village of Karameh on the East Bank opposite Jericho where a large guerilla base was located; a smaller force attacked three spots south of the Dead Sea. Backed by Jordanian tanks and artillery batteries, Palestinian guerillas fought a desperate battle against the invaders for over twelve hours. When the Israeli forces had withdrawn, Karameh was a heap of rubble, 150 Palestinians had been killed and over 100 taken prisoner. Israel gave her losses as thirty-two dead and seventy wounded, along with one plane and six tanks. Some observers believed, however, that the losses on the Israeli side were probably higher. The Chief of Staff, Major General Bar-Lev later announced that the back of Fateh had been broken. The political objective of the attack was intended as a warning to King Hussein that Israel would not tolerate his continued support of the commandos.

The Karameh episode did not fully live to Bar-Lev's expectations. In the one-month period prior to the attack, thirty-seven acts of sabotage by commandoes were committed. In August 1968, 103 guerilla raids took place, and exactly one year later, in August 1969, the number of operations was 480. Karameh, in fact, was a turning point for the resistance. Recruits flocked to the commando camps from all over the Arab world. This was gratifying but also a mixed blessing. Qualified instructors were at a premium and as the new recruits kept coming the quality of their training declined for some months before the situation was rectified. At the very peak of their strength the resistance had some 20,000 men under arms and another 20,000 trained as militia units.

In certain Arab circles these developments were viewed with consternation and alarm. Despite his past support and sympathy for the Palestinian cause, President Nasser judged the post-Karameh growth and popularity of the resistance as a threat to both his leadership and programme of political action. This period coincided with his War of Attrition against Israel along the Suez Canal. The purpose of this mini-conflict was to force a political settlement with Israel, through the mediation of the superpowers, in circumstances more favourable to the Arabs than those prevailing immediately after 1967. In the eyes of others, however, these were the moves of a tired man who might be prepared to compromise too much for too little in return.

If there was consternation in Cairo, there was growing alarm and fear in Amman. Since the June war King Hussein had not known a day's (or night's, for that matter) rest. With the new influx of refugees from the West Bank and Gaza his truncated kingdom was overwhelmingly Palestinian. While he still commanded the support of the army and the Beduin chiefs, the newest political force in the kingdom—the resistance—was almost completely outside his influence or control. His own

WHITHER PALESTINE?

position on the guerilla organizations ranged from open denunciation to grudging approval. Like Nasser, he sought a political solution based upon the November, 1967, resolution of the UN General Assembly, but his only means of pressuring the big powers was to warn them that if no alternative were left to him he would throw in his lot with the commandos.

In February, 1970, Hussein announced restrictions on the stockpiling, carrying and use of arms. The resulting clashes between the resistance and Jordanian security forces left at least thirty dead. After several frantic meetings between the two sides, Hussein stated that the restrictions were not aimed at the fidayeen but were intended as a reminder of existing laws and regulations. "The measures were not expected to meet such misunderstanding and uproar," he explained lamely. The restrictions were frozen and the King continued to walk his tightrope.

By the summer of 1970 Amman was entering the eye of a hurricane. The capital, like ancient Rome, huddles around seven hills. On one hill King Hussein had built one of his palaces. Opposite, on one of the largest hills in Amman, lay the Wahdat refugee camp known locally as the Republic of Palestine. It contained 70,000 inhabitants and all of the commando groups had offices inside the grounds. Once on republican territory a person was entirely free of Jordanian government control. The camp and the royal palace facing it symbolized the dual authority within the country as a whole.

Clashes between the army and the resistance became frequent. Each time, a cease-fire of sorts was arranged like a makeshift dressing over a festering wound. In June bitter fighting resulted in 1,000 dead on both sides. King Hussein knew that his sovereignty was compromised and that sooner or later he would have to crack down hard on the resistance. By August several of the fidayeen groups had also come to the conclusion that the Jordanian regime had to go. For his part, Yasir Arafat worked hard to stave off a head-on collision. Not out of any love for the King. Arafat would probably have welcomed his deposition and replacement by a more sympathetic regime; at the same time, he did not want the radical organizations in the resistance, like the PFLP, to force Fateh into an untimely confrontation when it would have to shoulder the main burden of the fighting.

As the showdown neared, references to Palestinian "terrorists" appeared in the government press while the slogan "All Power to the Resistance" was raised in Wahdat camp.

Wahdat camp was the site of an emergency session of the Palestine National Congress at the end of August. The resolutions of the Congress attacked the recent American peace initiative put forward by Secretary of State William Rogers. President Nasser had accepted the proposals and an "in-place" cease-fire was in effect along the Suez front at the time the Congress met. If the Congress reached any conclusion on the overall resistance attitude toward King Hussein, no indication of this was made public. The leaders of two small groups, Dr. Issam Sartawi and Ahmad Zaarour, were known to have urged patience with President Nasser. They argued that the Rogers peace plan would never work since the United States would not force Israel to withdraw from major portions of the occupied territories. In the atmosphere of heightened tension and expectancy the Congress seemed incapable of advising or adopting any concrete course of action.

George Habash's PFLP made its own point, stunning the world with its multiple skyjackings. Four planes were plucked out of the skies, three of which were taken to a disused airstrip in the Jordan desert. The fourth, a Pan-Am jumbo jet, was flown to Cairo and blown up—a symbolic protest to President Nasser for accepting the Rogers peace plan. The central committee of the PLO suspended the PFLP for these provocative acts but this did nothing to check the deteriorating situation in Jordan.

Precisely three weeks after the skyjackings Arafat and Hussein were in Cairo arranging a cease-fire to bring the carnage to an end. The sword of Damocles which had hung so long and so precariously over King Hussein's head was now firmly gripped in his hands. The Palestinian resistance, while not entirely eliminated, had been so severely mauled that it would not quickly recover from the blow. Estimates of casualties ranged between 10,000 and 20,000, the greatest numbers occuring among the Palestinian and Jordanian civilian population.

During the brief but violent conflict the only Arab country to side openly with the Palestinians was Syria, although to little avail. The combined Syrian and Palestine Liberation Army force which entered Jordan was checked and driven back by Jordanian armour. Even this support, however, did not emanate from wholehearted Syrian commitment to the Palestinian cause but rather from internal rivalries within the regime. The Syrian tanks were given no air cover because the Minister of Defense, over whose objections the intervention had been arranged, held sufficient power and authority to keep the air force grounded. The same man, Hafez al-Asad, who moved into the position of supreme control of Syria in November 1970, would intervene six years later in the Lebanese civil war against the Palestinians. Other Arab governments, notably Egypt, the Sudan and Tunisia, gave their moral support to the resistance, harshly rebuking Hussein for the atrocities perpetrated by his army. Libya and Kuwait temporarily suspended their payments to the Jordanian regime which had helped keep it afloat since the June war. But as one writer has acutely observed the Arabs pressured Jordan to end the war "short of extermination of the fidayeen."[11] In the Arab household the civil war was a deep embarrassment, but then, so were the Palestinians.

As the Palestinians sought to reorganize and unite their battered forces, Hussein's army set about its unfinished business of mopping up and restoring royal authority throughout the kingdom. The last guerilla camps were eliminated and the last armed fighter was driven beyond the frontiers by July 1971.

The Jordanian civil war was up to that moment the latest and perhaps the most critical phase in the Palestinians' long and bitter struggle for the restoration of their rights as a dispossessed people. Conflict and defeat have been their lot. But more than at any previous moment the civil war left them feeling isolated and very much on their own. The Jordanian episode also seemed to fit a single basic pattern of the Palestinians' story from their very first contacts with the Zionist settlers. That story is a story of denial. The Zionists denied the existence of a people and society in Palestine as they strove to transform it into a European Jewish enclave. Great Britain denied independence to Palestine alone among the mandated territories in the period after World War I. Finally, independent Arab governments which were incapable of successfully waging either war or peace with Israel on the Palestinians' behalf appeared by 1970 to deny them the only alternative of struggling on their own behalf. And yet, one inescapable fact remained. The Palestinians themselves, despite the grave setback in Jordan, continued to reject a fate designed and determined for them by others, whether Arab, Israeli, American or Russian. As the Arabs tried to blot out the bloody memories of Jordan and look to the future, the major imponderable in a world of imponderables was: whither the Palestinians?

The End is Prologue

The civil war gave rise to critiques of the resistance from all quarters both within and outside the movement. Grave mistakes had been made, to be sure. Swaggering, undisciplined rank-and-file guerillas acted as though they were a law to themselves. The need to build strong links with non-Palestinians had been played down or ignored, leading to the alienation of potential friends. The failure to perceive clearly or, worse, to act upon the knowledge that interests of state took precedence over intra-Arab issues reflected a failure to learn from bitter past experience. Specifically, the mainstream leadership had failed to determine (and hence act upon in its strategic planning) that coexistence with the Jordanian regime was doomed from the start. In the welter of criticisms some charged the resistance for its lack of a positive military-political strategy while others decried its over-emphasis on a military line and its consequent aversion to sound principles of political organization and its eschewing of any progressive ideological commitment. Finally, two radical critics, underscoring the basic weakness of the Palestine revolution, point in two quite different directions for the locus of the weakness. On the one hand, the resistance leaders' claims to have adopted revolutionary tactics and strategies different from those of even the most "progressive" Arab regimes is dismissed as mere pretension; in practice, the Palestinian leaders simply imitate the practices of the Arab regimes since they act within the same class limitations as the Arab ruling classes. On the other hand, it is argued that the Palestinian revolution lacks an accessible proletarianized labouring class which could make it the guiding force of the Palestinians in the same way that the workers of China, in spite of their numerical inferiority, were the guiding force of the Chinese revolution. In this view, the only true proletarianized segment of the Palestinian people is concentrated in the Galilee region of Israel and therefore totally isolated from other Palestinian social groups.

Each of these criticisms, judged in the context in which it is expressed, contains perceptive insights. Taken in their collectivity, they reflect the immense complexity of the nature and composition of the Palestinian nation. Briefly, there are three broad segments of the Palestinian people whose day to day lives are experienced in rather different ways. First, there is the so-called Arab-Israeli, the oppressed minority in the Jewish state which was once Palestine. Second, there is the Palestinian living directly under military occupation but still on a portion of Palestine. Third, there is the Palestinian in exile. Naturally, the experiences and expectations of Palestinians in one segment may vary from those in another segment. The refugee, who has formed the backbone of the armed struggle, is inspired by the idea of Return to the Land. The Arab-Israeli peasant, who may fortunately have retained some of his land, is compelled, on the other hand, to demand that all the rights and privileges enjoyed by Israeli Jews be extended to him as an Arab. Or, a bourgeois Palestinian living in Amman might support the resistance against Israel but withdraw that support once his material interests seem threatened by an overthrow of the monarchy. A bourgeois Palestinian in Nablus, on the other hand, might welcome Hussein's demise if a new regime would appear to bring his liberation from occupation one day nearer. All of these contrasting perspectives and conflicts of interest are part and parcel of the Palestinians' existential condition as a people. How immense then is the task of developing a revolutionary formula whose slogans would strike an immediate responsive chord in the heart of everyone. Moreover, each new success or setback in the evolving experience of the community has meant for different members of the Palestinian constituency either that new options were opened up or else other more tortuous paths were forced upon them.

The mood of despondency among the Palestinians following the civil war was coupled with the evident disarray within the ranks of Fateh. One faction seemed half-heartedly in favour of making compromises with the Arab regimes in order to keep their financial and political backing. This tactic, however, angered and alienated a younger, more militant group of the fidayeen. Michael Hudson had described two contradictory pressures confronting the resistance at this moment.[1] One was the outside pressure to "domesticate" the movement as the Arab regimes

THE END IS PROLOGUE

sought to ensure that it was kept closely under their planning and control. The counter-pressure came from within, toward a "radicalizing" of the resistance by going underground and waging a campaign of terror on all fronts. The first sign of this trend was the assasination of Jordanian Prime Minister, Wasfi Tal (November 28, 1971) in the foyer of the Sheraton Hotel in Cairo. A previously unknown group calling itself Black September claimed responsibility for the act.

With Jordan now a closed area to the resistance operations, their bases in Syria and especially in the Arqoub region of southern Lebanon became the last sanctuaries of the armed struggle. Lebanon presents a much more complex picture than Jordan, and it is appropriate here, by way of a short detour from the discussion, to sketch a few salient details of the Lebanese system.[2]

The foundation of the Lebanese political system is the National Pact. This informal agreement, drawn up in the last days of the French Mandate, divided the political spoils of national life according to the numerical size of the two main religious communities, Christians and Muslims. According to a census conducted by the French in 1932 (the results of which are today considered to have served France's cruder political interests) the various Christian sects *combined* gave them a slight majority over the Muslims. The Christian Maronite sect, traditionally pro-French and pro-western, possessed the largest single *minority*. The system, therefore, was a delicately balanced combination of several sectarian interests in which the Maronites were assured a paramount political role—which included the presidency of the republic. The Maronites, moreover, held a privileged position in the civil service; also, the commander-in-chief and many senior officer cadres of the army were Maronite. This sectarian (or vertical) division should not, however, obscure the importance of the economic, political and social power of landowning and commercial feudal interests which also divided the country horizontally into haves and have-nots, irrespective of religion.

Into this rather bewildering equation, place the Palestinians. Although Lebanon's ruling business interests benefited from the 1948 Palestine war (as a result of the Arab economic boycott against Israel), the country's population suddenly catapulted by ten per cent as hundreds of thousands of Palestinians, driven from or fleeing their homes during the war, became unwilling exiles upon her soil.

Barely a decade later, the contradictions of the National Pact were nakedly exposed during an outbreak of inter-communal fighting now referred to as the First Civil War of 1958. Once the crisis had passed, the Lebanese believed that they had learned a lesson, that such civil strife could not happen again. In the decade following 1958 this optimism seemed borne out as the economy forged ahead to unprecedented levels.

Several crucial lessons, however, had not been learned. The Lebanese government's short-sighted laissez faire approach to the economy also applied to the fields of social justice and welfare. While the civil war of 1958 was expressed in religious terms—Muslim against Christian—it could not conceal the underlying movement of discontent and demands for a more equitable disposal of the national wealth. The economy showed immense disparities between the agriculture and service sectors. For example, agriculture accounted for about 50% of the labour force while contributing only 11% to the national income; the service sector, on the other hand, accounted for only 14% of the labour force but contributed some 67% to the national income. In addition to income disparities there were growing regional disparities in development between the prospering, predominantly Maronite Mount Lebanon and the more backward agricultural south inhabited largely by poorer Shi'ite Muslims. Moreover, it was widely suspected that the demographic balance of population had shifted in favour of the Muslims. It was believed that the largest minority was no longer the Maronite sector but rather the far less privileged Shi'ite community. To say that the situation was "suspected" to have changed is to say that no one, except perhaps the Shi'ites, wanted to find out what the real score was by conducting a new census. The question was, simply, too explosive politically.

As in previous Arab-Israeli conflicts, Lebanon sat on the sidelines throughout the June war, 1967. Among the Lebanese masses, however, albeit with the notable exception of the Maronites, there was widespread sympathy for the Palestinian resistance which had bases on and ran operations from Lebanese soil. The Lebanese government watched these developments in nervous anticipation of Israeli retaliation which inevitably came.

THE END IS PROLOGUE

In October, 1969, a crisis erupted as the Lebanese security forces surrounded the Palestinian refugee village of Magdal Bani Salim in the south and opened fire on it. An army spokesman claimed that this was in response to gunfire from "a band of armed men." The incident touched off riots and demonstrations in the southern town of Sidon, in Beirut and Tripoli in the north—the last-named being in the hands of insurgents for a few days. An oil pipeline near Sidon was blown up; Palestinian guerillas and Lebanese soldiers sniped at each other in several districts; and, at the American University of Beirut, a pro-Palestinian demonstration was addressed by Laila Khalid, the young commando girl who had hijacked a TWA jet to Damascus the previous August. When peace was finally restored, the Lebanese commander-in-chief of the army, General Bustani, met with a delegation from Fateh in Cairo to hammer out an accord.

The Cairo Agreement of 1969 gave Fateh important military and diplomatic concessions. In return for a pledge to accept close supervision by the Lebanese authorities, the resistance gained free access to the "Arafat Trail" leading from Syria across the mountains into northern Israel. The Lebanese acknowledged that the Palestinian armed struggle was beneficial to the interests of Lebanon while the Palestinians noted that their revolution did not conflict with Lebanese sovereignty since they shared a common enemy. The Lebanese needed no reminding that the Zionists, as early as the Paris Peace Conference in 1919, had coveted the southern part of the country up to the Litani River, an area containing valuable water resources and fertile orchards.

The Cairo Agreement did not solve anything, at least in part because it did not anticipate the consequences of Black September in Jordan. Of necessity the resistance transferred more men and arms into Lebanon. Fearing a repetition of the events in Jordan, the Palestinians wanted to avoid if possible any friction with the host government. However, a familiar pattern of events recommenced. Fidayeen raids into Israel brought about massive Israeli retaliation in February and June, 1972. To facilitate their penetration raids of southern Lebanon the Israeli defence forces constructed armed observation posts and military roads *inside* Lebanon. Civilian casualties were high and for a few weeks the Palestinians suspended their operations from Lebanon and withdrew from the border area. All was quiet until mid-September when even harsher Israeli attacks were mounted in revenge for Black September's execution of the Israeli olympic team at Munich. The relatively small Lebanese army was helpless to prevent these invasions but it was the Lebanese government's generally indifferent attitude toward its southern inhabitants which provoked villagers to march upon Beirut in protest. Muslim feudal leaders were embarrassed and apologetic, while in Maronite quarters some cynically urged that the south could go to the devil or, better still, to the Israelis.

It was in these circumstances, as relations between government and the resistance grew more strained, that the resistance adopted a subtle change of tactics. Slowly it extended its role of support among the poorer classes of the Lebanese population, especially in villages of the south and the slum quarters of Beirut, while forging stronger links with organized leftist and progressive forces. The move was made in anticipation of the worst.

Suddenly, one evening in April 1973 the Israelis dealt a swift and heavy blow. Infiltrated agents caught three leaders of Fateh in an unguarded moment and gunned them down in their own apartments. It was rumoured that the wife of Muhammad Najjar, one of the victims, had also been killed because she recognized one of the assailants. It was not rumour, however, but plain fact that the Lebanese security forces did not lift a finger to apprehend the murderers. Lebanese President Sulaiman Franjieh brusquely dismissed Yasir Arafat's protestations with the remark, "We can't protect you; you will have to defend yourselves." Arafat accepted this for the veiled threat that it was and prepared his forces for the next confrontation with the Lebanese army, which came the following month and was the severest crisis to date. Though the actors may not have realized it then, these events were setting the stage for the second Lebanese civil war precisely two years later.

The October war of 1973 was hailed as a great Arab triumph, a shattering of the myths of Israeli invincibility. The main Arab participants, Egypt and Syria, had conceived the war as one of limited military objectives for the attainment of specific political targets; it was, moreover, regarded as the only means of breaking the no-war, no peace stalemate which had plagued these governments for so long. Military victory had restored pride and confidence in Arab capabilities. As the United States launched its peace initiative under the step-by-step supervision of Henry Kissinger, these regimes had a new straw to grasp at; thus, they began to perceive the Palestinian resistance, once a morale booster for their own disillusioned masses, as rather more of a liability than a benefit. In the strategy of the Arab governments the October war implicitly ruled out the future use of popular armed struggle as the sole weapon for the achievement of Palestinian political goals. The restoration of Palestinian rights was to be part of the overall objective of the Arab regimes, namely, the restoration of their own lands lost in the war of 1967, an objective which would be attained through the political process of eventual negotiation. This official thinking, however, might be considered by Palestinians to be a threat to their interests if it were judged (or proven) that the Arab governments could not obtain what was regarded as minimal for the needs of the Palestinian people, or, if it were suspected that their "rights" would be "restored" without the complete participation of the Palestinians themselves.

These difficulties were, in fact, appreciated in the Arab capitals. A consensus gradually emerged after the October war that if the Palestinians were to be urged to adopt a political path to a settlement, they should acquire a recognized and legitimate political personality. On the first anniversary of the October war of 1973, the Arab governments held a summit conference in Rabat, Morocco. There the assembled Arab nations resolved to "affirm the right of the Palestinian people to establish an independent national authority under the command of the Palestine Liberation Organization, the sole legitimate representative of the Palestine people in any Palestine territory that is liberated." In the same month the United Nations General Assembly formally invited the PLO to participate in its deliberations on the Palestine question. Consequently, on November 22, 1974, a week after Yasir Arafat had addressed the General Assembly, resolution 3236 was adopted which reaffirmed that the inalienable rights of the Palestinian people included (1) self-determination, (2) national independence and (3) the right to return to the homes and property from which they had been uprooted. A companion resolution on the same day granted the PLO observer status in all the sessions and work of the General Assembly.

Of the two organizations, the world body seemed to embrace the Palestinian cause more enthusiasticly than the Arabs themselves. The Rabat formula recognized the PLO's legitimate authority in any territory of Palestine that *is* liberated. Since no piece of Palestine was at that moment liberated, the door seemed to have been left open for anyone to walk in and supervise the shop *until* some piece of land was available for the PLO to look after. Certainly King Hussein construed the matter in this fashion. He argued that the West Bank should be placed as a "trust" in his hands until he could hand it over to the PLO upon the successful conclusion of a peace conference. The Palestinians could find little trust in their hearts for the Hashemite monarch. In fact, the point had been made earlier by the very Palestinians who mattered, those under occupation on the West Bank. The Palestine National Front, an underground body comprising all progressive elements active in the occupied territories, published a policy statement in December 1973. The Front emphatically expressed its support for the PLO as the legitimate representative of its people and denounced the regime in Amman for its repeated declarations of enmity to the Palestinians and their rights. The point was even more dramatically underlined during the municipal elections on the West Bank in 1976. The Israeli authorities confidently expected the traditional leadership with whom they had been dealing since 1967 to be returned easily. Massive and widespread demonstrations had erupted against the occupation and in the course of their savage repression by Israeli troops a number of Palestinians were killed. Israel badly needed a public "demonstration" that the riots were being instigated only by a handful of irresponsible hooligans. Hence the importance of the municipal elections. The National Front fielded candidates in every town and village all of whom were known to support the PLO—although it was imprudent to declare this publicly for fear of Israeli reprisal. By law it was illegal to support a "terrorist" organization, even if that organization had been recognized by the United Nations. As a warning to others, the Front candidate in Hebron, Dr. Ahmad Hamzeh, was deported. This object lesson backfired. Hebron elected the Front's second man and in eighty percent of the other municipalities the Front swept the traditional leadership from power. The Front was not merely "a suitcase full of phantoms" as one Israeli diplomat put it.

The international recognition of the PLO is perhaps the single most important accomplishment of the Palestinian resistance. The Palestinians, despite their numerous internal disputes, accept the PLO and its governing National Council as the only legitimate structure with authority to represent them in any discussion affecting their destiny. In Israel this development has also begun to have its effect. Not only fringe groups on the left but also important members of the establishment like Arie Eliav, the former secretary-general of the United Labour party, are now urging the Israeli government to adopt a more flexible policy toward the Palestinian aspiration of statehood. Change was reflected in other developments too. The Canadian government, submitting to organized Jewish pressure, "postponed" an international conference on crime because the PLO had been invited as observers. Some months later, the world Habitat conference on housing was held in Vancouver, Canada. Not only did a PLO delegation attend but the conference also passed a resolution condemming Zionism as a form of racism.

Thus, while international support for the PLO, notably in the Third World, continued steadily to grow, some Arab governments began to have uneasy second thoughts over their precocious protegée. In Syrian and Egyptian eyes primarily, both their own and the Palestinians' goals realistically meant some form of accomodation with the United States. One of the objectives of the October war had been to reach political ends by diplomatic means so as to avoid yet another costly conflict. President Sadat was personally convinced that the American president held all the trump cards in the game. Short of war, therefore, Arab leaders considered the Americans' "persuasive" power as the only effective means of moving Israel toward an acceptable settlement. The American strategy (which did not clash with the basic interests of the Arab confrontation states) was to squeeze Russian influence out of the area. In addition, the United States wanted to protect its oil interests by supporting such friendly regimes as Saudi Arabia whose oil revenues in turn had helped repair the losses suffered by the Arab states in the June War. This linkage of interests placed Washington in a strong position in the political bargaining process. The one potential area of conflict, of course, concerned the Palestinians. As Israel's most powerful backer, the United States was determined to see the PLO, with or without Arafat, trimmed down to pliable proportions. This did not necessarily clash with the interests of the Arab regimes. During the long weeks of Henry Kissinger's shuttle diplomacy following the October war, neither Egypt nor Syria was unduly concerned over the PLO's growing international popularity. Focus on the Palestinians helped underline the urgency in finding a solution to the Middle East conflict. However, both Arab regimes (together with Jordan and Lebanon) concurred that the resistance would have to be tamed and contained should it prove too stubborn an obstacle to a settlement favorable to their regimes. It was in the aftermath of the Arab successes of the October war, therefore, that the Palestinians, also riding high on a tide of international sympathy and approval, were about to face their most perilous trial.

By a fortuitous conjunction of circumstances created by the October war, various regional and international elements found a common ground of interest in attempting to crush, once and for all, the Palestinian resistance movement. The battleground for this showdown was to be the Lebanon, the last major sanctuary of the resistance; the opening act of this drama was the seemingly innocent signing of the second Sinai disengagement agreement between Egypt and Israel in September 1975.

The political gains of the agreement for President Sadat were negligible. The opposing forces in Sinai, Egyptian and Israeli, were merely redeployed with a United Nations buffer force in between. Israel continued to control the strategic Mitla and Giddi passes while Egyptian dependence upon the United States was symbolized by the American technicians who manned the early warning radar system in the passes. In return, Egypt received no firm assurances of a total Israeli withdrawal from Sinai, an objective which President Sadat has publicly reiterated he would never abandon. The Egyptian president, however, hoped these concessions would win favor for his policy of economic liberalization at home by demonstrating to American and European investors that their capital could play a decisive role in rebuilding Egypt along private capitalist lines. Some Egyptian political commentators have admitted privately that Egypt, in return for the illusory hope of rapid economic development, has in fact abdicated her traditional role of leadership in the arena of inter-Arab politics and chosen the road of isolationism.

This Egyptian retreat into isolationism in effect tacitly supported the American (and Israeli) aim of reducing Arab governmental support for the Palestinian resistance. The next stage of the scenario was to focus on the Lebanon where certain elements in the Maronite community were prepared to seize upon the new American penetration of the area and to exploit the Palestinian presence in a bid to ward off the challenges to its political and economic domination of the country. The Maronite contribution to this scenario was the proposed destruction of the resistance as a viable force in the Middle East conflict. After the major clashes between the Maronite-led Lebanese army and the resistance in May 1973, it would take little to ignite another explosion. In February 1975 an incident called the Protéine affair provided the spark and the prelude to the second Lebanese civil war.

Camille Chamoun, president of Lebanon during the civil war of 1958, was exploiting his still very considerable political power to establish a private company, Protéine, which would monopolize the traditional rights of independent fishermen along the coast. The fishermen reacted vehemently by striking and demonstrating in the southern port of Sidon; the disturbances, finally crushed by the army, left a number of civilians dead. The fishermen had been actively supported by elements of the PLO which espoused the cause of the most defenseless and oppressed segments of the population.

The whole affair underlined the increasingly cynical and corrupt approach to national problems by the Lebanese establishment both Maronite and Muslim. The situation was worsened, too, by the president, Sulaiman Franjieh, who had begun his political career as a mob enforcer in his native district of Zgharta and who could give no moral guidance to his people in time of crisis. Demands grew for reform of the political system: the reduction of the unlimited powers of the Maronite president, greater Muslim representation in parliament and a greater Muslim share in the workings of the army. Maronite leaders like Chamoun and Pierre Gemeyel, leader of the neo-fascist Kataib or Phalanges party, tried to maneuver around these challenges by making Palestinian interference in Lebanon's internal affairs *the* central problem facing the country. Next, the Phalanges, which boasted a highly organized and disciplined militia, escalated tensions into full-scale conflict. In mid-April Phalanges gunmen ambushed a bus returning to the Tell Za'atar refugee camp in Beirut and killed 27 of the Palestinian occupants. In the ensuing street fighting in Beirut (other battles took place in the towns of Tripoli, Sidon and Tyre) over 300 persons were reported killed.

That was merely the opening round. Eighteen months later, an estimated 30,000 people had lost their lives with tens of thousands more wounded or missing. Some say these figures are exaggerated. But no one is prepared to say by how much. The story they tell is one of property destruction, torture, murder, rape, kidnapping, looting and vengeance, only a partial catalogue of the customary terrors and tribulations of daily life. Another chilling figure of the civil war is that even before the invasion by the Syrian army (April-May 1976) there were an estimated 150,000 armed men in Beirut and the surrounding countryside, some ten times the size of the regular Lebanese army before it had disintegrated. One observer of the emergency sessions held at the Arab League in Cairo in June said the Arab foreign ministers were informed that possibly as many as 10,000 armed men were completely free agents, leaderless and under no one's control; this was simply one aspect of the chaos and confusion reigning in the country. Another is the constantly shifting pattern of alliances which at times became absurd. For example, Saudi Arabia, one of the most conserative and fundamentalist Muslim regimes, initially backed the equally fanatic Christian Maronite side because the Saudi government believed that the Phalanges and their allies were fighting communism. Then Saeb Salam, a feudalist Muslim leader and a former prime minister, flew to Riyad to explain that Muslims also were against the left as well as the Phalanges. The Saudis obligingly provided him with funds to establish his own militia.

Foreign observers have queried how the present has come about; many Lebanese also gaze in horror and shame at the spectacle. Like rumors of fear, theories "explaining" the civil war are legion. Their common denominator is that some "conspiracy" exists, the theories differing only with regard to who is plotting what against whom. Nevertheless, as far as the Palestinians' role in the conflagration is concerned, one can fairly easily identify the various interests acting both for and against them.

The Maronite leaders, from President Franjieh to the head of the Monastic Orders, Sherbal Kassis, wanted to scapegoat the Palestinians as the chief cause of all Lebanon's woes. Real political reform, economic and social justice were matters far from their concern; what did matter was the retention by the Maronite community of the privileges bequeathed them from the days of the French Mandate and the National Pact. Essentially, this entailed maintaining Lebanon's confessional political system, that is to say, the system of political privilege based upon religious affiliation. Why, the reformers demanded, should the president of Lebanon always be a Maronite Christian and the Prime Minister a Sunnite Muslim? Why should a modern, civilized society be founded upon obscurantist Medieval principles of religious sectarianism? This was the very question the Palestinians aimed at Israel where laws and social practices discriminated against its non-Jewish citizens of Palestinian origin. The concept of a democratic, secular state was indeed a challenge to the racial Zionist doctrines of ethnic and religious exclusiveness. The concept of a non-sectarian state, if applied in Lebanon, was revolutionary. The Maronites, therefore, posing in the guise of Lebanon's "true savior," sought to divert attention from the desperate need for reform by charging that the Palestinians were the major menace to the survival of the system. The Maronites' ultimate threat, if all else failed, was to fight for the partition of Lebanon and the creation of a Maronite state where the confessional, feudal system would be preserved in miniature.

The American and Israeli governments followed the opening phase of the civil war very closely but without public comment. Both governments, however, were anxious to see whether the

Maronite militias could deliver the goods—the crippling of the Palestinian resistance. Yasir Arafat, while repeatedly warning that the PLO would not tolerate a repetition of Black September in Jordan, placed his forces in a self-defense position as he tried to negotiate a settlement.

Throughout the summer of 1975 it became evident that agreement was impossible. Residents of many mountain resorts could hear the constant crackle of gunfire as militia groups trained in preparation for a resumption of the fighting. Of these groups, Pierre Gemeyel's Phalanges was the largest, best organized and disciplined; furthermore, it had experience in combat from its participation in the 1958 civil war. President Franjieh, also deeply involved, was funneling weapons and ammunition from army stores into the hands of the Phalanges and another militia group headed by his son Tony. Chamoun also headed a strong militia backed by a number of Maronite army officers who on their annual leave helped train recruits. The leaders of the Maronite establishment, despite petty personal differences between them, were able to demonstrate greater coordination and unity of purpose than their opponents.

The Muslim side was characterized by a much greater proliferation of militia groups each with quite a different ideological position. There were Nasserists, Ba'athists, Communists, and Progressive Nationalists; another group, founded by the Shi'ite religious leader Musa Sadr, was set up mainly to defend the Shi'ite quarters of Beirut which the Phalanges had time and again attempted to overrun and demolish. All of these militia groups were smaller, more poorly equipped and less experienced than their Phalanges adversaries. All of them stood for some degree of reform which would involve tampering with the arrangements of the National Pact. Hence, inevitably, these various segments of the Muslim Lebanese resistance came together under the banner of the Progressive Nationalist Forces and were linked to and supported by the Palestinian resistance. The Palestinians, in fact, helped train and equip many of the groups of the Progressive Forces.

When fighting broke out again on a major scale in September 1976 it was clear that the Maronite forces had not intended to single out only the Palestinians for attack. Muslims living in predominantly Maronite areas like Ashrifiya were driven from their homes, which were then destroyed. Commerical quarters where Muslim shopkeepers rented from Christian landowners were also destroyed. The Maronite objective in this stage of the civil war was to clean out any Muslim presence in the eastern half of Beirut, to extend territorially into the western half and thus divide the city by a line running from the port of Beirut east to Mount Lebanon; the northern areas of the country, where the majority of Maronites lived, would then become a secure enclave. The Maronite offensives were marked by unexpected ferocity. The small but densely populated slum quarter of Qarantina lay inside Maronite territory near the port. When the Phalanges attacked, beseiged and finally "liberated" the quarter, nearly 500 people had been killed including numerous elderly persons, women and children. The most savage day of the civil war was afterward labelled Black Saturday: in reprisal for the deaths of four Phalanges militia commanders, Phalanges forces rounded up all the Muslims they could find (religious affiliation being indicated on the Lebanese identity card) and brutally executed over 200 persons.

Black Saturday was a turning point in the war. Early in the new year (1976) the progressive forces and the Palestinians commenced a major counteroffensive driving the Maronites back from many positions they had captured. The Lebanese army which previously had attempted to supervise the endless string of cease-fires finally split when a young officer, Ahmad al-Khatib, formed a dissident force, the Lebanese Arab Army, and joined in with the progressives. The tide began to turn somewhat against the Maronites and leaders like Camille Chamoun appealed for Western intervention in the war.

These developments led up to the most dramatic turnabout of the war. Several governments were now decidedly nervous over the successes, however modest, of the Lebanese progressives and their Palestinian allies. On the military side it was clear that the Maronites could not deliver the goods unaided, although it was equally unclear whether their opponents would be able to take over the whole country. The last thing President Asad of Syria wanted to see was a radical reformist regime on his doorstep; nor did he need a powerful PLO which could operate freely outside of Syria's control and block the way to a settlement with Israel. King Hussein, who was providing training facilities, some equipment and intelligence advice to the Phalanges, wanted the PLO crushed for much the same reasons. The Lebanese situation worried the Americans and Israelis, too. If the Palestinians could not be routed or at least greatly weakened, it was imperative to prevent the progressives from seizing power and turning Lebanon into a confrontation state against Israel. Some means of support for the Maronites had to be found that would not involve direct American or Israeli military intervention. A highly placed diplomat at the Arab League in Cairo explained to me the background events leading up to the Syrian invasion of Lebanon. "The saddest of the many black days in our history," he said and sounded as though he meant every word.

Washington had made an offer which the Syrian president, Asad, being the practical man he is, could not refuse. The overall framework of a final settlement between Israel and her Arab neighbours would consist of a confederation of Arab States including Lebanon, Syria, Jordan and a Palestinian 'entity' of the West Bank and Gaza. Syria would be the senior partner of the confederation—a partial recreation of the Greater Syria existing prior to the British and French partition of the area after World War One. In return, Syria would receive generous American economic aid and Israel would be prepared to make negotiated concessions on the Golan Heights provided it was a strictly demilitarized zone. Lebanon's Maronites would be secure within a continuing religious sectarian system while King Hussein would safely retain his throne which in some other form of settlement he may well have lost. The Palestinian 'entity' would provide a measure of statehood to satisfy their national aspirations, while the PLO, provided it could be controlled or manipulated by Damascus, would still be recognized as the legitimate representative of the Palestinian people.

Syria's role in bringing about this settlement (which admittedly left many questions deliberately open and unresolved) was to "intervene" militarily in the Lebanon to back the Maronites and destroy the Lebanese progressive forces. Put in these terms the plan had a fine Machiavellian touch; Syria wanted to make it appear that she was intervening in a purely Lebanese civil

THE END IS PROLOGUE

war which in no way involved the Palestinians. President Asad apparently believed he could convince the PLO that Syria's move was intended only to end the bloodshed being spilt between brother Lebanese and was not aimed at the resistance as such. Israel, of course, was fully abreast of these proposals and arrangements. Tel Aviv agreed to provide the Maronites with as much military material (from light arms to heavy armour) as they required. Shipments could arrive up the coast from Israel to the Maronite-controlled port of Junieh. Despite official denials from Tel Aviv, the calculated indiscretions of Maronite leaders, evidence in the field and the admissions of Western diplomats in Cairo (unattributable, of course) confirm both Israeli and American involvement. Israeli aid, which was stepped up probably in early May (1976), has had a telling effect on the siege of the Tell Za'atar refugee camps—the last pocket of Palestinian resistance inside the Maronite enclave in Beirut.

When Mr. Dean Brown, the American Middle East envoy (who, it will be recalled, was American ambassador to Jordan during Black September 1970) left Damascus after lengthy discussions with President Asad, he was convinced Syria could pull off their "intervention" successfully within 72 hours. This timetable quickly went askew, partly from an initial hesitation on Syria's part as she entered Lebanon but also from the unexpectedly stiff resistance encountered from the progressive-Palestinian alliance supported by many ordinary Lebanese appalled at both the invasion itself and the behavior of the Syrian officers and men who were allowed to loot almost at random. Lebanese who have been in Damascus since the invasion report the markets full of stolen goods. Syria's publicly stated objective of end-the-bloodshed was belied by the massive bombardments of Palestinian refugee camps and the destruction of large areas of such towns as Tripoli and Sidon, the latter which until then had been the safest and most peaceful spot in the country.

The Syrian invasion undoubtedly complicated a situation of already bewildering complexity. The Palestinians (and their Lebanese allies) have suffered grievous losses which may well be irreparable. On the other hand, the heroic, bitterly stubborn and tragic defense of Tell Za'atar, the refugee fortress camp in Beirut, will inspire yet another generation of Palestinians who will refuse to forget. The problem will surely remain so long as there are only Zionist, Maronite or Syrian solutions to it. To write the final chapter of the Palestinian odyssey is impossible. The end of this present story is merely prologue to the next in their struggle for a rightful place in the community of nations.

Bibliography and Notes

Both the subject and the literature of the Arab-Israeli conflict (or the Palestine problem) are so vast that even a highly select bibliography would run to many pages. The avid student or scholar may wish to consult *Palestine and the Arab-Israeli Conflict: An Annotated Bibliography*, Edited by Walid Khalidi and Jill Khadduri, Institute for Palestine Studies, Beirut (1974) which cites 4580 items drawn from the literature in Arabic, Hebrew and the major European languages. In the bibliographical material provided below, the criteria of importance and current availability in English have largely guided the selection of items. The notes provide further sources, basically indicating the origin of quotations in the text. The whole of this section may be regarded as an introductory guide to the Palestine problem.

Chapter One

Arthur Herzberg has written an excellent essay on the historical development of Zionist ideology in his introduction to *The Zionist Idea*, New York (1966) which is an anthology of writings of the major Zionist thinkers. The diplomatic side of the Zionist movement has been treated in a short but penetrating work by Alan R. Taylor, *Prelude to Israel*, New York (1959). A good biography of the founder of Zionism is Desmond Stewart's *Theodor Herzl*, New York (1974), while the most recent exhaustive work on the movement as a whole is Walter Laqueur's *History of Zionism*, New York (1972). An invaluable selection of official British documents has been compiled and annotated by Doreen Ingrams, *Palestine Papers, 1917-1922: The Seeds of Conflict*, London (1972). *The Balfour Declaration*, by Leonard Stein, London, New York (1961) remains the most complete account of this controversial piece of paper. It should be read along with W. T. Mallison's article, "The Balfour Declaration: An Appraisal in International Law" in *The Transformation of Palestine: Essays in the Origins and Development of the Arab/Israeli Conflict*, Edited by Ibrahim Abu Lughod, Evanston (1971). This volume contains an excellent bibliography covering the entire history of the conflict; a second essay, relevant to the first chapter of this book, is Richard Steven's "Zionism as a Phase of Western Imperialism."

1. Hertzberg, *The Zionist Idea*, pp. 181-198, for the text of *Auto-Emancipation*.
2. *Ibid.*, pp. 200-230, for the text of *The Jewish State*.
3. Taylor, *Prelude to Israel*, p. 6.
4. *The Complete Diaries of Theodor Herzl*, Edited by R. Patai, New York (1960), Vol. I, p. 88, entry for 12 June, 1895.
5. Quoted by Hans Kohn, "Zion and the Jewish National Idea," reprinted from the *Menorah Journal* (1958) in A. R. Taylor and R. Tetlie, *Palestine: A Search for Truth*, Washington (1970).
6. Quoted in Michael Ionides, *Divide and Lose: The Arab Revolt of 1955-1958*, London (1960).
7. Weizmann's own account of his activities can be found in his autobiography, *Trial and Error*, New York (1966).
8. Weizmann, *Trial and Error*, p. 149.
9. H. F. Frischwasser-Ra'anan, *Frontiers of a Nation*, London, (1955), p. 80.
10. *Palestine: A Study of Jewish, Arab and British Policies*, published by the ESCO Foundation for Palestine, New Haven (1947), Vol. I, pp. 88-89. See also J.

M. N. Jeffries, *Palestine: The Reality*, London (1939), p. 129.
11. *Palestine: A Study . . .* , Vol. I, p. 91.
12. Weizmann, *Trial and Error*, p. 244.
13. *Palestine: A Study . . .* , Vol. I, p. 95.
14. Jeffries, *Palestine*, pp. 181-182.
15. Weizmann, *Trial and Error*, p. 207.
16. For a comment on Lord Balfour's private and personal position on the Balfour Declaration, see *Middle East Journal*, (Summer, 1968), pp. 340-345. The leading American Zionist, Justice Brandeis, expressed the following view in an interview with Balfour in 1919, "We are dealing not with the wishes of an existing community but are consciously seeking to re-constitute a new community and definitely building for a numerical majority in the future." Ingrams, *Palestine Papers*, p. 73.
17. *Documents on British Foregin Policy, 1919-1939*, eds. Woodward and Butler, First Series, Vol. 4 (1956), document 242, p. 345. Not all officials in either the British government or the Foreign Office were as shortsighted and indifferent to Palestinians as Lord Balfour. One official, George Kidston, commented on these views of Balfour in a memorandum: "Palestine is to go to the Zionists irrespective of the wishes of the great bulk of the population, because it is historically right and politically expedient that it should do so. The idea that the carrying out of either of these programmes will entail bloodshed and military repression never seems to have occurred to him." Ingrams, *Palestine Papers*, 74.

Chapter Two

For the nineteenth century background of the contemporary Middle East the following works may be recommended. The political history is outlined in P. M. Holt's *Egypt and the Fertile Crescent, 1516-1922*, New York (1969). A much fuller treatment will be found in the first part of A. L. Tibawi's *A Modern History of Syria, Including Lebanon and Palestine*, London (1969). The 1787 English edition of Volney's *Travels Through Syria and Egypt* has recently been reproduced by photo off-set and contains much valuable data on late eighteenth century Palestine. For the economic history of Syria there is Charles Issawi (Editor), *The Economic History of the Middle East, 1800-1914*, Chicago (1966), Part IV on Syria; see also the useful essay by Albert Hourani "The Fertile Crescent in the Eighteenth Century," in the same collection of readings. On the impact of Ottoman reforms in Palestine and related social and economic developments, see Moshe Ma'oz, *Ottoman Reform in Syria and Palestine 1840-1861*, Oxford (1968). Other works dealing with cultural and intellectual developments are A. L. Tibawi, *British Interests in Palestine, 1800-1901*, Oxford (1961); Albert Hourani, *Arabic Thought in the Liberal Age, 1798-1939*, London (1962) which contains an important chapter on Arab nationalism; Hisham Sharabi, *Arab Intellectuals and the West: The Formative Years, 1875-1914*, Baltimore (1970). For Arab views of Europe during the nineteenth century see Ibrahim Abu Lughod, *Arab Rediscovery of Europe*, Princeton (1963).

Chapter Three

The classic statement of the origins of the Arab nationalist movement and the relations between Britain, France and the Arabs during World War I is *The Arab Awakening* by George Antonius, New York (1965), who himself served in the Palestine Mandate government. See also Zeine N. Zeine, *The Struggle for Arab Independence*,

BIBLIOGRAPHY AND NOTES

Beirut (1960). A more recent account of the same period is Tibawi's *Modern History of Syria* (mentioned above, Chapter Two) in which the author has drawn heavily on hitherto unpublished documents of the British Foreign Office. *Backdrop to Tragedy: The Struggle for Palestine*, by W. R. Polk, D. Stamler and E. Asfour, Boston (1957) is useful. See also Isaiah Friedman, *The Question of Palestine, 1914-1918: British-Jewish-Arab Relations*, New York (1973) and Elizabeth Monroe, *Britain's Moment in the Middle East, 1914-1956*, London (1963).
1. Albert Hourani, "The Decline of the West in the Middle East" in *The Modern Middle East*, Edited by Richard Nolte, New York (1963), p. 39 and p. 41.

Chapter Four
1. David Ben Gurion, *Rebirth and Destiny of Israel*, New York (1954), pp. 7-27.
2. Greater detail on the early relations between Arabs and Zionists will be found in two articles by Neville Mandel, "Turks, Arabs and Jewish Immigration into Palestine, 1882-1914" in *St. Antony's Papers*, No. 17, Oxford (1965) and "Attempts at an Arab-Zionist Entente 1913-1914" in *Middle Eastern Studies*, I (1965), pp. 238-267.
3. Barnet Litvinoff, *The Road to Jerusalem*, London (1965), p. 132.
4. *Palestine: A Study* . . . , Vol. I, p. 131. On Zionist duplicity Alan Taylor has remarked that "Zionist vision and intent were concealed by an equivocation of statement and design. The statement of purpose always conformed to the morality of the world and the sympathies of each audience, while the design often did not." See his article, "Vision and Intent in Zionist Thought" in *The Transformation of Palestine*, pp. 9-26.
5. Quoted in W. F. Boustany, *The Palestine Mandate Invalid and Impracticable*, Beirut (1936), p. 136. In a memorandum to the British Foreign Office, Louis Bols reiterated his criticism, "It is manifestly impossible to please partisans who officially claim nothing more than a National Home but in reality will be satisfied with nothing less than a Jewish State and all that it politically implies." Ingrams, *Palestine Papers*, pp. 85-86. This is a clear example of what Taylor calls the "equivocation of statement and design."

Chapter Five
Two works for the period of the Mandate as a whole are Christopher Sykes', *Cross-Roads to Israel*, New York (1968) and John Marlowe's *The Seat of Pilate: An Account of the Palestine Mandate*, London (1959). Although Sykes' Zionist sympathies are evident, the book is very readable and balanced. The relevant parts of *The Transformation of Palestine* should be consulted, particularly Part II (Land and People) and Part III (Palestinian Resistance Under the Mandate). Very little has been written on how Palestinians personally viewed their dilemma and reacted to it. One book which helps fill the gap is *Palestine is my Country: The Story of Musa Alami*, by Geoffrey Furlonge, London (1969). Edward Atiyah's, *An Arab Tells His Story: A Study in Loyalties*, London (1946), is not readily available now, but still worth reading as a personal account. A documentary history from the pre-Mandate period to the June war of 1967 has been published by Walter Laqueur, *The Israel-Arab Reader*, New York (1969). A more important and useful anthology for the Mandate period is *From Haven to Conquest: Readings in Zionism and the Palestine Problem Until 1948*, ed. Walid Khalidi, Beirut (1971). A well reasoned and lucid challenge to the major myths of Zionist historiography is Maxime Rodinson's *Israel: A Colonial Settler State?*, New York (1973).

1. *Palestine: A Study...*, Vol. I, pp. 261-262.
2. Hertzberg, *The Zionist Idea*, p. 65.
3. *Palestine: A Study...*, Vol. I, p. 265.
4. F. F. Andrews, *The Holy Land Under Mandate*, 2 Vols., New York (1931), Vol. II, p. 86.
5. Great Britain, Commission on the Palestine Disturbances of 1929, *Report of the Commission* (Parliamentary Papers, Cmd. 3530, London, 1930), p. 129.
6. Andrews, *The Holy Land*, Vol. II, pp. 206-210.
7. Great Britain, Palestine Commission on the Jaffa Riots, 1921. *Palestine Disturbances of May, 1921: Reports of the Commissioners of Inquiry with Correspondence Relating Thereto* (Parliamentary Papers, Cmd. 1540, London, 1921), p. 57.
8. *Palestine: A Study...*, Vol. I, p. 272.
8a. *Ibid.*, Vol. II, pp. 619-621.
9. *Ibid.*, Vol. I, p. 159. See also Muhammad Asad's account in *The Road to Mecca*, London (1954), p. 94.
10. Arthur Koestler, *Thieves in the Night*, New York (1946), p. 38.
11. N. Bentwich and M. Kisch, *Brigadier Frederick Kisch*, London (1966), p. 98.
12. Hertzberg, *The Zionist Idea*, p. 616.
13. Ingrams, *Palestine Papers*, p. 32.
14. The figures in this paragraph are taken from Janet Abu Lughod's study of "The Demographic Transformation of Palestine" in *The Transformation of Palestine*, pp. 139-163. See also the article by E. Hagopian and A. B. Zahlan, "Palestine's Arab Population," *Journal of Palestine Studies*, No. 12 (Summer 1974), pp. 32-73.
15. Abu Lughod, "The Demographic Transformation," p. 142.
16. *Ibid.*, p. 147.
17. Albert Hyamson, *Palestine Under the Mandate; 1920-1948*, London (1950), Chapter 6.
18. Nevill Barbour, *Nisi Dominus*, London (1946), p. 156.
19. As observed by the Zionists' own commission of experts; cited in Andrews, *The Holy Land*, Vol. II, p. 147.
20. Marlowe, *The Seat of Pilate*, pp. 100-101.
21. Barbour, *Nisi Dominus*, p. 135.
22. John Ruedy, "Dynamics of Land Alienation" in *The Transformation of Palestine*, pp. 119-138.
23. In his account of the founding of the Jewish National Fund and its activities in land acquisition, Walter Lehn remarks, "It seems fair to conclude, therefore, that the J. N. F. was not at all successful in purchasing land from small Palestinian Arab landowners. Nevertheless, it was precisely these Palestinians who eventually paid the highest price for J. N. F. efforts to 'redeem' the land of Palestine." See *The Journal of Palestine Studies*, No. 12 (Summer 1974), p. 95 in the article entitled "The Jewish National Fund".
24. Great Britain, *Report on Immigration. Land Settlement and Development by John Hope Simpson* (Parliamentary Papers, Cmd. 3686-3687, London, 1930), Vol. I, p. 54.
25. Henry Rosenfeld, "From Peasantry to Wage Labour and Residual Peasantry: The Transformation of an Arab Village" in *Peoples and Cultures of the Middle East*, ed. Louise Sweet, Vol. II, pp. 156-157. Talal Asad has written an important critique of certain Israeli anthropological work on Arab villages. Asad's article deals with the changing class situation of Arab villagers under the Mandate and Israeli rule. See T. Asad, "Anthropological Texts and Ideological Problems: An

Analysis of Cohen on Arab Villages in Israel," *Review of Middle East Studies: I*, London (1975), pp. 1-40.
26. A. L. Tibawi, *Arab Education in Palestine*, London (1956), p. 103. The following figures indicate the impact of British colonial restrictions on Arab educational development and its encouragement of Jewish development. At the end of the Mandate period the Palestinian Arab student population was about 135,000, served by 827 schools; the ratio of students to the total Arab population was 9.2%. On the Jewish side there were about 109,000 students served by 794 schools, representing 16.7% of the total Jewish population. See Ibrahim Abu Lughod, "Educating a Community in Exile: The Palestinian Experience," *Journal of Palestine Studies*, No. 7 (Spring 1973) 94-111.

Chapter Six
The most detailed study of the political history of the Mandate from 1936-1948 is J. C. Hurewitz' *The Struggle for Palestine*, New York (1950). It contains an excellent bibliography for the period up to its publication in 1950. Shorter, but more up-to-date accounts providing somewhat different perspectives are the following: Ann Mosely Lesch, "The Palestine Arab Nationalist Movement Under the Mandate" in *The Politics of Palestinian Nationalism* by W. B. Quandt, F. Jabber and A. M. Lesch, Los Angeles (1973); David Waines, "The Failure of the Nationalist Resistance" and Barbara Kalkas, "The Revolt of 1936: A Chronicle of Events" in *The Transformation of Palestine*.
1. The story of illegal Jewish immigration into Palestine is told by Jon and David Kimche in *The Secret Roads*, New York (1955). Unfortunately, it is difficult to find.
2. Walid Khalidi, "Plan Dalet," *Middle East Forum*, Vol. 36 (November, 1961). See also Ben Halpern, *The Idea of the Jewish State*, Cambridge, Mass. (1961), p. 44 for the views of Chaim Arlosoroff.
3. Many of the details of the revolt have been taken from contemporary reports by the London *Times* correspondent in Palestine.
4. Hourani, "The Decline of the West" (see above Chapter Three).
5. *Jewish Chronicle*, 13 May, 1938.

Chapter Seven
There are now several works on the militarization of the Jewish community in Palestine and after. Yigal Allon's *The Making of Israel's Army*, New York (1971) is one.
1. Yehuda Bauer, "The Haganah, 1938-1946," *Middle Eastern Studies*, Vol. 2 (1966), pp. 182-210. See also J. C. Hurewitz, *The Struggle for Palestine*, New York (1950), pp. 93 and 109.
2. Arthur Koestler, *Promise and Fulfilment: Palestine 1917-1949*, New York (1949), p. 12.
3. J. and D. Kimche, *The Secret Roads*, New York (1955), p. 27.
4. *Ibid.*, p. 54.
5. Albert Hyamson, *Palestine Under the Mandate: 1920-1948*, London (1950), p. 150.
6. *Ibid.*, pp. 67-69.
7. See the article by Y. S. Brenner, "The Stern Gang, 1940-1948" in *Middle Eastern Studies*, Vol. 2 (1966), pp. 2-30.
8. Richard P. Stevens, *American Zionism and U.S. Foreign Policy, 1942-1947*, New York (1962), especially Chapters Five and Six.

Chapter Eight

Much of the fog which has surrounded the last months of the British Mandate has been brilliantly penetrated by Erskine Childers in his article, "The Wordless Wish: From Citizens to Refugees" in *The Transformation of Palestine*. Two other essays worth consulting for events of this period are "The Fall of Western Gaililee, 1948" by Nafez Nazzal, *Journal of Palestine Studies*, No. 11 (Spring 1974) and Elias Shoufani's "The Fall of a Village" in the *Journal of Palestine Studies*, No. 4 (Summer, 1972).

1. Netaniel Lorch, *The Edge of the Sword: Israel's War of Independence, 1947-1949*, New York (1961), p. 84.
2. *Ibid.*, p. 87.
3. Rony E. Gabbay, *A Political Study of the Arab-Jewish Conflict*, Paris (1959), pp. 76-77.
4. For more complete details, see Walid Khalidi's article, "Plan Dalet," *Middle East Forum*, Vol. 36 (November, 1961).
5. Walid Khalidi, "Why Did the Palestinians Leave?" *Middle East Forum*, Vol. 34 (July, 1959), p. 22.
6. Walid Khalidi, "The Fall of Haifa," *Middle East Forum*, Vol. 34 (December, 1959), pp. 22-34. For an account which differs from that of Khalidi, see Jon and David Kimche, *Both Sides of the Hill*, London (1960), pp. 118-124. Professor Khalidi's interpretation has not yet been successfully challenged.
7. *Ibid.*, p. 32.
8. Edgar O'Ballance, *The Arab-Israeli War, 1948*, New York (1957), p. 64.

Chapter Nine

For this and subsequent chapters, the reader may wish to consult parts of the following works for greater detail on different aspects of the story. Erskine Childers, *The Road to Suez: A Study of Western-Arab Relations*, London (1962), tries to dispel some of the myths which North Americans and Europeans have of the Arabs and of themselves regarding their relations with the Arab world. A penetrating study of the period from 1948 to the June war is that of Maxime Rodinson, *Israel and the Arabs*, London (1968). *The Covenant and the Sword: Arab-Israeli Relations 1948-1956*, London (1962) by Earl Berger, deals with the establishment and failure of the armistice agreements. In his work *The Arab-Israeli Dilemma*, Syracuse (1968), Fred Khouri has covered the three Arab-Israeli wars, making exhaustive use of United Nations' documents. Sami Hadawi, who was an official in the Department of Land Settlement under the British Mandate, has written an important book *Palestine: Loss of a Heritage*, San Antonio, Texas (1963). Hisham Sharabi's *Nationalism and Revolution in the Arab World*, New York (1966) is a good analysis. Constantine Zurayk's classic criticism of the Arab defeat in 1948 has been translated by Bayley Winder, *The Meaning of the Disaster*, Beirut (1956). The Palestinians' fate after 1948 is dealt with by Don Peretz in his *Israel and the Palestine Arabs*, Washington (1958).

1. Musa Alami, "The Lesson of Palestine," *Middle East Journal*, Vol. 3 (1949), pp. 373-405.
2. Malcolm Kerr, *The Arab Cold War 1958-1967: A Study of Ideology in Politics*, 2nd. Edition, London (1967), pp. 150-151. A third edition appeared in 1971.
3. A. H. Abidi, *Jordan: A Political Study, 1948-1957*, London (1956), p. 50.
4. *Ibid.*, pp. 26-38.
5. United Nations press release, 11 February, 1957.

Chapter Ten

In addition to Peretz' book mentioned above (Chapter Nine), three other works, all with the same title, *The Arabs in Israel*, provide useful material on the Arab Israeli community. The first by Walter Schwartz, London (1969) is well balanced and describes the impact on the Palestinians resulting from their sudden transformation to a minority. The second book by Jacob Landau, Oxford (1969), contains good analysis of Arab voting patterns in Israeli elections. The last book is by Sabri Jiryis, an Arab Israeli lawyer. It contains penetrating and sometimes bitter criticisms of Israeli government policies concerning the Arab minority but it is meticulously documented and gives details not to be found elsewhere. A second, enlarged edition, was published by the Monthly Review Press, New York (1976). The first edition appeared in Beirut in 1968.

1. *Jewish Observer*, 9 November, 1956.
2. *Jewish Observer*, 16 November, 1956.
3. *Jerusalem Post*, weekly airmail edition for 23 October, 1967.
4. Rony E. Gabbay, *A Political Study of the Arab-Jewish Conflict*, Paris (1959), p. 153.
5. Peretz, *Israel and the Palestine Arabs*, p. 36.
6. Walter Laqueur, *The Israel-Arab Reader*, New York (1969), pp. 162-163.
7. *Haaretz*, 29 June, 1973.
8. Uri Davis, "The Law of Return: Its Implications and place in Israeli Zionist Society," paper presented to the Palestine Colloquim in Brussels, May, 1976.
9. Joseph Ryan, "Refugees Within Israel," *Journal of Palestine Studies*, No. 8 (Summer, 1973), pp. 55-81.
10. For details, see Sabri Jiryis, "The Land Question in Israel," *Middle East Research and Information Project* (MERIP), No. 47 (1976).
11. Peretz, *Israel and the Palestine Arabs*, p. 150.
12. Quoted in Jiryis, "The Land Question," p. 13.
13. Jiryis, *The Arabs in Israel*, Beirut (1968), p. 5.
14. *Ibid.*, p. 21.
15. *Ibid.*, p. 43.
16. *Ibid.*, p. 52.
17. *Ibid.*, p. 46.
18. *Ibid.*, pp. 92-118 for details from the court records.
19. *Ibid.*, p. 140.

Chapter Eleven

The June war produced a crop of "instant books" naturally lacking in historical perspective or analytical value. Future historians may regard them as interesting examples of the near hysteria and manic elation surrounding the war which successfully managed to cloud the central issues of the conflict. More sober and detached are two works which trace the background to the June war, Walter Laqueur's *The Road to Jerusalem: Origins of the Arab-Israeli Conflict 1967*, New York (1968) and Nadav Safran, *From War to War: The Arab-Israeli Confrontation 1948-1967*, New York (1969). Two other works covering other aspects are Theodore Draper's *Israel and World Politics: The Roots of the Third Arab-Israeli War*, New York (1967) and Michael Howard & Robert Hunter, *Israel and the Arab World: The Crisis of 1967*, London, Institute of Strategic Studies, (1967). To achieve a balanced perspective of the June war, each or all of the above should be read along with *The Arab-Israeli Confrontation of June 1967*, Edited by Ibrahim Abu Lughod, Evanston (1970) which contains a number of excellent essays.

The Fall of Jerusalem, by Abdullah Schleifer, New York (1972) is a moving account of this sensitive aspect of the conflict by a very acute observer. Another, much overlooked, problem is treated by Peter Dodd & Halim Barakat, *River Without Bridges: A Study of the Exodus of the 1967 Palestinian Arab Refugees*, Beirut, Institute for Palestine Studies (1968).

Two recent personal accounts by Palestinians are by Fauzi al-Asmar, *To Be an Arab in Israel*, London, Frances Pinter (1975) and Fawaz Turki, *The Disinherited: Journal of a Palestinian Exile*, New York (1972). John Davis, who has had long experience with the Palestinian refugees, wrote *The Evasive Peace: A Study of the Zionist-Arab Problem*, London (1968).

A full account of the Israeli occupation has not yet been written. Shabtai Teveth's *The Cursed Blessing*, London (1970), covers only the first two years and is mainly a eulogy of Dayan's policies. Israeli lawyer, Felicia Langer, has written a first hand account of the treatment of Palestinian civilian and commando prisoners in *With My Own Eyes: Israel and the Occupied Territories, 1967-1973*, London (1975). The story of Israel's annexationist designs is well treated by Israeli journalist Amnon Kapeliouk, *La Fin des Mythes*, Paris (1975) and hopefully it will soon be available in English.

The following readers contain much additional material: Arieh Bober (Editor), *The Other Israel: The Radical Case Against Zionism*, New York (1972); Russell Stetler, (Editor), *Palestine: The Arab-Israeli Conflict*, San Francisco (1972); Uri Davis (Editor et al.), *Israel and Palestinians*, London (1975).

1. See Ahmed Khalidi, "The War of Attrition," *Journal of Palestine Studies*, No. 9 (Autumn, 1973), pp. 60-87.
2. Doreen Ingrams, *Palestine Papers, 1917-1922: The Seeds of Conflict*, London (1972), p. 150.
3. Amos Elon, *The Israelis: Founders and Sons*, New York (1971), p. 325.
4. *Ibid.*, p. 324.
5. *New Outlook*, Vol. 18 (May-June, 1975), p. 34.
6. On this point see Amnon Kapeliouk, *La Fin des Mythes*, Paris (1975), pp. 183-222.
7. David Hirst, "Rush to Annexation: Israel in Jerusalem," *Journal of Palestine Studies*, No. 12 (Summer, 1974), pp. 3-31.
8. Shabtai Teveth, *The Cursed Blessing*, London (1969), p. 30.
9. Israel Shahak, "Interview," *Journal of Palestine Studies*, No. 15 (Spring, 1975), pp. 3-20.
10. *Yediot Aharanot*, 31 October, 1969.
11. *Haaretz*, 8 January, 1974.
12. *Maariv*, 23 November, 1973.
13. *Haaretz*, 30 November, 1973.
14. *Davar*, 12 October, 1974.
15. Noam Chomsky, "Israeli Jews and Palestinians: Reflections on a National Conflict," *Holy Cross Quarterly*, (Summer, 1972).
16. *Davar*, 29 November, 1973.
17. *Maariv*, 26 September, 1971.
18. Felicia Langer, *With My Own Eyes*, London (1975), p. 111 quoted from a report of the League of Civil Rights.
19. Muhammad Farah, "Legal Status of Israel and the Occupied Territories,"

Association of Arab-American University Graduates, *Information Papers*, No. 15 (April, 1975).
20. *Ibid.*
21. Kapeliouk, *La Fin des Mythes*, p. 38.
22. *Mahaniam*, (April, 1969).
23. The details of this paragraph are taken from the excellent account by Sheila Ryan on "Israeli Economic Policy in the Occupied Areas," *Middle East Research and Information Project* (MERIP), Report No. 24 (1974).
24. *Haaretz*, 7 November, 1972; *Davar*, 8 November, 1972.
25. *Hotam*, 14 February, 1975.
26. *Al-Hamishmar*, 30 January, 1975.
27. Mordechai Nahumi, "Israeli as an Occupying Power," *New Outlook*, Vol. 15 (June, 1972), p. 33.
28. Michael Adams, "Signposts to Destruction: Israeli Settlements in the Occupied Territories," pamphlet published by the Council of the Advancement of Arab-British Understanding, n.d. (ca. 1975).
29. *Ibid.*, p. 6.
30. Shabtai Teveth, *The Cursed Blessing*, London (1970), p. 15.

Chapter Twelve
Accounts of the rise of the Palestinian resistance are of very uneven quality. The few listed here have been selected from what is now a considerable body of literature. John Cooley's *Green March, Black September: The Story of the Palestinian Arabs*, London (1973) is a readable journalistic treatment which contains interesting details on many of the Palestinian personalities behind the resistance. *The Palestinian Resistance* by Gerard Chaliand, London, Penguin (1972) is critical and perceptive. Dana Schmidt's *Armageddon in the Middle East*, New York (1974) contains three chapters on the guerilla movement. *Strike Terror: The Story of Fateh*, New York (1970) is by Israeli journalist Ehud Yaari. Edgar O'Ballance, the British military historian has written a ponderously detailed work called *Arab Guerilla Power 1967-1972*, London (1974). *Laila's Hijack War*, London (1970) by Peter Snow and David Phillips is a colourful account of the young female hijacker, Laila Khalid.

An attempted academic treatment of the resistance is made by a former Israeli Military Intelligence chief, Y. Harkabi, *Fedayeen Action and Arab Strategy*, London (1968) which should be read alongside of Hisham Sharabi's *Palestine Guerillas: Their Credibility and Effectiveness*, Washington (1970). Sharabi's book, *Palestine and Israel: The Lethal Dilemma*, New York (1969) is also useful. Noam Chomsky's *Peace in the Middle East?* presents the views of a radical American Jewish intellectual. A radical Arab perspective is set out in Fawwaz Trabulsi, "The Palestine Problem: Zionism and Imperialism in the Middle East," *New Left Review*, 57 (September-October, 1969), pp. 53-90. Finally, some critical reviews of the resistance in light of the Jordan civil war are Samir Franjieh, "How Revolutionary is the Palestinian Resistance: A Marxist Interpretation," *Journal of Palestine Studies*, No. 2 (Winter, 1972) and Michael Hudson, "The Palestinian Resistance: Developments and Setbacks, 1967-1971," *Journal of Palestine Studies*, No. 3 (Spring, 1972) and Sadik al-Azim "The Palestinian Resistance Movement Reconsidered" in E. Said and M. Suleiman, (editors) *The Arabs Today*, Columbus (1973).

1. See Walid Kazziha, *Revolutionary Transformation in the Arab World: Habash and his Comrades from Nationalism to Marxism*, London (1975).

2. Ibrahim Abu Lughod, "Altered Realities: The Palestinians Since 1967," *International Journal*, Vol. 28 (Autumn, 1973), p. 659. The whole issue is entitled *The Arab States and Israel*.
3. William Quandt, "Political and Military Dimensions of Contemporary Palestinian Nationalism," in *The Politics of Palestinian Nationalism*, by W. Quandt, F. Jabber and A. M. Lesch, Los Angeles (1973), p. 91.
4. *Ibid.*, p. 102.
5. See also Davis' personal account "Journey out of Zionism: The Radicalisation of an Israeli Pacifist," *Journal of Palestine Studies*, No. 4 (Summer, 1972), pp. 59-72.
6. *Le Monde Diplomatique*, March, 1969.
7. Bassam Sirhan, "Palestine Refugee Camp Life in Lebanon," *Journal of Palestine Studies*, 14 (Winter, 1975), p. 101.
8. Abu Lughod, "Altered Realities," p. 661.
9. *Davar*, 12 December, 1972.
10. *Maariv* Supplement, 15 December, 1972.
11. Quandt, "Political and Military Dimensions of Contemporary Palestinian Nationalism," p. 128.

The End is Prologue
1. Michael Hudson, "The Palestinian Resistance: Developments and Setbacks 1967-1971," *Journal of Palestine Studies*, No. 3 (Spring, 1972), pp. 83-84.
2. On the background to the Lebanese civil war see Kamal S. Salibi, *Cross Roads to Civil War*, New York (1976).

General Index

Abandoned Areas Ordinance, 126
Abdul Hadi, Auni, 76
Abdullah, King, 101, 103, 104, 112, 114, 115, 172
Absentee Property Regulations, 125
Adams, Michael, 153
Alami, Musa, 108, 118
Alami, Zuhayr, 178
Alexander, D. L. 24
Allon, Yigal, 166
All-Palestine Government (1948), 113, 115
Almogi, Joseph, 127
Aloni, Shulamit, 162
Anglo-French Declaration, 42, 45
Anglo-Jewish Association, 24
Arab Development Society, 118
Arab Higher Committee, 74, 76, 77, 79, 84, 96, 97, 113
Arab Israeli War (1948), 95-104
Arab League, 86, 97, 101, 113, 114, 179
Arab (Palestine) Congresses, 54, 57, 60, 61, 113, 115
Arafat, Yassir, 10, 175, 178, 183, 184, 188, 191, 200, 201, 208
al-Ard (The Earth), 137
Arendt, Hanna, 16
Army of Liberation, 96
Aruri, Tayseer, 157
Asad, Hafez, 193, 209, 210, 211
Asquith, Herbert, 20, 37
Atallah, Antoun, 148
Attlee, Clement R., 93

Balfour, Arthur, 26, 27, 28, 45, 52
Balfour Declaration, 22, 23, 27, 45, 51, 53, 59
Bar-Lev, Major General, 190
Basle Congress, 16, 17
Bassett, J. R., 41
Ben Gurion, David, 47, 63, 72, 78, 87, 88, 90, 91, 94, 101, 102, 108, 121, 122, 123, 128, 129, 131, 136
Bernadotte, Folke, 113, 115

Bevin, Ernest, 91
Biltmore Conference, 88
Black September, 197, 199, 200, 211
Bols, Louis, 50, 51
Brinton, John, 32
Brit Shalom, 62
British Government, 11, 21, 26, 40, 41, 45, 53, 55, 57, 59, 73, 76, 78, 82, 83

Cairo Agreement (1969), 199
Chaliand, Gerard, 184
Chamberlain, Joseph, 17, 18
Chamoun, Camille, 205, 208, 209
Chomsky, Noam, 150
Churchill, Winston, 55, 58
Committee on Illegal Immigration (Mossad), 88
Conjoint Committee, 24, 26
Covenant of the League of Nations, 43, 44

Davis, John, 118
Davis, Uri, 182
Dayan, Moshe, 114, 124, 139, 146, 151, 159, 161, 166, 168
Democratic Popular Front, 188
Dreyfus, Alfred, 14
Dreyfus, Charles, 27

Eban, Abba, 123, 139, 142, 152
Eder, Dr., 61, 62
Egypt-Israeli Armistice Agreement (1949), 103
Elon, Amos, 144
English Federation of Zionists, 25
Eshkol, Levi, 122, 146
Eytan, Walter, 121

Fateh, 175, 176, 181, 183, 185, 188, 189, 190, 191, 200, 203
Faysal, King, 110
Franjieh, Sulaiman, 200, 205, 207, 208

Gafni, Shraga, 161

Gaza Congress, 115
Geneva Convention, 147, 158
Georges-Picot, M., 21, 24

deHaas, Jacob, 26
Habash, G., 154, 174, 188, 189, 192
Haganah, 63, 78, 87, 88, 89, 90, 91, 92, 95–101
Hammond, Laurie, 78
Hamzeh, Ahmad, 159, 203
Hawari, Loutfiya, 157
Hawatmeh, Nayif, 188
Haycraft Commission, 56, 61
Herzl, Theodore, 11, 14, 15, 16, 17, 18, 19
Hirst, David, 147
Histadrut, 67, 72
Hitler, 85, 86, 89, 90
Hope Simpson, Sir John, 67, 68, 69
Hourani, Albert, 44, 78
Hudson, Michael, 196
Hussein ibn Ali, Sherif, 39–41, 54
Hussein, King, 166, 174, 190, 191, 192, 202, 210
Husseini, Hajj Amin, 71, 73, 74, 79, 83, 113, 171
Husseinis, 81, 84
Hyamson, Albert, 89

Irgun, 90, 91, 92, 98
Israel Government Yearbook, 121
Israeli Defense Laws, 130–133
Israeli Defense Ministry, 131, 141, 165
Israeli Frontier Force, 134, 189
Israeli Government, 114, 120, 121, 127, 129, 145, 147

Jabotinksy, Vladimir, 62
Jarring, Gunnar, 180
Jerusalem, 30, 143, 146, 147, 148, 149, 151
Jewish Agency, 53, 62, 63, 64, 66, 72, 73, 76, 79, 83, 86, 87, 90, 95, 97, 101, 119
Jewish Federation of Labor, 67
Jewish immigration, 64–66, 71, 82, 88
Jewish National Colonizing Corporation, 25
Jewish National Fund, 67, 69, 74
Jewish National Home, 22, 27, 28, 45, 48, 49, 51, 53, 55–70, 80, 82, 89, 95, 108, 119, 133
Jewish Settlement Police, 86
Jiryis, Sabri, 131, 137
Jordan, civil war, 189, 192–193, 195
June War (1967), 69, 117, 122, 139, 141, 142, 143, 145, 146, 150, 152, 167, 174, 176, 177, 185, 193, 198

Kafr Birim, 124–125
Kafr Qassim, 134–136
Kan'an, Hamdi, 155, 156
Kapeliok, Amnon, 160
Kenon, Amos, 155
Kerr, Malcolm, 110
Khalid, Laila, 199
al-Khatib, Rauhi, 146, 147
Kimche, Jon and David, 88, 89
Kisch, Frederick, 62
Kissinger, Henry, 201, 204
Klatzkin, Jacob, 54
Koestler, Arthur, 87
Kollek, Teddy, 149
Koussa, Elias, 97

Labouisse, Henry, 116
Landau, Eli, 187
Langer, Felicia, 157
Law of Return, 124, 134
Lawrence, Thomas Edward, 40
Lebanon, civil war, 193, 197–199, 200, 204, 205–212
Leibovitch, Yeshayahu, 150
Levy, Shabatai, 97
Lloyd George, David, 19, 22, 26

MacDonald, Ramsay, 66, 72
Mandate (Palestine), 30, 44, 45, 53–70, 72, 74, 80, 81, 83, 88, 90, 95–105, 114, 140
Mandate Defense Laws, 129
Mapai, 128, 131, 136, 137
Mapam, 128, 136, 137
Maqi, 134, 137
McMahon, Henry, 39
Meir, Golda, 114, 125, 152
Mills, Eric, 144
Montagu, Edwin, 26
Montefiore, Claude, 24
Mossad (Committee on Illegal

INDEX

Immigration), 88
Moyne, Lord, 90
Muslim-Christian Associations, 54

Nahmani, Joseph, 126
Nahumi, Mordechai, 165
Narkis, General, 187
Nashashibis, 81, 84
Nasser, Gamal Abdel, 107, 109, 140, 141, 173, 176, 190, 192
National Defense Party, 84
Nationality Law, 134

O'Ballance, Edgar, 101
October War (1973), 150, 159, 167, 200, 201, 203, 204
Oliphant, Laurence, 31
Oz, Amos, 144

Palestine, 15-18, 21, 22, 25, 27, 28, 29-38
Palestine Arab Party, 84
Palestine Government, 66, 88
Palestine Liberation Army, 177, 192
Palestine Liberation Organization, 160, 176, 177, 182, 184, 187, 188, 192, 201, 202, 204, 205, 210
Palestine National Charter, 182
Palestine National Front, 202
Palestine War (1948), 68, 95-104, 105, 107, 108, 111, 113, 197
Palestine Zionist Executive, 63
Palmach, 87, 95, 99
Paris Peace Conference (1919), 43, 51, 108, 199
Partition Resolution (1947), 94
Patria, 89
Peres, Shimon, 132
Peretz, Don, 126
Pinsker, Leo, 13, 14, 46
Popular Front, 154, 175, 188, 189, 192

Qasim, Abdul Karim, 109, 110
Qassam, Izzadin, 74

Ra'anan, Frischwasser, 22
Raqah, 137
Rhodes, Cecil, 18
Rogers, William, 141, 192
Rothschild, Edmund, 33
Rothschild, Walter, 26

Sacher, Harry, 62
Said, Nuri, 103, 111
Saleh, Abdel Jawad, 156
Salman, Yaacov, 146
Samuel, Herbert, 51, 52, 53, 54, 72, 83
Sapir, Pinhas, 168
Sartawi, Issam, 192
Scott, C. P., 19, 21
Shaath, Nabil, 182
Shabat, Ibrahim, 127, 128
Shahak, Israel, 147
Shamgar, Meir, 147
Shapiro, Jacob, 129
Sharett, Moshe, 123
Sharif, Zeef, 147
Shaw Commission, 62, 66
Shukayri, Ahmad, 176, 177, 178
Sixth Zionist Congress, 18
Soviet Union, 92
Special Committee on Palestine, 93
Stanhope, Lady Hester, 31
Stern Gang, 90, 91, 92
Stone, I. F., 140
Storrs, Ronald, 70
Suez Canal, 17, 20, 21, 141, 173
Supreme Muslim Council, 71, 72, 79, 83
Sykes, Christopher, 145
Sykes, Mark, 21, 24

Tal, Wasfi, 197
Taylor, Alan R., 15
Tell Za'atar, 206, 211
Thomas, Lowell, 40
Toledano, Shmuel, 187
Truman, Harry, 93, 123

UN General Assembly, 115, 146, 170, 171, 183, 201
UN Palestine Commission, 94
UN Security Council, 140
United Arab Republic, 109-110, 173, 174
United Nations, 93, 95, 97, 101, 102, 103, 113, 114
United Nations Works Relief Agency, 112, 113, 115-116, 117
United States, 100, 109, 111, 113, 123

Unterman, Chief Rabbi, 146
Urbach, Ephraim, 150

War of Attrition, 141, 190
Wauchope, Arthur, 73, 89
Weizmann, Chaim, 13, 19, 21, 24, 25, 26, 27, 28, 49, 50, 54, 62, 63, 64, 66, 144
White Paper, 72, 77, 82, 83
Wilson, Woodrow, 26
Wingate, Orde, 87
Wingate, Reginald, 41

World War I, 11, 20, 33, 39, 106, 109
World War II, 83, 85, 107, 109, 111
World Zionist Organization, 11, 16, 49, 53, 63, 89, 121

Yishuv, 63, 67

Zaarour, Ahmad, 192
Zangwill, Israel, 62
Zionism, 12-28, 54, 146, 150, 151, 170
Zionist Commission, 49, 50, 51, 61
Zionist Congress, 16, 62, 73, 78